DAILY LIFE OF

CHRISTIANS IN
ANCIENT ROME

**Recent Titles in the
Greenwood Press "Daily Life Through History" Series**

DAILY LIFE OF

CHRISTIANS IN

ANCIENT ROME

JAMES W. ERMATINGER

The Greenwood Press "Daily Life Through History" Series

GREENWOOD PRESS
Westport, Connecticut • London

Library of Congress Cataloging-in-Publication Data

Ermatinger, James William, 1959–
    Daily life of Christians in ancient Rome / James W. Ermatinger.
        p. cm. — (The Greenwood Press "Daily life through history" series,
    ISSN 1080–4749)
    Includes bibliographical references and index.
    ISBN 0–313–33564–8 (alk. paper)
    1. Church history—Primitive and early church, ca. 30–600.   2. Rome—
History—Empire, 30 B.C.–476 A.D.   3. Christian life.   I. Title.
    BR170.E76   2007
    274.5'63201—dc22   2006027920

British Library Cataloguing in Publication Data is available.

Library of Congress Catalog Card Number: 2006027920
ISBN: 0–313–33564–8
ISSN: 1080–4749

First published in 2007

Greenwood Press, 88 Post Road West, Westport, CT 06881
An imprint of Greenwood Publishing Group, Inc.
ww.greenwood.com

Printed in the United States of America

The paper used in this book complies with the
Permanent Paper Standard issued by the National
Information Standards Organization (Z39.48–1984).

10   9   8   7   6   5   4   3   2   1

To Angela, Michelle, and Ian

Contents

PREFACE

Books dealing with Christianity fill libraries, both public and private, throughout the world with literally tons of information. Works arguing both for and against Christ's divinity and discussing Christianity's history, the missions of early Christians, and Christianity's impact continually appear and add to the already existing volumes. Scholars and amateurs alike constantly challenge each other in promoting both plausible and fantastic theories and notions about Christ, early Christians, and Christianity in general. The general public interest in Christianity has not diminished and is unlikely to do so any time soon. So why should another work exist on the subject? One reason is to explore the differences between Christians and pagans in their daily life. Another reason is to examine how Christianity developed and identified itself in a hostile environment. As such, this present work is not a history of Christianity; rather, it attempts to place the Christians within the framework of Roman society, although historical events and periods are not ignored. Likewise this book is not a discussion of Christian theology. While theological disputes are touched on, I feel it best to allow theologians to argue the merits of different views, especially since by the 2nd century c.e. there were over 20 varieties of Christianity in existence. The central aspect of this book examines Christians' daily life during the Roman world, especially in the city of Rome and before the legalization of Christianity.

There are numerous works also on Roman daily life. Rome's admission of new groups, how the Romans viewed urbanization, the development of Roman cities, the workings of the Roman family, and many other topics have been explored extensively. Why then is there another book on the daily lives of Christians? Although not a detailed account of the daily life of urban populations—for this, one is referred to the excellent work in this series by Gregory Aldrete, *Daily Life in the Roman City: Rome, Pompeii, and Ostia*—this present book attempts to show how Christians lived in the city, primarily in Rome. The numerous works that discuss Christianity often ignore the daily life of individuals—how they lived and how they interacted with each other and different groups. These divergent components are crucial in understanding Christian society and its religious beliefs. What makes this book different from other works on the daily life of ancient Romans is that I have attempted to show not only the similarities between Christians and non-Christians but also the major differences. Determining these major differences is the key to understanding Christian daily life.

The daily life of Christians is fascinating because this group existed as a persecuted minority believing in a set of beliefs alien to the general Roman population. Christian apologists attempted to define who they were to counter the generally negative views spread through the pagan community. Using literary and archaeological sources I hope to show the differences and similarities in daily life between Christians and their neighbors.

In order to place Christians within the context of Roman society, I have included Biographies and Points in Time. These Biographies describe certain individuals, both Christians and non-Christians, who influenced society and therefore daily life. Drawn from throughout the imperial age, they further paint a picture of Roman society. Analogous to the Biographies are the Points in Time. These accounts, usually from the ancient literature, attempt to place the chapter subject within the context of Roman history and society. By using the two sidebars together, a fuller understanding of Christian daily life occurs.

The book is organized into 10 chapters in 3 sections. The first section describes the setting of Christianity in the Roman world and attempts to answer the question, what made Christians unique? Chapter one details the two saviors of early Christian history: the first emperor, Augustus, who restored order, and Jesus of Nazareth. Placed within the historical context are the Points in Time—Augustus' own words on how he brought peace to the empire and what peace would look like to a provincial inhabitant. The chapter then explores the reasons why Christianity was adopted by non-Jews. Chapter two examines the city of Rome. With Biographies from architects and a first-century C.E. writer and Points in Time from ancient catalogues and descriptions of the city, a general overview of the city is given. Chapter three discusses the general history of pagan religions, especially the so-called mystery religions, in Rome. Although by no means exhaustive, the information attempts to show that Christianity was not the only religion counter to the traditional Olympian religion and its despairing view of the afterlife. That these pagan sentiments were strong is indicated in the Point in Time describing the battle between Christians and pagans over the famous statue of Victory erected by Augustus in the Senate House and removed by Christian emperors. The two leading opponents, Ambrose and Symmachus, are described in their respective Biographies. This first section ends with chapter four describing Rome's initial contact with the Christians. In addition to exploring the debate among early Christians concerning their Jewish identity, this chapter describes Nero's persecution of the Christians after a great fire in Rome, using an ancient account, and includes biographies of Nero and Paul, who was executed during this first persecution.

The second section of the book explores the daily life of Christians in Roman society and attempts to answer the question, what made Christians different? Chapter five examines the private daily life of Christians and looks at their family size, occupations, housing, furniture, methods of reckoning time, food, and clothing. Although these attributes were not substantially different from those of pagan Romans, Christian moral behavior was quite different, especially when Christians came from the elite class. Using two late-contemporary Christians, Marcella and Jerome, a portrait of how the different sexes viewed Christian life is also given. Chapter six examines the public life of Christians, including a more specific examination of occupations such as weaving, banking, and the military and the interactions among Christians and pagans associated with taverns, baths, and the games. This latter interaction provides a Point in Time about the circus. In addition to the occupations and interaction, this chapter also examines how Christians interacted with the government. Two leading examples of individuals in the late empire who involved themselves in public life were Augustine and Cassiodorus. Chapter seven explores the interaction of Christians with pagans. This interaction was an extension of the private and public lives of Christians and pagans. The Point in Time is an archaeological site that points to the disturbances caused by the persecutions, the greatest interaction between Christianity and pagans. This chapter focuses mainly on the persecutions, since these events were the most visible and violent happenings, with the Biographies focusing on a persecutor and a martyr.

The final section of the book explores the particulars of Christianity. Here the central question asked is, what did it meant to be a Christian? Chapter eight discusses the general religious life of Christians. After exploring Christianity's Jewish origins and the rise of the house churches, a general examination of Christian churches, especially after Constantine legalized Christianity, is provided. Associated with this description is the development of the general feasts, which had elements of both Judaism and paganism. The full development of Christian ideology is seen in the Point in Time, Constantine's conversion and the establishment of state protection for Christianity. Since most of the religious training took place within the family, a further examination of family life is offered. Finally, the conflict between the legalized Christian religion and the state is described in the two Biographies: Theodosius, a Catholic who was admonished by the church, and Theodoric, an Arian who coexisted with the church. Chapter nine examines Christianity and its beliefs in the afterlife and how this differed from paganism. Crucial to this discussion is the difference between pagan and Christian burial customs. Where and how Christians buried their dead completes this discussion. The Point in Time, a description of Christian tombstones, coupled with the Biographies of two Christians who were active in preserving the memory of the Christian martyrs, helps explain the differences between Christians and non-Christians. The final chapter discusses the impact of Christianity from antiquity to the modern age. This is particularly seen in the evolution of the pilgrimage—how Christians in the medieval world and afterwards used such pilgrimages for religious piety and how the city of Rome used them to revitalize their city through tourism. This particular component is still seen today.

This book then attempts to create a multifaceted approach to the daily life of Christians that will spark debate and more research. How individuals worked, ate, worshipped, and enjoyed themselves in the past has always fascinated modern society. We often take for granted certain "necessities" such as television, automobiles, and microwaves, without fathoming how earlier societies survived. Like the ancient pagan Romans, modern societies view new religions with suspicion and occasionally with fear. While we often profess toleration, a noble attribute, we are quick to sneer at and ridicule others' beliefs and customs. In other words, much has not changed since the Romans first came into contact with the Christians. This work attempts to cast some light on how a persecuted sect of Judaism lived and functioned in a totalitarian society.

Acknowledgments

I would like to thank my wife, Angela, who read, commented on, questioned, and discussed this manuscript. Michael Hermann of Greenwood Publishing Group suggested the work and patiently answered all my questions. Mariah Gumpert, acquisitions editor at Greenwood, oversaw the completion of the manuscript giving much needed advice. Michael Gunn from the Walters Art Museum, Baltimore Maryland, and Patricia Woods from the St. Louis Art Museum helped in the acquisition of photographs for this work. Gregory and Alicia Aldrete kindly let me reproduce their drawings and images; I would like to thank the American Philosophical Society for allowing me to reprint selections from Aelius Aristides' oration *On Rome*. Dalton Curtis of the Department of History at Southeast Missouri State University read parts of the manuscript and made helpful suggestions. Larry Easley of the Department of History at Southeast Missouri State University executed the map under the vaguest of my suggestions. I would like to thank Martin Jones, dean of the College of Liberal Arts at Southeast Missouri State University, for providing assistance. My daughter Michelle suggested photographs and pieces of art to be included in the manuscript, and my son Ian frequently asked the crucial question "Why" when I related aspects of the book. Although all of these individuals helped, I assume full responsibility for the material in this book. All attempts have been made to find the rightful copyright holders, and if I have omitted anything or made a mistake please contact me so that I may rectify the error.

CHRONOLOGY

(Dates C.E. unless otherwise noted)

31 B.C.E.	Augustus defeats Cleopatra and Antony; establishes Roman Empire
31 B.C.E.–14 C.E.	Rule of Augustus as Rome's first emperor
6–4 B.C.E.	Birth of Christ
14 C.E.	Death of Augustus, who is then declared a god
14–37	Rule of Tiberius
29	Death of Christ
34	Conversion of Saul, who takes the name of Paul
37–41	Rule of Caligula
38	Riots in Alexandria, Egypt, between Jews and Greeks
41–54	Rule of Claudius and his edict concerning riots in Egypt of 38
45–47	Paul's first journey
49	Claudius expels Jews (possibly Christians) from Rome
50	Council of Jerusalem
50–53	Paul's second journey

1

INTRODUCTION

This chapter discusses early Christian history within the context of the Roman Empire. Augustus established the empire and was viewed by many contemporaries as Rome's savior for ending a century of civil war. This chapter discusses Augustus' achievements through his own words, a brief history of imperial Rome, a provincial's view of the city of Rome, and the growth of early Christianity, including why it was successful. This chapter also provides a brief overview of Roman imperial history.

If an individual living in the Roman Empire in 200 C.E. had been asked who Rome's savior was, the answer would have been the emperor Augustus, who had brought peace and prosperity back to the Roman world after a century of civil war. But by 400 C.E. the emperors themselves had proclaimed a new savior, a criminal from the distant land of Palestine crucified about 30 C.E., Joshua Bar Joseph, better known as Jesus. The religion that Jesus' followers established, Christianity, would become the official religion of the Roman Empire.

IMPERIAL HISTORY

Augustus became the savior of the Roman world, and under his rule Jesus was born in Palestine. The empire then became interconnected with Christianity, for under Augustus' successor, his stepson Tiberius, Jesus' ministry began and ended with his Crucifixion. Augustus' creation of the empire then coincided with the establishment and growth of Jesus' mission.

Rome: Statue of She Wolf. James W. Ermatinger.

AUGUSTUS' OWN VIEW OF HIS PLACE IN HISTORY

It is difficult to know how emperors desired to be remembered. However, for the emperor Augustus, a remarkable record discovered in Turkey records his personal achievements and how he wished to be seen. The following extract from Augustus' own record of achievement presents the ideas that Augustus fostered and promoted, indicating how he wanted the Roman world to view him:

THE ACHIEVEMENTS OF THE DIVINE AUGUSTUS

Below is a copy of the acts of the Deified Augustus by which he placed the whole world under the sovereignty of the Roman people, and of the amounts which he expended upon the state and the Roman people, as engraved upon two bronze columns which have been set up in Rome.

3 Wars, both civil and foreign, I undertook throughout the world, and when victorious I spared all citizens who sued for pardon. The foreign nations which could with safety be pardoned I preferred to save rather than to destroy. The number of Roman citizens who bound themselves to me by military oath was about 500,000. Of these I settled in colonies or sent back into their own towns, after their term of service, something more than 300,000, and to all I assigned lands, or gave money as a reward for military service. I captured six hundred ships, over and above those which were smaller than triremes.

13 Janus Quirinus, which our ancestors ordered to be closed whenever there was peace, secured by victory, throughout the whole domain of the Roman people on land and sea, and which, before my birth is recorded to have been closed but twice in all since the foundation of the city, the senate ordered to be closed thrice while I was princeps.

20 The Capitolium and the theatre of Pompey, both works involving great expense, I rebuilt without any inscription of my own name. I restored the channels of the aqueducts which in several places were falling into disrepair through age, and doubled the capacity of the aqueduct called the Marcia by turning a new spring into its channel. I completed the Julian Forum and the basilica which was between the temple of Castor and the temple of Saturn, works begun and far advanced by my father, and when the same basilica was destroyed by fire I began its reconstruction on an enlarged site, to be inscribed with the names of my sons, and ordered that in case I should not live to complete it, it should be completed by my heirs. In my sixth consulship, in accordance with a decree of the senate, I rebuilt in the city eighty-two temples of the gods, omitting none which at that time stood in need of repair. As consul for the seventh time I constructed the Via Flaminia from the city to Ariminum, and all the bridges except the Mulvian and the Minucian.

25 I freed the sea from pirates. About thirty thousand slaves, captured in that war, who had run away from their masters and had taken up arms against the republic, I delivered to their masters for punishment. The whole of Italy voluntarily took oath of allegiance to me and demanded me as its leader in the war in which I was victorious at Actium. The provinces of the Spains, the Gauls, Africa, Sicily, and Sardinia took the same oath of allegiance. Those who served under my standards at that time included more than 700 senators, and among them eighty-three who had previously or have since been consuls up to the day on which these words were written, and about 170 have been priests.

26 I extended the boundaries of all the provinces which were bordered by races not yet subject to our empire. The provinces of the Gauls, the Spains, and Germany, bounded by the ocean from Gades to the mouth of the Elbe, I reduced to a state of peace. The Alps, from the region which lies nearest to the Adriatic as far as the Tuscan Sea, I brought to a state of peace without waging on any tribe an unjust war. My fleet sailed from the mouth of the Rhine eastward as far as the lands of the Cimbri to which, up to that time, no Roman had ever penetrated either by land or by sea, and the Cimbri and Charydes and Semnones and other peoples of the Germans of that same region through their envoys sought my friendship and that of the Roman people. On my order and under my auspices two armies were led, at almost the same time, into Ethiopia and into Arabia which is called the "Happy," and very large forces of the enemy of both races were cut to pieces in battle and many towns were captured. Ethiopia was penetrated as far as the town of Nabata, which is next to

Meroë. In Arabia the army advanced into the territories of the Sabaei to the town of Mariba.

34 In my sixth and seventh consulships, when I had extinguished the flames of civil war, after receiving by universal consent the absolute control of affairs, I transferred the republic from my own control to the will of the senate and the Roman people. For this service on my part I was given the title of Augustus by decree of the senate, and the doorposts of my house were covered with laurels by public act, and a civic crown was fixed above my door, and a golden shield was placed in the Curia Julia whose inscription testified that the senate and the Roman people gave me this in recognition of my valour, my clemency, my justice, and my piety. After that time I took precedence of all in rank, but of power I possessed no more than those who were my colleagues in any magistracy.

35 While I was administering my thirteenth consulship the senate and the equestrian order and the entire Roman people gave me the title of Father of my Country, and decreed that this title should be inscribed upon the vestibule of my house and in the senate-house and in the Forum Augustum beneath the quadriga erected in my honour by decree of the senate. At the time of writing this I was in my seventy-sixth year.

Augustus, *Res Gestae Divi Augusti*, trans. Frederick W. Shipley, Loeb Classical Library (London: Heinemann 1924).

The early emperors, the Julio-Claudians (Augustus, Tiberius, Caligula, Claudius, and Nero), implemented and developed this new imperial ideology, a rule of one absolute leader. As the remnant of the old republic and its families died out during the next few decades, Augustus' military dictatorship became more evident, especially seen in the emperors Caligula and Nero. But these emperors did provide an environment that allowed Christianity to foster, providing most notably peace, security, and a common unified political, social, and economic system. The infamous negative traditions relating to these emperors' private lives are only one side of the coin, for inscriptions, papyri, and archaeological material indicates that these early emperors actually had the best interests of their subjects in mind. They may have humiliated the Senate; however, they lavished the crowds with their gifts of cheap food, games, and public works, which reinforced the imperial ideas of peace, prosperity, and security.

TWO SAVIORS OF THE ROMAN WORLD

Augustus

Augustus, born Gaius Octavius (63 B.C.E.–14 C.E.), changed his name to Gaius Julius Caesar after Julius Caesar, who had adopted him in his will, was assassinated. However, Gaius Octavius is better known as Augustus, the name given to him in 27 B.C.E. by the Roman Senate. His mother, a niece of Julius Caesar, reared him after his father's death in 58 B.C.E., and Julius Caesar promoted him into public life, having Octavius accompany him to Spain in 45 B.C.E. and sending him to Apollonia in Epirus to complete his studies. Octavius, residing in Apollonia when Caesar was assassinated in 44 B.C.E., returned to Italy to claim his financial and political inheritance. He first battled Marc Antony, Julius' lieutenant, and then joined with him to combat Brutus and Cassius, Caesar's assassins. Octavius joined with Antony and Marcus Lepidus to create the Second Triumvirate, or rule of three. When Julius Caesar was declared a god in 42 B.C.E., Octavius became, in effect, the son of a god by virtue of his adoption, which gave him even more prestige. The triumvirate then defeated Brutus and Cassius at Philippi in Macedonia in 42 B.C.E. Octavius then married Scribonia, a relative of Sextus Pompey, who had rallied to Sicily senators opposed to Caesar and the subsequent triumvirate and who had begun to terrorize the grain ships heading to Rome. The marriage produced Octavius' only child, a daughter named Julia. Divorcing Scribonia in 40 B.C.E., Octavius married Livia Drusilla, who would remain his wife until his death.

Antony had married Octavius' sister Octavia, with whom he had two daughters, Antonia Major and Antonia Minor. However, in the East, Antony had become enamored of Cleopatra and had abandoned Octavia. Octavius' general Agrippa successfully defeated Sextus Pompey and removed Lepidus from power, leaving only Antony opposed to Octavius. In 31 B.C.E. Octavius and Antony met at Actium, and Octavius, with Agrippa leading his fleet, routed Antony, who now fled to Egypt with Cleopatra, where they both committed suicide the following year. Seizing Egypt and its resources, Octavius demobilized a sizable number of troops, giving them land and money as rewards. Upon returning to Italy, Octavius made a series of political settlements, which guaranteed his power. To ensure that his hold on power was supreme, Octavius held the power of a tribune, which gave him the right to veto any political and legal act and the power to introduce legislation; he held the power of a consul, without holding the office, which gave him the right to command the armies; and because of his personal wealth, he controlled the financial resources of the empire. With these powers Octavius held complete control of the state. In 27 B.C.E. he became known as Augustus, signifying his having saved the Roman state. The period after 27 B.C.E. saw the increase of the empire into the Balkans and Germany. His public life proved the message that he had brought security, prosperity, and peace to the Mediterranean world.

His family life, however, was not as successful. Augustus began the process of planning his succession after 27 B.C.E. He married his daughter Julia to his nephew Marcellus. After Marcellus' death in 23 B.C.E., Augustus gave her in marriage to his general Agrippa. Since Agrippa was only an *equites*, unsuitable in the Senate's eyes to succeed the emperor, Augustus adopted Agrippa and Julia's sons Gaius and Lucius as his own sons. Agrippa died in 12 B.C.E., and Augustus forced Julia to marry Tiberius, his stepson, who was made to divorce his wife Vispania. The marriage between Julia and Tiberius was not happy; soon Julia was accused of adultery and banished to a small island. Tiberius blamed by Augustus for not being a dutiful husband, now went into voluntary exile. With the deaths of Gaius and Lucius, however, Augustus recalled Tiberius, since he was the only individual of age and competence upon whom Augustus could rely. He then adopted Tiberius as his successor.

Augustus died in 14 C.E. He could be ruthless and manipulative and worked his subordinates hard. He himself worked relentlessly, but his accomplishments matched his efforts. He added more territory to the Roman state than anyone before or after, especially in Germany, on the Danube, and in the East. He reformed the financial and tax system, making it more equitable and fair, especially for the provinces. Augustus' long rule, over 40 years, produced a period of internal peace and prosperity, allowing him to be seen as Rome's savior.

Jesus

Just as Augustus was seen as savior of the Roman world, another individual, Jesus, born under the rule of Augustus, would be seen as the religious savior of the world. Joshua Bar Joseph, better known as Jesus, was born in Judea under the reign of Augustus and Herod the Great around 6–4 B.C.E. Surprisingly little is known of his life, with almost nothing about his preministry time. Two authors even present different stories concerning his birth. Matthew stated that Jesus was born under Herod (before 4 B.C.E.) and was taken by his family to Egypt before returning to their home town of Nazareth after Herod's death. Luke indicated that Jesus was born under the rule of Augustus when Quinirius was governor of Syria, suggesting a birth date after 6 C.E. The only other information concerning Jesus' life before his public ministry was a visit to Jerusalem he made when he was about 12. Many have argued that he began his ministry around the age of 30, but it could have been earlier or later. Luke also recorded that he began his ministry in the 15th year of Tiberius, or 29 C.E.

The major thrust of the Gospels, or stories about Jesus, is his public ministry. An attempt to discuss his ministry life is hampered again by a lack of credible information. For instance, there is no indication that Jesus married, although it is evident that he knew several women. Some believe that he had natural brothers, including James the Greater, but the evidence is mainly an interpretation of Greek words that may mean a natural brother, a cousin, a distant relative, or even a fellow villager. His ministry is said to have lasted 3 years, but again, an examination of the texts indicates a ministry covering 3 Passovers—a time as short as 2 years—while some scholars even argue that his ministry may have lasted only 18 months. Jesus was initially arrested and charged by the Jewish authorities with blasphemy, but since only the Roman authorities could execute a criminal, a further charge of treason was added. The Roman governor Pontius Pilate was not initially swayed by the Jewish authorities, but finally decided that Jesus was guilty of treason and ordered him executed. Jesus' followers believed that he rose from the dead after 36 hours and later ascended into heaven. It is this belief that started the new religion of Christianity.

The canon of the New Testament says very little about Jesus' personal life. Tradition holds that he did not marry. The last mention of his father Joseph is when Jesus is 12, when the New Testament relates the story of Jesus teaching the elders in the temple, and it may be assumed, since his mother is mentioned as being his companion during Jesus' ministry, that Joseph was already dead. Jesus learned his trade from Joseph, a carpenter. This occupation would have made him a skilled craftsman, or from the middle class. He had studied the rabbinic sources and preached in the synagogues, indicating a familiarity with Jewish teachings, and he is described, even by his enemies, as a learned man.

Jesus' ministry stressed an internal struggle between good and evil, practice versus form, and the simplicity of life. It is apparent that Jesus regarded wealth with disdain and urged his followers to be like little children in their faith. His compassion and integrity won over many converts and followers, which led to his rising popularity. It was in part this popularity that caused some Jewish leaders to become worried about the threat he represented to their authority, leading them to file charges against him.

These two individuals, Augustus and Jesus, living nearly contemporaneously with each other in the same political system, influenced the future of Christianity and the Roman world. Both individuals and their messages tied the two together. At the same time that Christianity developed, the Roman Empire underwent changes in political ideology. The first emperor, Augustus, proclaimed that he had restored the Roman Republic. This fictitious proclamation was meant to highlight Augustus' return to the old system of Roman self-governance. In reality, the empire Augustus created was a military dictatorship. Augustus, however, had ended a century of civil wars, which had depleted and demoralized the state. Ruling from 31 B.C.E. to 14 C.E., longer than any other emperor, Augustus brought stability, if not freedom, to the Mediterranean. In fact, most inhabitants of the Roman Empire never had political freedom; this was reserved for the small percentage of senators, who often abused their position for personal gain. Augustus provided security for the entire Roman world, which allowed individuals to pursue their profession, trade, studies, and pleasures without the threat of violence.

The ruthless emperor Nero, the last of the Julio-Claudians provoked the Jewish state into rebellion by planning to introduce a statue of himself into the Jewish temple, which the Jews regarded as idolatry; he also upset many of the senior military commanders by executing a popular general named Corbulo. General dissatisfaction grew as Nero's behavior made him increasingly unpopular. The empire was further jolted with the rebellion of Galba, governor of Spain, in 68, which forced Nero to flee Rome and ultimately to commit suicide.

Galba's ascension to the position of emperor showed three things: First, one no longer had to be a Julio-Claudian; second, one did not have to be in Rome; and third, the army had immense power and could make and, as seen shortly later, unmake emperors. After a quick succession of emperors (Galba, Otho, and Vitellius) each supported by the military, the army in Judea proclaimed its own commander, Vespasian, emperor. Fighting against the Jewish rebels, Vespasian was aided by allies in Rome, the Danube region, and Egypt. Taking control of Egypt and its vital grain trade, Vespasian caused panic in Rome with the threat of interruption of the grain. The Roman mob, relying on free and cheap grain, rioted and caused the crowd to turn away from Vitellius and toward Vespasian. Arriving in Rome with troops augmented by the army on the Danube, Vespasian established a new ruling family or dynasty, the Flavians. Vespasian (69–96) continued to place more power in the hands of the emperor at the expense of the Senate and Italian aristocrats. The Senate, which continued to have political rivals, became more interested in fostering its own financial gain. Senators began amassing land and economic power, since

Head of a Young Man. Saint Louis Art Museum.

property and money were potentially safer than political clout. Although some emperors confiscated individual senators' holdings, most were content to allow the senators to concentrate on economic gains, since such a pursuit distracted them from the emperor's solidification of political power. Vespasian's son Domitian concentrated even more political power in his own hands. Although viewed as a "bad" emperor, Domitian was not the same as Caligula or Nero, who were seen as both "bad" and "insane." Domitian was a brutal man who realized that with the backing of the army he firmly controlled Rome. His brutality however, caused his own family and household to fear for their lives, prompting his assassination in 96 c.e.

The new emperor, Nerva, chosen by the Senate, faced the serious prospect of a civil war, since the army had respected and liked Domitian. Facing the possibility of civil war and assassination, Nerva, who had no children, adopted the general Trajan, which pacified the military. After Nerva died,

Trajan became emperor without incident. Trajan began an active military agenda, first in Dacia (modern Romania) and then in Mesopotamia. Suffering a stroke, the childless emperor adopted his kinsman Hadrian as emperor. Hadrian, not a militaristic emperor, abandoned the imperialism of Trajan and concentrated on securing the empire's frontiers. His activities included the construction of Hadrian's Wall in Britain, the creation of the *limes,* or frontiers, in Germany, traveling throughout the empire (as witnessed by coins celebrating the provinces), and continuing to concentrate power in the emperor's hands. His adoption of Antoninus secured the smooth transition of power, even though the Senate disliked Hadrian. Antoninus, realizing that the Senate's dislike of Hadrian resulted from the emperor's continual travels and living outside of Rome in his palatial villa at Tivoli, remained in the city of Rome, rarely traveling. Under Antoninus the empire reached its zenith of prosperity and security. Antoninus gave his daughter Annia Galeria Faustina to Marcus Aurelius in marriage and then adopted Marcus Aurelius as his heir. This new emperor, a philosopher, would break the pattern of adoption by promoting his own son Commodus as emperor. Marcus Aurelius faced increased problems: frontier disruptions, the plague, and a decline in the population. His son Commodus, an erratic emperor who became more interested in public games, neglected the frontiers.

This period from Nerva to Commodus, an age when the best men suited to rule were adopted and elevated to power, became known as the Age of the Antonines. The Antonine period (96–180) witnessed even more power in the hands of the emperors, although the populace and especially the Senate had economic prosperity and stability. The emperors Nerva, Trajan, Hadrian, Antoninus, and Marcus Aurelius have traditionally been viewed as the acme of Roman civilization and peace; these individuals became known as the good emperors, in part due to adoption for their successors. The full extension of Roman peace (Pax Romana) was now realized. With the absence of civil wars, Rome expanding on some frontiers, the Senate pacified, and society accustomed to emperors ruling in place of elected officials, the full economic benefits of Augustus' empire began to accrue. Trade increased dramatically, bringing more economic prosperity to the empire and its inhabitants. New trade items from distant lands became more common. With economic prosperity society became more tolerant and willing to accept new ideas, including the ideas promoted by Christianity. Although there existed some persecutions, society was willing to accept new ideas, including this new religion. This period witnessed the full blessing of imperial peace as seen in Aristides' *Praise of Rome.*

LATER IMPERIAL HISTORY

Commodus, similar in temperament to Domitian, abandoned his father's campaign in the north and became known as a gladiator rather than a ruler. Nevertheless Commodus reigned for 12 years before being

Bust of an Unknown Man. Saint Louis Art Museum.

A PROVINCIAL'S VIEW OF ROME

The following excerpt from Aelius Aristides' 26th oration praises the city of Rome and its position in the empire. The passage reflected how a visitor viewed the city, especially the impact the size and complexity made on guests. This image must have been felt by many who arrived in the capital throughout its imperial history, and still effects modern visitors.

6. ... For beholding so many hills occupied by buildings, or on plains so many meadows completely urbanized, or so much land brought under the name of one city, who could survey her accurately? And from what point of observation?

7. Homer says of snow that as it falls, it covers "the crest of the range and the mountain peaks and the flowering fields and the rich acres of men, and," he says, "it is poured out over the white sea, the harbors and the

shores." So also of this city. Like the snow, she covers mountain peaks, she covers the land intervening, and she goes down to the sea, where the commerce of all mankind has its common exchange and all the produce of the earth has its common market. Wherever one may go in Rome, there is no vacancy to keep one from being, there also, in mid-city. 8. And indeed she is poured out, not just over the level ground, but in a manner with which the simile cannot begin to keep pace, she rises great distances into the air, so that her height is not to be compared to a covering of snow but rather to the peaks themselves. And as a man who far surpasses others in size and strength likes to show his strength by carrying others on his back, so this city, which is built over so much land, is not satisfied with her extent, but raising up on her shoulders others of equal size, one over the other, she carries them. It is from this that she gets her name, and strength (*rômê*) is the mark of all that is hers. Therefore, if one chose to unfold, as it were, and lay flat on the ground the cities which now she carries high in air, and place them side by side, all that part of Italy which intervenes would, I think, be filled and become one continuous city stretching to the Strait of Ontranto.

9. Though she is so vast as perhaps even now I have not sufficiently shown, but as the eye attests more clearly, it is not possible to say of her as of other cities, "There she stands." Again it has been said of the capital cities of the Athenians and the Lacedaemonians—and may no ill omen attend the comparison—that the first would in size appear twice as great as in its intrinsic power, the second far inferior in size to its intrinsic power. But of this city, great in every respect, no one could say that she has not created power in keeping with her magnitude. No, if one looks at the whole empire and reflects how small a fraction rules the whole world, he may be amazed at the city, but when he has beheld the city herself and the boundaries of the city, he can no longer be amazed that the entire civilized world is ruled by one so great.

10. Some chronicler, speaking of Asia, asserted that one man ruled as much land as the sun passed, and his statement was not true because he placed all Africa and Europe outside the limits where the sun rises in the East and sets in the West. It has now however turned out to be true. Your possession is equal to what the sun can pass, and the sun passes over your land. Neither the Chelidonean nor the Cyanean promontories limit your empire, nor does the distance from which a horseman can reach the sea in one day, nor do you reign within fixed boundaries, nor does another dictate to what point your control reaches; but the sea like a girdle lies extended, at once in the middle of the civilized world and of your hegemony.

11. Around it lie the great continents greatly sloping, ever offering to you in full measure something of their own. Whatever the season make grow and whatever countries and rivers and lakes and arts of Hellenes and non-Hellenes produce are brought from every land and sea, so that if one would look at all these things, he must needs behold them either by visiting the entire civilized world or by coming to this city. For whatever is

grown and made among each people cannot fail to be here at all times and in abundance. And here the merchant vessels come carrying these many products from all regions in every season and even at every equinox, so that the city appears a kind of common emporium of the world.

12. Cargoes from India and, if you will, even from Arabia the Blest one can see in such numbers as to surmise that in those lands the trees will have been stripped bare and that the inhabitants of these lands, if they need anything, must come here and beg for a share of their own. Again one can see Babylonian garments and ornaments from the barbarian country beyond arriving in greater quantity and with more ease than if shippers from Naxos or from Cythnos, bearing something from those islands, had but to enter the port of Athens. Your farms are Egypt, Sicily, and the civilized part of Africa.

13. Arrivals and departures by sea never cease, so that the wonder is, not that the harbor has insufficient space for merchant vessels, but that even the sea has enough, <if> it really does.

And just as Hesiod said about the ends of the Ocean, that there is a common channel where all waters have one source and destination, so there is a common channel to Rome and all meet here, trade, shipping, agriculture, metallurgy, all the arts and crafts that are or ever have been, all the things that are engendered or grow from the earth. And whatever one does not see here neither did nor does exist. And so it is not easy to decide which is greater, the superiority of this city in respect to the cities that now are or the superiority of this empire in respect to the empires that ever were.

Aelius Aristides, "The Ruling Power," trans. James H. Oliver, *Transactions of the American Philosophical Society* (Philadelphia: The American Philosophical Society, 1953), pp. 896–897.

assassinated in the palace by an athlete, Narcissus, in the service of Laetus, *Praetorian prefect*, and Marcia, the emperor's mistress. The civil war following Commodus' death ultimately saw the dominance of Septimius Severus and the establishment of the Severan dynasty. Septimius embarked on an ambitious attempt to expand the empire by attacking both the Parthian East and the Britons in the northwest. Septimius, who had no use for the Senate, advised his sons Caracalla and Geta to reward the military and ignore the Senate as a way of solidifying their power. Caracalla, after murdering his brother, continued to grasp more power. Caracalla is best remembered for extending Roman citizenship to all free-born citizens, which would include free-born Christians. Caracalla's own murder placed the weak and erratic Elagabalus on the throne. Elagabalus attempted to introduce a new religion based on the Syrian god of the sun in Rome, which produced a backlash, resulting in his assassination. His cousin Severus Alexander attempted to restore sanity to the empire but ultimately was murdered in a military coup in 235. This ended the Severan dynasty and plunged Rome into a 50-year decline where numerous emperors and pretenders fought for control, leaving the empire in near ruins. For the next 50 years the empire was attacked both from within and without.

The empire witnessed foreign invasions from the Germanic tribes in the north and the revived Persian Empire in the East. The Germanic tribes had begun to coalesce into larger entities, making them both more dangerous and political. With their gathering of power the tribes potentially posed an increased danger for the Romans; but with this coalescing into larger and more stable tribes, Rome could negotiate with them easier. The Rhine then became less of a threat and more settled, which in turn freed some of Rome's military resources for other areas. During the 3rd century the problems shifted from the Rhine to the Danube, where the Germanic tribes were not as well organized, forcing Rome to expend more energy. In the East the Persians overthrew the Parthians, becoming the new threat to Rome's Syrian frontier. During this unstable time some emperors sought to explain away the troubles visiting the empire by blaming insidious

Belt Section with Medallions of Constantius II and Faustina I. The Walters Art Museum, Baltimore.

groups who undermined the Roman state. The emperor Decius (250) blamed Christians and ordered a religious test, universal sacrifice, and punishment for any who refused to sacrifice. After the emperor's death in an attack by the Goths, the Roman authorities abandoned their campaign against the Christians until 257, when Valerian sought to resurrect the charges. His defeat, capture, and death by the Persians ended this persecution of the Christians. Valerian's son and successor Gallienus focused on external threats rather than the social and religious problems. With a series of military emperors, Aurelian, Probus, and Carus, culminating with Diocletian in 284, Rome survived the chaos but was a greatly altered state. Society was now modeled on a military camp.

CHRISTIANITY

It is within this history that a generation after the death of Jesus Christianity began to flourish. Between Jesus' death and the council of Antioch, in the mid-40s c.e., when Christianity was clearly identified as a distinct religion, the new religion was considered by its members to be the fulfillment of Judaism rather than a new religion. Since Jesus was a Jew and preached to the Jews, Christianity was closely linked to Judaism. Early Christian missionaries, being Jews, interacted at first with the Jewish communities in the empire's cities. This was only natural and gave them common ground with other groups in the provinces in which Jews were a minority. These missionaries would preach in the local *synagogues,* arguing that Jesus was the Jewish Messiah. Among the Jews, however, resistance to Jesus being the Messiah was often encountered, and early on, the Christians or the church gained converts from non-Jews. A question soon arose among the followers of Jesus: Were non-Jewish converts required to convert to Judaism first before they became Christians? This debate had specific ramifications, since for a Gentile male to convert to Judaism required the painful act of circumcision.

At the council of Antioch, Peter, the leader of this new group, reaffirmed the ideas presented earlier in Jerusalem that a new believer did not have to first become a Jew to become a follower of Jesus, or of Christianity. By declaring this precept, Peter now created a new religion, one based upon following Jesus rather than on Judaism. The new missionaries, especially Paul, reached out to Gentiles, non-Jews, bypassing the Jewish communities.

How did this new religion spread? What were the forces that helped or hurt the spread? These questions are crucial for understanding the growth of Christianity. Interestingly, the spatial diffusion of Christianity follows patterns similar to other phenomenon such as diseases or marketing, where geographers have developed theories concerning spatial diffusion. These theories in turn help explain the spread of Christianity. Through a series of questions that are generally based on the spread and adoption of a phenomenon, relating specifically to early Christianity, the characteristics of spatial diffusion and adoption of Christianity can be examined and explored.

The first series of questions relate to the origins of the phenomenon. Geographers first ask, is the phenomenon adoptable? This is important, since in order for a phenomenon to succeed, it must be adoptable, especially initially. As a phenomenon, religion can clearly be adopted, and the growth of Christianity attests to this situation, since it could be adopted readily. Second, did the phenomenon arise at one location? To understand a phenomenon's spatial geography, especially how and why it spread, the location of its origin is crucial. If something arose in more than one location it would be difficult to determine how the phenomenon spread. If, however, the phenomenon arose in one area its diffusion can be studied to help determine who, where, why, and how it was adopted. Since Christianity arose in Palestine, a well-defined location from which it spread, its diffusion and adoption can be ascertained. Third, what is the location and status of adoption by the population? Knowing the location of the adoption helps explain the paths of the phenomenon. The status of the adopters further helps explain those who might adopt the phenomenon. Status of adoption includes those who possess the characteristics (adopters), those who do not possess the characteristic but could (susceptible), and those who are not susceptible. For Christianity the population was easily defined as Christian and non-Christian, with the latter being further divided into those who might become Christian and those who would not.

The next group of questions relate to those who adopt the phenomenon. Fourth, what is the means of communication or contact between either individuals or groups of individuals? Knowing the means of communication will allow one to know how the phenomenon spread. Christianity in its early stages used the Jewish synagogues, allowing it access to individuals who were non-Christians but who might be susceptible to the new religion due to their common historical and religious bond. After this initial stage local churches and missionaries allowed for contact with both individuals and groups. Fifth, what is the spatial distribution of adopters and those susceptible? Also important and connected with this phenomenon is the likelihood of each person being contacted by the other, which is dependent upon the ease or difficulty in making contacts. In other words, how easy is it for those who are Christians to interact with those who might become Christian? This is crucial for the spread of Christianity, since if individuals are too far away, then spreading is too difficult. For Christianity this spatial distribution was dependent upon the routes of missionaries and their ability to attract converts. Associated with this ability was the level of resistance to the new religion associated with the sixth question: What is the level and variability of adopter enthusiasm, the persistence of adopters contacting others, and the resistance of the susceptible population? Since Christianity was not a legally recognized cult and was subject to persecution, this phenomenon varied from region to region and over time. Some regions produced a high level of adopter enthusiasm, while in other areas it was slow. In addition, some time periods and regions witnessed little resistance to Christianity, while in other periods and/or regions persecutions existed.

A series of questions can be asked pertaining to what factors help or impede the new phenomenon. Seventh, what were the minimum economic barriers for acquiring the characteristic? In other words, was the adoption of Christianity based upon economics, class, or payments? Since Christianity accepted all individuals who believed in its message regardless of social or economic position, Christianity could appeal to any class. This was different than some of the other religions where converts were screened based upon class or ability to pay. Eighth, what is the relative attractiveness and life expectancy of the characteristic? In other words, why would someone join, and would it be merely a fad? As a religion that offered hope and eternal salvation for all individuals, Christianity could be seen as attractive, with long-lasting possibilities. Ninth, what is the degree to which the phenomenon is appropriate to the susceptible population? A crucial element was a Christian's ability to live up to its faith ideologies. Christianity, through its missionaries and then leaders, clearly gave examples that made it appropriate to those who might convert.

Finally, a set of questions discuss how the phenomenon spread. Tenth, is the process better described by a deterministic or stochastic structure—how much uncertainty surrounds the decision? Since Christianity spread from Palestine it was heavily dependent upon the geographical terrain, competing religions, and strength of its missionaries. It was therefore stochastic, since the religion had to compete with and faced opposition from other religions. Eleventh, are there formal "propagators" or "promoters" of the phenomenon? In order to be promoted and to spread, Christianity had to have a clear idea of its promoters, those who had authority to discuss and transmit the religion in everyone's name. Christianity had a clear missionary system along with a hierarchy that clearly delineated the propagators or promoters (missionaries) from those susceptible (converts). Finally, are there competing phenomena? This in turn would guide the missionary activities, since some areas had competition from other religions or sects. Christianity had to compete not only with non-Christian groups, but with competing sects within Christianity.[1]

An examination of the early missionary sites that show acceptance to Christianity shows that they follow a traditional pattern of spreading to key cities and moving on to other key cities, before spreading to rural regions. This distribution pattern, hierarchical spatial distribution, produced a situation in which Christianity became a religion of urban dwellers of major cities, mainly situated on trade routes. Rural regions, hard to access even with the Roman road structure, would receive missionaries only later. This should not be surprising, since rural areas tend to be more conservative, avoiding change, while urban areas, with contact with other regions, are more likely to experiment and accept new ideas. During the next three centuries Christianity spread throughout the Roman world, following this model and pattern. Paul, however, did journey inland into rural regions, and he approached the cities there by a single route, the major and only real north-south inland route which tied the interior of Asia Minor together. This region had a large number of Jewish inhabitants who had lived in the area for nearly two centuries. In addition, Paul was urged to travel into the interior by Sergius Paulus, proconsul and governor of Cyprus, who recently converted to Christianity hailed from and may have had a number of family, friends, and clients still present and perhaps receptive to the new religion.

Christianity became one of many new religions competing with the traditional Greco-Roman Olympian beliefs, which had stressed public

Ostia: Roadway. James W. Ermatinger.

sacrifice for the public good and safety, with no concept of heaven or eternal salvation for most individuals. After death, individuals would travel to the underworld, Hades, without any prospect of leaving. This did not mean that Greco-Roman society viewed that individual as "evil," as modern society views hell; it merely meant that all individuals went to Hades. Only by being declared a god or goddess could one avoid eternity in Hades. During the period from 300 B.C.E. to 100 C.E. several new religions sprang up to supplement this old philosophy, specifically regarding personal salvation. These new religions, classified as mystery religions, promised their members eternal salvation. By believing in these new deities, an individual could avoid eternity in Hades. As time passed, and with the development of philosophy, individuals began to ask fundamental questions such the reason for their existence and what happened to them after they died. The traditional Olympian religion could not offer answers about life and death, but the mystery religions did.

Entrance into these mystery religions involved a complicated set of rituals and initiations, where the individual would be admitted into the mysteries or wonders of the new religion. To obtain admittance one had to pay an initiation fee; in some ways an individual's salvation became tied to their ability to achieve enlightenment, which was often based on one's finances. Although Christianity was not a mystery religion and did not require an entrance fee, it nevertheless had similarities with mystery religions, especially in offering eternal salvation. Christianity stressed that any individual could achieve salvation, allowing for all levels of society to be rewarded in the afterlife, even slaves. Like the mystery religions, Christianity offered a potentially better afterlife, making it appealing. This appeal accounts for some of the growth in the new religion as it spread throughout the empire. In addition Christianity presented a very clear approach: One can believe only in its one God. Unlike other religions, including mystery religions, which allowed for multiple beliefs and conflicting views, Christianity was simple. By accepting Christianity one did not have to worry about the other religions and gods. Christianity took the guess work out of believing.

Christianity spread first to the eastern Mediterranean, as seen through the Acts of the Apostles with Paul and his followers' missionary activities. Preaching in cities such as Antioch, Ephesus, Thessalonica, Corinth, Philipi, Athens, and numerous other sites, these missionaries helped Christianity take root. What is remarkable about Paul's missionary activities is that he traveled not only to large cities and coastal cities as would be expected, but he also journeyed into the interior of Asia Minor (modern Turkey). In two journeys he went through the heart of Asia Minor, making contact with Jewish elements and converting some to Christianity. These sites soon grew, and by the end of the 1st century Christianity was so firmly established in the interior of Asia Minor that Pliny, writing a letter to the emperor Trajan, would comment that the number of Christians was large in his province, a minor one at that. In the West both Peter and Paul traveled to Rome, and Paul supposedly went to Spain, although there is little to suggest that this is true. By the end of the 1st century, Christianity was established in numerous coastal towns along the Mediterranean, although it was strongest in the East. In the second century Christianity spread along traditional trade routes to North Africa, Gaul, the Black Sea, and Egypt, as well as inland. Christianity again followed typical patterns of spatial distribution; chief cities received missionaries first since there was more of a chance to convert individuals in a higher population density. From these chief cities Christianity spread to the 2nd-tier cities, often bypassing nearby smaller towns and villages. Afterwards there was a "backfilling" of these smaller cities and villages. The 2nd century witnesses the spreading to the 2nd-tier cities, while the 3rd century saw the backfilling. Throughout this process, however, the number of Christians remained a small percentage of the Empire's population, no more than 10 percent by 300 C.E.

Debate on the number of Christians has been extensive, but without census figures, it is nearly impossible to estimate their number. Even after Constantine legalized and favored Christianity in 312 C.E., the number of Christians in cities was not great, and even less in the countryside. In essence Christianity remained a small minority until continual imperial pressure, laws, and patronage supplanted paganism. Christianity was then tied closely to imperial history, especially in its success in increasing throughout the empire in the 4th century.

What allowed Christianity to take root and develop was the Roman peace (Pax Romana) that Augustus had established. Before Augustus, the continual internecine wars of the republic, the numerous client states, and corrupt Roman politicians and bureaucrats made life precarious for Christians. With Augustus' supremacy and the rise of the empire, civil wars rarely occurred, client kingdoms were absorbed, and corrupt politicians and bureaucrats were curtailed. The empire produced a system allowing for the relative easy exchange of goods, ideas, and people from Britain to Asia Minor. In many ways Christianity could not have thrived without the Roman Empire. Since Rome ruled and governed Palestine, Jesus' message was within the sphere of Roman life. If Jesus' ministry had occurred 50 or 100 years earlier it would have been an internal Jewish religious issue held within the boundaries of a Jewish kingdom. Given Christianity's inability to spread throughout Jewish Palestine before 300 C.E., even under Roman rule, it is doubtful if it could have spread at all if Palestine were not Roman.

The peace of Augustus also allowed for the existence of economic and social movements. The empire produced economic opportunities, and the general economic health of the empire increased. At the same time, society became more stabilized, and Roman citizenship expanded, becoming important and sought after since it afforded more rights and protection, as seen in the case of Paul. From Augustus to Marcus Aurelius, the Roman world enjoyed peace, prosperity, and stability, which allowed Christianity to grow.

With the death of Marcus Aurelius, Rome faced new problems, both internal and external. Internally, a series of weak rulers and civil wars nearly destroyed the empire. Emperors such as Commodus, Caracalla, and Elagabalus produced situations that encouraged distrust, fear, or apathy, leading to assassinations and civil war. Emperors such as Septimius Severus, Gallienus, and Aurelian came to the throne through civil war. In addition to these internal political problems society suffered from a loss of confidence in the economic system. With numerous usurpers, the local population was forced to supply their armies with more and more produce. With various groups vying for power, the local population was caught in the middle and suffered. If a city or village supported one group and that group lost, the city or village was often plundered or punished with increased taxes.

Externally, Rome faced a slew of foreign invaders from the northern Germanic tribes, the Eastern Persians, and nomadic desert tribes. These problems had an adverse effect on society. Fearful of both internal and external problems, many sought to blame some person or a group. Instead of being more tolerant, Roman society became more suspicious and intolerant. This intolerance gave rise to the *persecutions,* attacks made on Christians because of their religious beliefs and an attempt to eliminate the Christians.

This attempted elimination might be through converting Christians back to paganism, and if this was not successful, through death. The Roman persecutions of the Christians began as early as Nero, who blamed Christians for setting fire to the city of Rome, and continued through the 2nd century. These persecutions, however, were locally inspired and were not the result of a concerted plan by the central government. Such attacks tended to be against select elements of Christians by local communities. However, during Decius' reign (249–251) the persecutions were intended to be empire-wide, planned for a specific purpose: to purge society of unbelievers who caused the gods of Rome to punish the empire. The persecutions involved universal sacrifice: At a particular time inhabitants were to assemble in the towns and offer sacrifice. In return, the individuals received receipts indicating that they had sacrificed, with the date and place and the names of witnesses. Individuals without a certificate would be compelled to sacrifice, and if they refused they would be punished. This program did not end until the death of Decius.

The 3rd century saw a transformation of Roman society from the prosperous, peaceful, tolerant, and low-taxed environment of the 2nd century to a period of chaos, fear, and uncertainty. The century witnessed economic upheavals, increased taxation, and repressive regimes that attempted to control Roman society. Sections of the empire broke away in civil war, creating disruptions in trade and central authority. Finally, in the late 3rd century a series of soldier emperors—Aurelian, Probus, Carus, and Diocletian—successfully restored the Roman state, but it was altered. The state now looked rigid, like a military camp. Although the empire was restored it was no longer as tolerant or as prosperous as before. Cities struggled to maintain their infrastructure, while wealthy individuals sought the safety of flight into the rural settings away from taxation and forced public service.

During this period Christianity prospered, since it offered an explanation for these troubles. God was punishing Roman society for its wickedness. More importantly, Christianity argued that it did not matter what happened to individuals during their lifetime, since the true reward occurred in the afterlife. This philosophy allowed individuals to accept the disasters that befell society. Roman officials argued that Roman society suffered because of unbelievers, who must be punished. In 303 Diocletian inaugurated the last persecutions, which ultimately ended with the victory of Constantine, a Christian convert.

After the retirement of Diocletian in 305, a period of civil unrest among the co-emperors occurred. During this time the sons of two emperors, Maxentius in Rome (Maximian's son) and Constantine in Gaul (Constantius' son), declared themselves emperors. The two represented the religious climate of the early 4th century—Maxentius a follower of the pagan Sol Invictus (the unconquered sun) and Constantine a recent convert to Christ. Constantine's victory over Maxentius not only established the Constantinian house, which would rule over the empire for the next 50 years, but the triumph of Christianity over paganism. Constantine promoted Christianity, and within a century the new religion had achieved preeminence in Roman society, although in the city of Rome there remained a strong pagan influence among the aristocracy. Rome's imperial history after the victory of Constantine is tightly connected with Christianity. The once persecuted religion now became the official state religion. Individuals quickly learned that by converting to this new religion there were more opportunities for advancement and wealth.

NOTE

1. Questions from Richard Morrill, Gary L. Gaile, and Grant Ian Thrall, *Spatial Diffusion,* Scientific Geography Series, Vol. 10 (Newbury Park, CA: SAGE, 1988), pp. 21–22.

2

THE CITY OF ROME

In order to understand Christian daily life in Rome, it is crucial to examine the city of Rome and its environs. The major regions of Rome as set up by the first emperor Augustus provide the framework for this chapter. Augustus' 14 regions and their relative positions in relation to the Tiber River allow modern students to understand the layout of the city. In addition to the city's layout, this chapter places many of the pagan and Christian buildings in each region. Finally, the chapter ends with a description of the Christian organization together with a description of the imperial offices that oversaw the city.

The modern city encompassing ancient Rome is surprisingly small compared to London, Paris, or New York, about 3–5 km by 3–5 km. In fact one can walk from the top of the Janiculum Hill on the southwest across the Tiber to the Villa Borghese in the northeast in about two hours. A visitor in 300 C.E. would have passed the docks on the Tiber, crossed one of the bridges, seen the theatre of Marcellus or the theatre of Balbus, passed through the imperial *fora,* seeing numerous temples and the Coliseum, and gone on to the baths of Diocletian and the Praetorian camp at the city's edge. The city of Rome had grown tremendously throughout the last century of the republic and the first century of the empire. The vivid description of the city life of the poor by Juvenal attests to the tremendous problems facing this immense city.

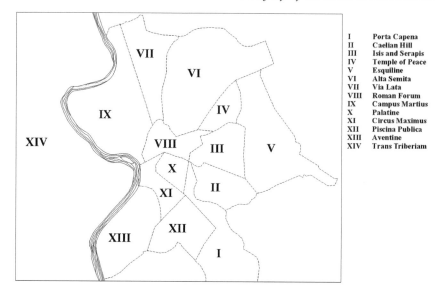

I	Porta Capena
II	Caelian Hill
III	Isis and Serapis
IV	Temple of Peace
V	Esquiline
VI	Alta Semita
VII	Via Lata
VIII	Roman Forum
IX	Campus Martius
X	Palatine
XI	Circus Maximus
XII	Piscina Publica
XIII	Aventine
XIV	Trans Triberiam

The Fourteen Regions of Augustus' Rome. Courtesy of Larry Easley.

Descriptions concerning the city of Rome come from a variety of literary sources. The best description depicting the cramped quarters and the hard life of Rome's inhabitants comes from Juvenal. But before Juvenal wrote, two professional administrators had used their training to help define Rome's infrastructure, Vitruvius and Frontinus. Both men left works that dealt with the architecture of the city: Vitruvius, a general history of architecture, and Frontinus, a work on aqueducts.

Vitruvius (1st century B.C.E.)

Marcus Vitruvius Pollio (ca. 80 B.C.E.- ?) a Roman writer, architect, and engineer, was active in the last part of the 1st century B.C.E. A Roman citizen from Campania, he may have served under Julius Caesar in Spain, Africa, and Gaul. He was probably an army engineer constructing siege weapons. After Caesar's death Vitruvius worked on the water supply of Rome under Octavian (Augustus). His work on the *Ten Books of Architecture*, dedicated to Augustus, is the only work on architecture from classical antiquity and was meant to be a handbook for Roman architects. In his work he mentioned that he worked on the basilica at Fanum Fortunae in the modern town of Fano, but the basilica has disappeared. Vitruvius compiled much of his information from other works and existing architectural and engineering practices and his work covered most aspects of architecture. Although Roman architecture was based on the Greek concept, Vitruvius sought to show how architecture could be used for the new Roman order. His book explored such ideas as city planning, building materials, temples and the use of the Greek orders, public and private buildings, decoration, timepieces, and building engines. Vitruvius influences the Renaissance architects Alberti, da Vinci, and Michelangelo. His age and year of death are unknown.

Frontinus (late 1st century C.E.)

Sextus Julius Frontinus, born in Gallia Narbonensis, began his career in the military, serving first as a cavalry officer. A senator, he became praetor in 70 C.E. and consul in 73 C.E. His military experience and his support for the emperor Vespasian propelled him into the governorship of the frontier province of Britain in 74 C.E., where he defeated the Silures and other Welsh tribes, constructing a legionary camp at Caerleon with smaller auxiliary forts throughout the region. He completed his service in Britain in 77 C.E.

After his successes in Britain, Frontinus most likely served Vespasian's son and emperor, Domitian, in the early 80s in his war against the Chatti in Germany. His success in these endeavors led to his appointment in 85 C.E. by Domitian as proconsul of Asia, a prestigious post. For the next decade Frontinus is absent in any records and most likely spent his time writing his military strategy works and his land-surveying book. He was also a member of the College of Augurs, which may date from this period.

With the assassination of Domitian, Frontinus once again comes into the public life under the emperor Nerva. He was elected to a board to examine ways to reduce public expenses. This board most likely gave him access to the emperor, and in 97 he was made *curator aquarum,* the individual in charge of the aqueducts. This job would lead to his most famous work on the water supply of Rome, a history and description of the laws and architecture of Rome's aqueducts. His appointment probably arose from his experience as a land surveyor, his distinguished record in the military, and as an author on military strategy.

He was consul for the second time in 98 C.E. and consul for the third time in 100, both under the new emperor Trajan. He died in 104. An influential senator, he served the Flavians (Vespasian, Titus, and Domitian) and the early Antonines (Nerva and Trajan), and he may have even served Nero.

Juvenal (2nd century C.E.)

Decimus Junius Juvenalis, a satirist from the city of Aquinum, is best known for his picture of Rome. Although his work indicates a retelling of individuals found in Tacitus and Martial, he nevertheless vividly described Rome in 9 of his 15 surviving poems. His life for the most part is obscure, and the few details that can be gleamed from his writings and other authors indicate that he viewed the corruption of the city with distaste. He had knowledge of Egypt, but it is impossible to determine when and if he visited the province. His sixth satire was an attack on women, but again, it is unclear if he viewed all women negatively, or if this was merely an example of stock attacks against notorious women. He wrote most of his works between 110 and 130 C.E.

LAYOUT OF ROME

The layout of the ancient city skirted the Tiber River, which ran roughly north to south as it flowed towards the sea, emptying at Rome's port Ostia, about 15 miles away. Traveling downstream, the right bank contains the Vatican and Janiculum Hills and the Trans Tiberim region, or modern Trastevere, Augustus' 14th region. Located here were Hadrian's mausoleum, the modern Castel San Angelo, and numerous tenements, more than in any other region.

The left or eastern bank of the Tiber had been early Rome's boundary, and the area contained Augustus' other 13 districts or region. Augustus' 14 districts became the wards for city planning and safety during the empire. Sailing downstream one would see on the left, in the north, Augustus' mausoleum, Domitian's stadium, and the Pantheon located in the Campus Martius. Further downstream lay the portico of Octavia with the Theatre of Marcellus and the still extant round temple to Hercules. Moving further downstream, after passing the Capitoline Hill, Palatine Hill, and the Circus Maximus one sees the Aventine Hill rising sharply toward the sky.

While the city and the river are closely interconnected, Rome is always known for its hills, the fabled seven, although there are actually more. These hills ring the city and provided a natural barrier against invasion and other dangers. During the early republic the Capitoline, Palatine, and Aventine hills provide protection in central Rome. But the hills also promoted danger, especially disease, since water flowed into the valleys where it was often trapped in marshes, promoting malaria, a disease marked by recurring chills and fevers. Rome did not rid itself of this disease carried by mosquitoes living in swamps until the modern age.

By the time of Augustus the marshes had been drained, and the hills became centers of religion, politics, and power. The valleys, home to most of the urban poor, were more crowded and full of noise and filth, while wealthy individuals built their houses on the hills with better living conditions.

The Christian city of Rome in the 4th century was a sight to behold, having reached its architectural zenith. Christianity and paganism existed side by side, not always harmoniously, but at least tolerating each other. This spectacle may be seen in the work of Ammianus Marcellinus given in the accompanying Point in Time.

Although only a cursory description of the Christian city can be made, its size and complexities can be noted so that one can understand how everyday Christians might have lived. The 14 regions were each divided into associated districts or wards, *vici,* which contained local shrines. Each

---

EMPEROR CONSTANTIUS II VISIT TO ROME, 357 C.E.

13. As he went on, having entered Rome, that home of sovereignty and of all virtues, when he arrived at the rostra, he gazed with amazed awe on the Forum, the renowned monument of ancient power; and, being bewildered with the number of wonders on every side to which he turned his eyes, having addressed the nobles in the senate-house, and harangued the populace from the tribune, he retired, with the good-will of all, into his palace, where he enjoyed the luxury he had wished for. And often, when celebrating the equestrian games, was he delighted with the talkativeness of the common people, who were neither proud, nor, on the other hand, inclined to become rebellious from too much liberty, while he himself also reverently observed a proper moderation.

14. For he did not, as was usually done in other cities, allow the length of the gladiatorial contests to depend on his caprice; but left it to be decide by various occurrences. Then, traversing the summits of the seven hills, and the different quarters of the city, whether placed on the slopes of the hills or on the level ground, and visiting, too, the suburban divisions, he was so delighted that whatever he saw first he thought the most excellent of all. Admiring the temple of the Tarpeian Jupiter, which is as much superior to other temples as divine things are superior to those of men; and the baths of the size of provinces; and the vast mass of the amphitheatre, so solidly erected of Tibertine stone, to the top of which human vision can scarcely reach; and the Pantheon with its vast extent, its imposing height, and the solid magnificence of its arches, and the lofty niches rising one above another like stairs, adorned with the images of former emperors; and the temple of the city, and the forum of peace, and the theatre of Pompey, and the odeum, and the racecourse, and the other ornaments of the Eternal City.

15. But when he came to the forum of Trajan, the most exquisite structure, in my opinion, under the canopy of heaven, and admired even by the deities themselves, he stood transfixed with wonder, casting his mind over the gigantic proportions of the place, beyond the power of mortal to describe, and beyond the reasonable desire of mortals to rival. Therefore giving up all hopes of attempting anything of this kind, he contented himself with saying that he should wish to imitate, and could imitate the horse of Trajan, which stands by itself in the middle of the hall, bearing the emperor himself on his back.

Ammianus Marcellinus, *The Roman History of Ammianus Marcellinus* 16.10.13–15, trans. C. D. Yonge (London: George Bell and Sons, 1894), pp. 101–102.

vici had two superintendents, freedmen elected by the ward's inhabitants, who oversaw 48 quartermasters who helped provide supplies for the vici. These superintendents and quartermasters assured that their local regions remained safe and were supplied with grain and water.

By Augustus' time and throughout the imperial period, Rome was well supplied with water. In fact, not until the 20th century would Rome again have the quantity and quality of water ancient Rome had. Rome received its water from a variety of sources: rain water, wells, and aqueducts. Rain water was irregular and insufficient to supply imperial Rome's constant water needs. Nevertheless, the occasional rains recharged some of the cisterns, garden basins, and *impluvium* in private homes as well as providing the occasional water to clean the city streets. These downpours could create enough force to drive refuse into the sewers and out into the Tiber.

Wells provided some of Rome's water needs, but again were unable to support the growing needs of an increased capital's population. During the early republic, rainwater filling local cisterns and wells probably was sufficient, but by 350 B.C.E. Rome needed more fresh water. Roman engi-

Monumental Gate with Aqueduct. James W. Ermatinger.

neers constructed aqueducts, which brought water into Rome due to the increased demand for water.

By Augustus' death there existed seven major aqueducts. The oldest, Appia (312 B.C.E.) supplied the city with 73,999 cubic meters per day and flowed from Porta Maggiore to Porta Capena via the Caelian Hill (Caelian Region), then to the cattle market by the Tiber via the Aventine Hill (Region XIII). The Old Anio (272 B.C.E.) from the Anio River entered Rome at the Porta Maggiore and skirted the Esquiline Region (III) to the Viminal (Region IV), delivering 176,000 cubic meters of water per day. This aqueduct supplied the region known as the *subura*, with its heavy concentration of population, with its water. When Rome increased its population during its rise to empire (200–133 B.C.E.) two more aqueducts were constructed: the Marcia (144 B.C.E.), also running from the Porta Maggiore to the Esquiline and Viminal, with a branch that ran to the Capitoline, carrying 187,000 cubic meters of water per day, and the Tepula (126 B.C.E.) carrying only 17,800 cubic meters, which supplied the subura. In 33 B.C.E. the aqueduct Julia, carrying 48,000 cubic meters, joined with the Tepula and likewise supplied the subura with its water. The emperor Augustus constructed two more aqueducts: the Virgo (19 B.C.E.), which carried 100,000 cubic meters to the Campus Martius, and the Alsietina or Augusta (2 B.C.E.), carrying only 16,000 cubic meters, which served the naumachia, a large manmade lake for sea battles, across the Tiber in the 14th region.

The emperor Claudius built the Claudia aqueduct (38–52 C.E.) where its arches can still be seen at the Porta Maggiore, with 184,000 cubic meters coming in and going to the Caelian Hill. Claudius also built the New Anio, paralleling the Old Anio, which supplied water to the northeast, delivering 190,000 cubic meters of water per day. To supply water for the mills on the Janiculum and the Trans Tiberim (Region XIV), the emperor Trajan constructed the aqueduct Traiana (109 C.E.). To supply his baths, Caracalla constructed the Antoniana in 210 C.E., actually a branch of the Marcia that took water away from its previous distribution. Finally, Severus Alexander (225 C.E.) constructed the Alexandrina to supply water for the reconstructed baths of Nero in the Campus Martius.

As discussed, Rome received over one million cubic meters of water everyday by the early 3rd century. Water served nearly every region of the city, since small pipes branched off from the aqueducts supplying mansions, local fountains, and pools *(lacus)* in each region. These fountains and pools allowed the local inhabitants without private indoor plumbing to receive fresh water daily. These fountains and pools also allowed Rome's fire department, the *vigiles,* to fight fires in the city.

The 14 regions of Rome, moving from the north to the south along the river and inland from west to east, were the Campus Martius (IX), Via Lata (VII), Temple of Peace (IV), and Alta Semita (VI) in the north. In the center the Circus Maximus (XI) lay along the river south of the Campus Martius, while the Forum Romanorum (VIII) and Palatinus (X) lay in the center south of the Temple of Peace; to the east lay the Esquiline (V), south of the Alta Semita, with the region Isis and Serapis (III) just south of the Esquiline. Moving downstream past the Circus Maximus stood the Aventine (XIII) region alongside the river, with the Piscina Publica (XII) inland and central south of the Palatine, and the Caelian Hill (II) and Porta Capena(I) further east south of Isis and Serapis. Therefore, districts I, II, III, V, VI, VII, IX, and XIV (on the opposite bank), were all outside the old republican Severan wall of the fourth century B.C.E., while the Aurelian wall of 270 C.E. enclosed all 14 districts. One could cross the river from region XIV on the right bank to the city proper by several bridges. These regions each had their own flavor, which added to Rome's distinction and influenced the inhabitant's lives.

To understand the city and the daily life of its Christian inhabitants, an examination of the 14 regions is needed. The city could have grown either across the river, up the Janiculum, or north along the river into the Campus Martius, which often flooded. Region IX, the Campus Martius, developed during the late republic and early empire. The largest region on the left bank, the Campus Martius was also the newest. This region witnessed numerous construction projects, most notably the theatres of Pompey and Balbus, the baths of Agrippa and Nero, the mausoleum of Augustus, the stadium of Domitian, and Hadrian's Pantheon. Interspersed were numerous temples, shrines, baths, and living quarters.

Rome: Theatre of Marcellus. James W. Ermatinger.

To the east of the Campus Marius lay region VII, the Via Lata or the Broad Street, containing numerous parks, some temples, and villas for wealthy Romans. One monument, the Portico of Vispania, named for Agrippa's family, supposedly contained a map of the Roman world. In this region there was also the pig market, since pork was a major staple in Rome. Pigs were herded through the streets and into the city where they were butchered. On the far eastern side, Region VI, the Alta Semita, meaning High Land, ran on top of the Quirinal Hill. This area had the Porta Collina, with the Praetorian Guard's camp built under the emperor Tiberius (14–36 C.E.). Standing on the Quirinal, one would have seen the great Gardens of Sallust. Perhaps the most imposing structure in this region was the Baths of Diocletian, which lay south of the gardens and covered 28 1/2 acres of land. This immense structure, like the gardens, could be enjoyed by all classes. The baths allowed everyone welcome relief from Rome's heat and dirt.

The next region south along the Tiber was the Circus Maximus (XI), with docks serving Rome. Goods from all over the empire, carried on and off by slaves and day laborers, were transported to warehouses and shops and then resold to the local merchants who set up shops here or carried them through the city to other regions. But what dominated this region was the great racetrack, the Circus Maximus, where not only chariot and horse races took place, but also gladiatorial combats and hunts. The great racetrack stood between the Palatine Hill on the north or left side, walking from the Tiber, and the Aventine Hill on the right or south. A wall with concrete and stones on the lower levels and wood on the top over 90 feet high and nearly 100 feet wide was built to house the seating. The seating capacity approached 250,000 spectators. The race course was over 2,000 feet (nearly .4 mile) long and almost 400 feet (.075 miles) wide. In the middle was the *spina,* or dividing wall, which had an Egyptian obelisk, now in the Piazza del Populi. Here the four great teams competed for their fans, who screamed, bet, and enjoyed themselves. The Circus allowed most Romans the opportunity to relieve themselves of the daily tedium of life, as sports and television do for contemporary people. Inland from the Circus Maximus and slightly north stood Region VIII, the Roman Forum, and Region X, the Palatine, the historical and political center of Rome.

The Roman Forum, originally a swamp, became the original political, religious, commercial, and social center of Ancient Rome, with the Palatine Hill on the south and the Capitoline Hill on the west. Over time the Romans under the monarchy drained the valley, making it the meeting place in the early republic. The Arch of Titus provided a dramatic entry into the Forum from the Sacred Way at the northeast, and moving to the southeast, then turning left to the southwest corner before turning left again and running back to the northwest near the entrance were the Temple of Romulus, the Temple of Antoninus and Faustinus, the Basilica Julia, and the Curia, or Senate House, before going through the Arch of Septimius Severus on the far end of the Forum. From the Arch of Septimius Severus in the south- east corner to the forum's southwest corner lay the Temple of Saturn and Temple of Vespasian on the right or the outer side and the rostra on the left or inner. Overlooking these structures on the Capitoline were the great temple of Capitoline Jupiter, Juno, and Minerva on the eastern side and the Tarpeian Rock on the western. Built into the hill beneath the Temple of Capitoline Jupiter was the Tablinum, or record hall. In the Forum moving from the southwest corner to the northwest corner one would pass the Basilica Aemilia, the Temple of Castor, and the Vestal Virgin complex of the Temple and House, to name just a few sites. These sites promoted the traditional daily religious and political life of the ancient Romans.

The Forum was the political heart of Rome. The Senate House allowed the collective wisdom of Rome during the republic to debate political policies, which led to the establishment of the empire. The *rostra,* or speak- ing platform, witnessed great politicians such as Cicero, Cato, Caesar, and Augustus convincing the people of their policies. The basilicas served a dual function, as court houses and business centers, for in and around these great buildings Roman commercial life and social interactions flourished. The Forum, however, soon became too crowed and congested for all these transactions. To help alleviate this overcrowding, Julius Caesar built a new forum next to the Roman Forum and named it the Forum of Caesar. Augustus, Vespasian, Domitian, and ultimately Trajan followed by building imperial fora. These fora not only provided space but allowed the region to become an open urban park. They also separated the political-commercial sectors of the city from the residential environment. These fora, to the north of the Roman Forum, were finally enclosed late in antiquity by the Basilica of Maxentius (312 C.E.), an immense structure that completed the old Roman Forum. Vespasian's Temple of Peace, one of the imperial fora, gave the name to the region encompassing the imperial fora.

The Palatine hill lay to the south of the Roman Forum between the Roman Forum and the Circus Maximus. The Palatine during the republic housed both the rich and poor in a conglomeration of houses. Under the empire successive rulers beginning with Augustus and ending with Domitian erected palatial houses or palaces. By the end of the 1st century C.E. the entire hill overlooking the Roman Forum to the north and the Circus Maximus to the south and joined by a bridge to the Capitoline had become the emperor's private estate. To provide water for the emperor's palace the Aqua Claudia was extended, the remains of which can still be seen. Even the large hall built by Domitian dwarfed the Curia or Senate House, and the emperors had a private viewing box for the circus extended from the palace. Legend has it that Nero dined while the crowd eagerly waited for the start of the race, which could only begin with the emperor present, and, when the crowd grew restless he dropped his napkin *(mappa)* out of a window to signal the start of the race. Ever since then, the dropping of the napkin or waving the flag has signaled the start of the race; even modern NASCAR races begin with this ancient Roman custom.

To the east of the Roman Forum and the Palatine lay region III—Isis and Serapis—and region II, the Caelian Hill. Region III included the Coliseum and Oppian hill. The region received its name from two temples honoring the two Egyptian gods Isis and Serapis, both of whom competed with Christianity and offered an alternative. The region had the Portico of Livia (wife of the emperor Augustus), which was over 300 feet long and 225 feet wide. The portico, one of many in Rome, provided shops and covered ways so consumers could purchase their goods without the elements distracting them. Nearby was the area that provided an interesting example of public versus private space, the estate of the emperor Nero.

The great fire of 64 C.E. destroyed most of this region. Nero decided to rebuild the area; however, instead of giving it back to the people, he decided to construct private buildings for himself on the ruins. On the site of the fire Nero also laid out extravagant private gardens, a lake with a colossal statue of himself, and a new palace, the Domus Aureus, or Golden House. The people of Rome, not pleased with this decision, spread rumors that Nero had actually set the fire so he could appropriate the land (see below). After Nero's death, the Flavians—Vespasian and his sons Titus and Domitian—converted Nero's private estate into a series of public sites. The private gardens, which formerly only the emperor could use, became the large public gardens of Vespasian's Temple of

Peace, located in Region IV (see above). The private lake was drained and replaced by the public Flavian Amphitheater—better known by the colossal statue of Nero, now transformed into the god Helios—and later named the Coliseum. And Nero's private house, the Domus Aureus, was filled in and covered with dirt to become the foundations for the baths of Titus and later the Baths of Trajan. Neither bath survived, but through a stroke of luck, Nero's Golden House did and can now be viewed today, albeit underground. This region then was quickly transformed in a short period of 40 years, from Nero through the Flavians, from a public tenement district, to a private imperial estate, to a public entertainment district.

To the west of the Coliseum at the edge of the Roman Forum stood the Temple of Venus and Rome, an immense structure where two cellae holding the cult statues stood back to back. Just outside the Coliseum were the *meta sudans,* or sweating fountain, and the arch of Constantine, commemorating the Christian emperor's victory over Maxentius.

To the north of the Coliseum lay subura, where the poor lived, in districts IV and VI. Businesses in the subura included wool makers, glassmakers, bronze smiths, pottery workshops, and clothing factories. These shops were small family operations, usually run out of the first floor of *insulae,* apartment houses. Here all sorts of people worked and eked out a living. Nearby were the taverns, which sold drinks, quick food, and sexual pleasures. The city was constantly at odds with legal and illegal

Rome: Arch of Constantine. James W. Ermatinger.

activities, and subura was the center. But the area was also crucial, since it provided Rome with the necessary labor force and consumers, important components in any city and economy.

To the south of the Coliseum lay Region II, the Caelian Hill, with the immense Temple of the Deified Claudius (Caligula's successor). This district had headquarters for the *frumentarii,* or supply soldiers of wheat, who later became the dreaded secret police. The most important building, however, was the great market built by Nero. With its immense dome, the market became one of the most famous bazaars of ancient Rome, and this entire region became one of Rome's most important commercial centers. Also in Region II was the Lateran district, which in later times would house the great basilica known as St. John Lateran.

The final third of Rome, further south on the left bank of the Tiber, contained regions XIII (Aventine), XII (Piscina Publica), and I (Porta Capena). The Aventine, named for the Aventine Hill, was the chief river port of Rome, since the river traffic coming up the Tiber from Ostia would unload its wares there. Pulled with ropes by donkeys and oxen, the small river barges would rest on either bank where their cargo was unloaded. The shore line, dotted with numerous docks and granaries, offices, and warehouses, became the great granary for Rome and the commercial and government distribution source. Here grain, wine, olives, and olive oil contained in amphorae were unloaded. Many of the remnants of these amphorae were piled high in a systematic rubbish heap, the Mons Testaceus, which ultimately reached a height of nearly 200 feet and an area of about one-third of a mile in diameter. Although the state funded grain importation, there was still much profit in its import with private sup-plementary shipping. The amphorae were unloaded where the customs officer, a government accountant, removed the two stamped handles of each amphora, one handle staying at the office where they were counted and divided into separate piles for each shipper, the other handle acting as a receipt for buyer. The goods were then taxed. For large shipments the bullion remained in Rome and was merely credited from one account to another, much the way modern commodity brokers work. The Aventine Hill had extensive mansions with an intermixing of housing for the poor. On the top of the Aventine stands the 4th century basilica Santa Sabina. At the bottom of the Aventine at the river side was the great Porticus Aemila, the immense commercial center, 1,500 feet by 200 feet and two stories high, which provided an immense number of stores.

To the east of the Aventine was Region XII, the public pool. The area was poorer than most, but it held many of the city's small workshops. At the eastern edge of the region were the baths of Caracalla, built about 215 C.E.

Finally, at the far end was Region I, the Capena Gate district, which opened onto the old Appian Way, Rome's most famous highway. The Appian Way was lined with ancient tombs, including the catacombs, and with numerous taverns, brothels, and hotels to accommodate travelers.

As it enters the city the road crossed the Almo stream, sacred to Cybele. Outside the Porta Capena, the gate into the old city, stood the temple to Honor and Virtue, restored at the end of the Second Punic War (204 B.C.E.). The district provided a link to the land-based economy, the Appian Way and the interior farms, with the sea-based economy from the Tiber. Not far from the Tiber, goods were brought overland into Region I from the areas neighboring Rome and then through the city via Regions XII and XIII to the Tiber. From there the barges were reloaded and floated with the current downstream to Ostia and to the rest of Mediterranean.

The final district, Region XIV, the Trans Tiberim on the left side of the Tiber, had the mausoleum of Hadrian, now Castel San Angelo, which dominated the river view. Also nearby was the Vatican Hill and the region where Peter supposedly met his death. This area also had the naumachia. Further south was Trans Tiberim—modern Trastevere—with the Janiculum Hill overlooking the city. The area was lined with store-rooms and granaries as well as apartment houses, mainly occupied by foreigners. On the Janiculum were located numerous mills supplied with water from the Aqua Trajani, which powered the water wheels to grind the wheat. Also along the river to the south were the gardens of Julius Caesar. This district was where many of the working poor lived, including a large number of Jews and presumably early Christians.

REGIONARY CATALOGUE OF ROME

In the 4th century a list was drawn up detailing the various regions of the city and their monuments. A portion, with the summary appendices, is given below.

CATALOGUE OF THE 14 REGIONS OF THE CITY WITH OFFICIAL STATISTICS

Region 1 Capena Gate
Contains: Temple of Honor and Virtue; (vale of) the Muses; Fountain of Prometheus; Bath (private) of Torquatus; Baths of Severus and Commodus; Square (area) of Apollo and Sples; Street of Glassmakers; Square of Peasants' cloth market; Post Station (open area) of Caesar; Baths of Abascantus and Mamertinus; Carriage Square; Temple of Mars; Almo Stream; Arch of Divine Verus and Trajan and Drusus; 10 quarters; 10 shrines; 48 quarter managers; 2 superintendents; 3250 apartments (insula); 120 Mansions; 16 public granaries; 86 baths (private); 81 fountains; 20 bakeries; contains 12,211 1/2 feet.

Region II Caelian Hill
Contains: (Temple of) Claudius; Great Market; Brothel zone office; Grotto (Atrium) of Cyclopes; Station of 5th squad of police and firemen (Vigiles);

Head of Africa School; Street of Sacred Tree; Provincial Soldier Camp; House of Philip; House of Victiliana; Morning Gladiatorial school and Dacian [school]; Morgue (stripping of armor); Weapons polisher; Golden Dining Hall (Gleaming Gold); 7 quarters; 7 shrines; 48 quarter managers; 2 superintendents; 3600 apartments (insula); 127 Mansions; 27 public granaries; 85 baths (private); 65 fountains; 15 bakeries; contains 12,200 feet.

First Appendix

Libraries 28; Obelisks 5: 1, 2 in circus maximus, 2 lesser has 87 1/2 feet, major has 122 1/2 feet. In Vatican one, 75 feet high, In Campus Martius one, 72 1/2 feet high, 5, 6, In Mausoleum of Augustus 2 each 42 1/2 feet high; Bridges 8: Aelius, Aemilius, Aurelius, Mulvius, Sublicius, Fabricius, Cestius and Probi.

Second Appendix
Horum Breviarum

2 Capitolia; 2 Circus; 2 Amphitheaters; 2 colossus; 2 marble columns; 2 Markets; 3 Theaters; 4 Schools (for Gladiators); 5 naumachia; 15 Fountains (Nymphaean); 22 great equestrian (statues); 80 gold gods (statues); 74 ivory (statues); 36 marble arches; 37 gates; 423 quarters; 423 shrines; 672 quarter managers; 29 superintendents; apartments for the total city 46,602; mansions 1790; 290 public granaries; 856 baths; Putea Fountains 1352; 254 bakeries; 46 brothels; public latrines quod est sicessos 144; Praetorian cohorts 10; urban cohorts 4; watchmen 7; of whom are guards 14; vexilla common 2; camp of equitum singularium II; camp of Peregrina; of Ravennatium; of litter-bearers; Silicariorum (funeral bearers); Misenatium; Letter-carriers; Assistants of sacrifices; Tables of oil for the whole City 2300.

CHRISTIAN ORGANIZATION

The Christian hierarchy used the city's division for its own purposes. Around 250 c.e. the church had divided the city into 7 ecclesiastical regions, which probably corresponded to combining two of Augustus' 14 regional districts into one, similar to Augustus' disposition of the vigiles. In fact the church might have used Augustus' own system of vigiles for their ecclesiastical regions. In each district a deacon took charge, looking after the poor and collecting church revenues. Also connected with this arrangement were the cemeteries, at least one per region.

The Christian community's size in Rome and other cities is difficult to determine precisely; however, there are some pieces of information that help. For the year 250, 25 *tituli*, or parish churches, existed in the 7 ecclesiastical regions. Eusebius reported that there were 46 priests, 7 deacons, 7 subdeacons, 42 acolytes, 52 exorcists, lectors, and porters with the offertory supporting 1,500 widows, sick, and poor. For Antioch Syria in 350 c.e. John Chrysostom tells of 100,000 Christians, with 3,000 being poor. If the proportion of total Christians to poor was the same for Rome, there would have been about 50,000 Christians in Rome in 250, or between 5 and 10 percent of the population, a reasonable figure. A catalogue, similar to the 4th-century regionary catalogues of Rome's buildings, is given in the Chronicle of Zachariah of Mitylene from the 6th century, with some added Christian attributes.

EMPEROR

CHRONICLE OF ZACHARIAH OF MITYLENE 6TH CENTURY

CHAPTER XVI

Now the description of the decorations of the city, given shortly, is as follows, with respect to the wealth of its inhabitants, and their great and pre-eminent prosperity, and their grand and glorious objects of luxury and pleasure, as in a great city of wonderful beauty.

Now its pre-eminent decorations are as follows, not to speak of the splendour inside the houses and the beautiful formations of the columns in their halls and of their colonnades and of their staircases, and their lofty height, as in the city of wonderful beauty.

It contains 24 churches of the blessed apostles, Catholic churches. It contains 2 great basilicae, where the king sits and the senators are assembled before him every day. It contains 324 great spacious streets. It contains 2 great capitols. It contains 80 golden gods. It contains 64 ivory gods. It contains 46,603 dwelling-houses. It contains 1797 houses of magnates. It contains 1352 reservoirs pouring forth water. It contains 274 bakers, who are constantly making and distributing annonae to the inhabitants of the city, besides those who make and sell in the city. It contains 5000 cemeteries, where they lay out and bury. It contains 31 great marble pedestals. It contains 3785 bronze statues of kings and magistrates. It contains, moreover, 25 bronze statues of Abraham, Sarah, and Hagar, and of the kings of the house of David, which Vespasian the king brought up when he sacked Jerusalem, and the gates of Jerusalem, and the gates of Jerusalem and other bronze objects. It contains 2 colossal statues. It contains 2 columns of shells. It contains 2 circuses. It contains 2 theatres and one. It contains 2 amphitheatres. It contains 4 beth ulde. It contains 11 imfiya. It contains 22 great and mighty bronze horses. It contains 926 baths. It contains 4 orbilikon. It contains 14 tinon enkofitoriyon. It contains 2 parenamabole of special bronze horses. It contains 45 sistre. It contains 2300 public oil-warehouses. It contains 291 prisons or aspoke. It contains in the regions 254 public places or privies. It contains emparkhe, who guard the city, and the men who command them all are 7. The gates of the city are 37. Now the circumference of the whole city is 216,036 feet, which is 40 miles; the diameter of the city from east to west is 12 miles, and from north to south 12 miles.

But God is faithful, who will make its second prosperity greater than its first, because is the glory of all the might of the dominion of the Romans.

The Syriac Chronicle Known as that of Zachariah of Mitylene, trans. F. J. Hamilton and E. W. Brooks (London: Methuen, 1899), pp. 317–319.

The emperor held the real power in Rome, both the city and the empire. Augustus had seized power through a military coup and continued to hold power through a series of republican offices hiding his true source of power, the army. Later emperors realized that the army held the key to power and courted them accordingly. Augustus created the Praetorian Guard, a force of 12,000 men who not only protected him, but provided the emperor with a large force in the capital to prevent rebellion. The Praetorian Guard soon realized its tremendous power and used it. If the guard backed the emperor, a problem rarely existed. Throughout the empire's history, from 31 B.C.E. down to 400 C.E., no riot removed an emperor unless the guard allowed it. The emperor and his bureaucracy ensured the smooth running not only of the empire but of the city as well.

One of Augustus' greatest accomplishments for the city's protection was the creation of a permanent fire/police department. During the late republic, Rome suffered from continual civil disturbances by rival faction members. In addition, Rome did not have a fire department. In the 70s B.C.E. the wealthy banker Crassus used his slaves to combat fires, but not for a noble reason. If a fire broke out (and he was often accused of starting them) his slaves arrived but did not put the fire out until Crassus had arrived and bought the property for far less than it was worth. The property would then be "saved," repaired, and sold for a handsome profit. For his part, Augustus instituted a group that would not only fight fires but would act as local policemen.

When Augustus divided the city into 14 regions, each region had quarters (vici) or blocks that totaled 262 for the city. Associated with each quarter was an *aedicule,* or small temple, which housed the Lares, or gods of the neighborhood. Each quarter had two superintendents whose chief duty was to look after the Lares, compile the local census figures, and act as local judge for petty crimes. This would alleviate the central administration of many of the mundane criminal acts. The local police, however, were the vigiles, or watchmen, a combination of firemen and policemen. There were seven cohorts; each patrolled two regions and had a police station and two watch houses, one for each region. Each cohort originally had 560 men but later had 1,120 men, making a total of 7,840 vigiles for the city. These men were not the legionary citizens, but rather freedmen divided into centuries (groups of 100) commanded by a centurion with a tribune over the entire cohort, similar to the military units of the legions. The vigiles patrolled the streets, especially at night, in small groups, and would put any arrested criminals in lockup in the station. Each station had a professional torturer to extract confessions from the prisoners. If the crime was minor, the local region prefect would try them; if major, the offender was sent to the prefect *Vigilum,* the prefect of the watch, or to the city prefect. The prefect of the watch was second only to the city prefect in municipal power. A further force was the Urban Cohort, composed of four cohorts, each of 1,000 men, who were intermediary between the Praetorian and vigiles and supplied backup for either group. Like the Praetorians, who were Roman citizens, the members of the Urban Cohort were from Italy and could be promoted to the guard.

The city prefect's main job was to ensure the city's safety. He would not only try cases of importance, but attempted to ensure that cases never reached him. For example, he would constantly be on the watch for illegal societies. The Romans had a sort of national paranoia; they distrusted any gathering of people. For example, consider a volunteer fire department. On the surface, it would appear that an organization created to fight fires and thus save the city would be welcomed; but, on the contrary, Rome would even ban such an organization as a threat to civil order. Pliny, writing in the early 2nd century C.E. as governor of Bithynia, modern Northern Turkey, asked if a fire department could be established. The enclosed Point in Time is his letter to the emperor Trajan and the emperor's response.

CITY MAGISTRATES

ROMAN FEAR OF GROUPS: VOLUNTEER FIRE DEPARTMENT

LETTER 42: TO THE EMPEROR TRAJAN

While I was making a progress in a different part of the province, a most extensive fire broke out at Nicomedia, which not only consumed several private houses, but also two public buildings; the town-house and the temple of Isis, though they stood on contrary sides of the street. The occasion of its spreading thus far was partly owing to the violence of the wind, and partly to the indolence of the people, who, manifestly, stood idle and motionless spectators of this terrible calamity. The truth is the city was not furnished with either engines, buckets, or any single instrument suitable for extinguishing fires; which I have now, however, given directions to have prepared. You will consider, Sir, whether it may not be advisable to institute a company of firemen, consisting only of one hundred and fifty members. I will take care none but those of that business shall be admitted into it, and that the privileges granted them shall not be applied to any other purpose. As this corporate body will be restricted to so small a number of members, it will be easy to keep them under proper regulation.

LETTER 43: TRAJAN TO PLINY

You are of opinion it would be proper to establish a company of firemen in Nicomedia, agreeably to what has been practiced in several other cities. But it is to be remembered that societies of this sort have greatly disturbed the peace of the province in general, and of those cities in particular. Whatever name we give them, and for whatever purposes them may be founded, they will not fail to form themselves into factious, assemblies, however short their meetings may be. It will therefore be safer to provide such machines as are of service in extinguishing fires, enjoining the owners of houses to assist in preventing the mischief from spreading, and, if it should be necessary, to call in the aid of the populace.

Pliny the Younger, letter 43: Marcus Tullius Cicero, *Letters of Marcus Tullius Cicero, with his treatises on friendship and old age,* trans. E. S. Shuckburgh; *Letters of Gaius Plinius Caecilius Secundus,* trans. William Melmoth, rev. F.C.T. Bosanquet, with introductions and notes, Harvard Classics Vol. 9 (New York: P. F. Collier, 1909).

This type of response influenced Roman policy with other groups, in particular the Christians, who were seen as potential terrorists. Rome's structural paranoia would always view these groups with caution and fear. Although the emperor recognized the problem of fires, he nevertheless worried that these societies would undermine the state. The city prefect then had to ensure that secretive groups, such as Christians, were not permitted to establish themselves. The city prefect also attempted to ensure peace by preventing riots, most of which occurred due to a scarcity of food, often only a rumor, which caused panic, often driving up prices. The prefect attempted to keep these prices down. Other officials in Rome who helped ensure the city's smooth running were the "curators of public works," who maintained the buildings, especially temples and city buildings, and, if needed, repaired them. The prefect of the grain supply ensured that the city was fed with cheap grain, helped by the "official grain measurers" and "grain warehouse overseers" in Ostia. Finally, the "Board for the Tiber, River-Banks, and Sewers" attempted to prevent floods, recover the city from floods, and keep the sewers from backing up, for obvious health reasons. The aqueducts were overseen by "supervisors of the water supply" who were usually professional engineers.

In addition to the imperial and municipal government, the Senate still existed during the empire. This board, however, had lost most of its political power when Augustus seized power and now merely became a pool for imperial bureaucrats. The Senate still had its prestige, but it traded its political power for economic power. Although there was no set number of senators, Augustus reduced its number to about 600, and that number usually remained. By the end of the empire, the Senate had become a body overseeing the province of Italy, but holding no real power.

The city of Rome became the largest metropolitan city in the ancient world. The reforms Augustus made assured that Rome functioned, even if the emperor was not actively involved in the city's government. Merchants from all over the empire supplied the city with needed goods and luxury items. One of the by-products of this mercantile activity was the importation of new religions, including Christianity.

3

COMPETITION WITH OTHER RELIGIONS

Christianity was not the only religion that existed in the Roman world. In addition to the state religion focusing on the Olympian gods, mystery religions competed for followers. These powerful forces focused on worshipping various gods including Fortune, Dionysus, Asclepius, Cybele, Isis, and Mithras, as well as the imperial ruler cult, all of which offered their followers a chance for immortality, in contrast to the stark state religion. Unlike these religions, which allowed for multiple beliefs and membership, Christianity believed in its exclusiveness, offering its followers a distinct and uncompromising setting, monotheism. In addition to exploring these religious cults, this chapter concludes with a discussion of the final conflict between Christianity and pagan Rome witnessed in the debate over the removal of the Statue of Victory from the Senate House in the late 4th century C.E.

ANCIENT RELIGION

In the early empire the variety of religions and cults allowed individuals the opportunity to explore contrasting philosophies and beliefs in a vibrant setting. For the early Christians their everyday life came into contact with these different forces that would influence both Christianity and paganism. Examining the various religions and cults existing in the 1st and 2nd centuries allows the modern viewer to understand the dynamic forces that shaped Christianity over the next few centuries. The creation of the Roman Empire caused the breakdown of geographical and social barriers in the Mediterranean, allowing the varied ideas to move easier across space and society. With the region's political unification, competition moved from the political/military sphere to the philosophical/religious realm. When Augustus fixed the frontiers, the push to obtain souls replaced the push to obtain land.

In ancient society the gods consistently interacted with humans directly. The traditional Roman religion focused on state rituals that would ensure the state's safety, producing an ideology that the gods would favor Rome if the city and its inhabitants performed the correct sacrifices in an exact fashion. During the modern age many have argued that ancient pagans did not sincerely believe in their religion. Christians, the winners in this religious war, propagated this assumption to further discredit paganism. Current evidence and scholarly thought now argue that most inhabitants had a true belief in the gods of Rome where the gods altered events in people's lives. This alteration could be beneficial or not depending on how the gods behaved.

The public rituals were therefore crucial, and the priests, *flamens,* performed these acts providing a direct link between the people and the gods. The priests were typically nobles who viewed their role as flamens as an important public office. An example of how important and related these pagan flamens were to Christianity can be seen in several canons from the Christian Council of Elvira in early 4th-century Spain. The canons clearly showed that some Christians had become or had held the office of pagan flamens. That the council had to make several distinctions among the flamens also indicated that this was not an isolated or unique occurrence, but rather well known and perhaps even common among the upper class. As more and more pagans became Christian, some converts may have desired to retain their political and social prestige, which included holding pagan offices.

The flamens offered sacrifices for the city. Their job ensured that the sacrifices occurred, assuring that the state prospered, since the gods were pleased. The state religion embodied the people's patriotism for the state. While modern viewers might scoff at this idea, one merely has to look at modern war memorials and public displays, which although not exactly religious, nevertheless have quasi-religious sentiments and attributes often provoking an emotional response promoting national identity and fervor.

The emperor Augustus made great use of the traditional Roman religion in his restructuring of the state. Augustus honored the gods, proclaiming that they had helped him in his struggle over Antony and Cleopatra. During his reign Augustus constructed and repaired numerous temples. One of his most famous monuments was the golden statue of Nike, the goddess of victory, in the Senate House, commemorating his victory over Cleopatra and ending the century of civil war. This golden statue remained in the Senate House as a symbol of Rome's victory over the enemies of

Funerary Bust of Priest Yedi-bel. Saint Louis Art Museum.

Rome until the late 4th century. During his lifetime Augustus was honored as a savior, Sebeste, in the Roman world, and after his death he was deified. Temples were erected to him and to Rome.

The state religion, however, did not address the universal concern of what happened after death. The state religion promoted the empire's safety rather than that of the individual. In the state religion, after death individuals merely went to the underworld unless they were declared a god or goddess. This situation produced a feeling of helplessness and despair among many individuals, that the gods and goddesses were uncaring in their daily lives. To counter this sense of emptiness many individuals looked more to Fate or Fortune. Fate could strike one down or raise one up. Fate was praised and cursed, for it was seen as fickle, but it directly interacted with individuals. While its name was invoked, it was also feared. Numerous statues have Fortune or Tyche, a female goddess, holding a cornucopia, the symbol of plenty. Pliny the Elder in the enclosed Point in Time

Isis Fortuna. The Walters Art Museum, Baltimore.

related the current philosophy about Fortune's power.

This idea of Fortune naturally led many to examine other concepts or beliefs of the afterlife. During the two centuries after Augustus the Mediterranean witnessed a proliferation in the number and vitality of the mystery religions. These religions, which offered a chance at immortality at least for the soul, differed from magic, which might protect you or alter your fate during your lifetime. In all cases there was the process of initiation and secrecy.

The key to immortality was knowledge, or gnosis, with those seeking this knowledge called Gnostics and the philosophy or religion called Gnosticism. By obtaining this knowledge through reason, one would learn the way to salvation. To obtain this gnosis a messenger or teacher imparted this knowledge. This messenger had to know and be known by the god who gave the knowledge. These in turn allowed the messenger or "anointed one" to control the flow of information and ultimately decide who would receive the knowledge. Often associated with Gnosticism was the concept of duality: Good versus evil. This duality came from the Oriental religions such as the Persian Zoroaster. Examples of the mystery religions that existed in the Mediterranean World included those honoring Dionysus, Asclepius, Cybele, Isis, and Mithras. These in turn influenced the growth and perception of the Imperial Cult celebrated in Rome since the foundation of the empire.

DIONYSUS

Originally the celebration at Eleusis from the 7th century B.C.E. honored Persephone and her marriage to Pluto and the cycle of autumn and

---

A ROMAN HOMAGE TO FORTUNE

Among these discordant opinions mankind have discovered for themselves a kind of intermediate deity, by which our scepticism concerning God is still increased. For all over the world, in all places, and at all times, Fortune is the only god whom every one invokes; she alone is spoken of, she alone is accused and is supposed to be guilty; she alone is in our thoughts, is praised and blamed, and is loaded with reproaches; wavering as she is, conceived by the generality of mankind to be blind, wandering, inconstant, uncertain, variable, and often favouring the unworthy. To her are referred all our losses and all our gains, and in casting up the accounts of mortals she alone balances the two pages of our sheet. We are so much in the power of chance, that change itself is considered as a God, and the existence of God becomes doubtful.

Pliny the Elder, *The Natural History,* trans. John Bostock and H. T. Riley (London: Taylor and Francis, 1855), p. 1023.

---

spring. Later the celebration became associated with Dionysus or Bacchus and was associated with orgies, which often challenged local morality. Dionysus' introduction into Italy in 186 B.C.E. caused great alarm in the Senate due to a conspiracy called the Bacchanalia (see chapter 4), leading to his celebrations being curtailed. The celebration became popular during the first two centuries after Augustus. The initiate would become Bacchus himself. Although the particulars about the initiation are lacking, it is clear that those who believed in Bacchus were saved while those who did not would be damned. Bacchus rewarded believers with salvation while he punished unbelievers. It appears that the cult of Dionysus was for the upper class and was associated with senses, especially drinking and sex. With its abandonment of morality, Bacchus faced a strong struggle with the other mystery religions and Christianity, which focused on morality and individual personal salvation.

ASCLEPIUS

A popular religion known as Aesculpaius sprang up surrounding Asclepius, the god of healing, who came to Rome from Epidaurus in Greece early in the 3rd century B.C.E. at the request of the ancient Roman Sibyl or prohpetess. Asclepius was a particular favorite among the army, and shrines to him existed throughout the Roman Empire including Spain, Britain, and Dacia (Romania). As servants of the god of healing, the priests were well versed in traditional medicine, helping patients with physical and mental illnesses. But the belief in the god himself also argued for curative powers, with prayers being offered to Asclepius for help in all illnesses. Throughout the empire there were shrines erected to the god, especially around sites near springs and wells.

Zeus Serapis. Saint Louis Art Museum.

CYBELE

This cult, which came to Rome from Asia Minor in 204 B.C.E., celebrated the exuberance of the mystery cults in gruesome detail. After seven days of fasting, and a procession with a recently cut pine tree—the symbol of the dead god Attis—the Day of the Blood occurred, where priests would cut themselves and novices would castrate themselves. An art relief showed the high priest holding in his right hand fruit and branches of the pomegranate, which symbolized life and resurrection, and in the left hand the pine cone, the symbol of fertility. Roman officials attempted to subdue the frenzy, especially castration, and it appears that the priests ultimately were no longer eunuchs, although in some instances castration still continued. Adherents to the cult came from the upper classes, and even the emperor Antoninus Pius and his wife Faustinus were firm believers, although probably not fanatics. An example of this fanaticism and perhaps in response to the ban on castration were the celebrations of the Taurobolium (when a bull was used) or Criobolium (when a ram was used), where initiates would descend into a hole under which the bull or ram was slaughtered on a grill, with the animal's blood pouring over them through the grate. The initiates would receive the blood into their mouths, noses, ears, and all over their bodies. Initiates would then be reborn forever. Since these initiates had to pay for the animals, and especially since the bull was preferred, the followers were probably from the upper class. Evidence exists for this cult throughout the empire, with the last rites taking place on the Vatican hill in the 4th century C.E., after the legalization of Christianity.

ISIS

While these other mystery religions were extremely popular, Isis and her worship became universal throughout the empire, existing in nearly every province. Although her shrines were often destroyed in the city of Rome during the chaotic civil wars when Cleopatra and Antony vied for power against Octavian, by the time of Gaius (Caligula) her worship was well established. Together with Osiris, the god of the underworld who accompanied Isis and represented rebirth, this mystery religion offered the initiate a chance to descend into Hades and, upon meeting the gods, overcome death and attain immortality. The lure of Isis lay in the promise that she could conquer Fate and provide immortality. No longer would people be obliged to live and, upon dying, have no further life, since Isis promised the initiate that they would move beyond the mundane world and find fulfillment. This fulfillment appealed to all regardless of their social, gender, or economic position.

These ideas are best seen in the novel by Apuleius, *The Golden Ass,* which tells the story of Lucius, who has searched far and wide for some type of fulfillment. Believing in Fate, Lucius soon realizes that his life is inextricably bound to the whims of the goddess. It is Isis who relieves Lucius of his burden and in so doing frees him so that he may overcome death and, therefore, Fate.

These mystery religions all had similar traits, such as orgiastic ceremonies, intermixing of the sexes, and the view that they had an undisciplined approach to life. These concepts made many conservative Romans nervous, remembering the Bacchanalia conspiracies that had threatened the republic. One group, however, that was soon admired for its strict discipline was the worshippers of Mithras.

MITHRAS

Competing with Christianity's notion of moral austerity, especially in contrast to the frenzy habits of cults like Cybele or Dionysus, was the ancient cult of Mithras. A popular cult disseminated by the army, Mithras argued for a duality, a world with good and evil. Originally Indian, the religion found a stronghold in Persia, where Mithras searched for goodness, fighting for the god Ahura-Mazda against the dark side, embodied in the evil god Ahriman. Mithras' labors involved two deeds, wrestling with the sun and thus becoming its friend, and capturing and sacrificing a bull to bring about a renewal in agriculture. This symbolism was not Persian, but Hellenistic, and spread to the Roman world from Cilicia in Asia Minor. The image of the Mithraean labors can be seen in many sculptures, especially from the Western Empire. As this rite spread westward the importance it placed upon the sun increased. Mithras was seen by the Romans as a Persian cult, since the Magi were responsible for its sacrifices. Unlike the other mystery religions where there was an annual death and rebirth festival, Mithras had conquered death completely. Mithras was not a god, but rather a guide for humanity to lead those who believed to the path of light. The cult had a strong set of ethical behaviors, which further separated it from the other mystery religions.

The artistic motif of Mithras in the Roman world was not Persian, but rather Phrygian, from Asia Minor shown by the style of his cap on numerous pieces of art. Most likely it spread from Trapezus on the Black Sea in the north, which was known as a strong center for Mithras throughout Asia Minor, before being adopted by the Romans from Cilicia in the south in the 1st century B.C.E. Mithras was often depicted as a horseman, again representative of the region's history regarding horses. Asia Minor was also a center for the Magi, as attested by the early church fathers.

The religion appears to have been solely for men, since there was no symbol or representation for women. The seven grades for initiates were masculine, and there was no professional priestly class, for those who presided over the ceremony appear to have been elected for that occasion from the membership. The shrines were placed underground and were rectangular, with a niche in the far end where the motif of Mithras slaying the bull was usually placed. On either side of the hall were a series of steps or benches. There was a pit in the floor where the initiate was laid. In one initiation the individual had his hands tied with chicken intestines and was thrown across a pit filled with water. There may have been human sacrifice in this cult, but it is not known for sure, since Christians may have spread that rumor to discredit it.

The city of Rome had at least 45 Mithraea, (pl. of Mithraeum, a cave or building imitating a cave where participants met and worshipped), and throughout the West numerous sites have remains of Mithraea. The religion in particular flourished where the army promoted and established it. But the religion was not limited to just the military, for it existed and flourished in coastal towns throughout the Mediterranean such as Alexandria, Carthage, and Ostia. Since Mithras stressed a contract between the initiate and the gods, it was favored by merchants, who operated in a similar fashion. Unlike Christianity, however, Mithras became a religion exclusively for the middle and upper class.

Mithraists (followers of Mithras) were allowed to practice their religion without government interference. This may have been due to the fact that it did not admit women and that it was popular among the military. It seems to have been seen as a burial club, like other mercantile guilds or organizations. The army was the chief means by which Mithraism propagated. As the empire in the West weakened during the 3rd century, Mithras became stronger, a bulwark for Rome, like a soldier, and was seen as an alternative to the frenzied religions of the Mediterranean. Associated with the military, Mithras termed each of its initiates a soldier, and urged them, like soldiers, to be strong, chaste, and politically involved. Unlike Christianity, whose members also struggled against the frenzied behavior of the Mediterranean mystery cults by retreating into the desert as aesthetic hermits, Mithras believed that its individuals had to be an active member of society.

The rise of these new religions within the army potentially allowed for society to have a new state religion. The connection between the sun god and the army, through Mithras, fostered the worship of Sol Invictus, the unconquered sun. Aurelian may have attempted to produce a new state religion based upon the rites of Sol Invictus, which Maxentius may have further used to counter Constantine's newfound favoring of Christianity. Maxentius failed to triumph for Sol Invictus against Constantine's Christianity at the battle of the Milvian Bridge, which ended the official political avocation of Sol Invictus; however, the rites and religion persisted. Although Mithras had power, rigorous morality, and intensity, it did not appeal to everyone and in fact it excluded half of the population—women—outright, which hampered a sustained propagation. Without a professional priestly class, openness to the lower classes, and means of sustained propagation, Mithras could not become the universal religion needed to provide society with its spiritual needs.

IMPERIAL CULT

Beginning with the emperor Augustus, Rome witnessed the importation of a Hellenistic idea of the imperial cult. Although Augustus forbade the outright worship of himself in the West, he did not forbid the practice in the East. The original ideology focused on the benefits for the empire from the emperor himself, focusing on his ability to deliver peace and prosperity. Although some emperors, such as Caligula and Nero, misused the concept, most viewed the imperial cult as a means to unite the different groups of the empire. By providing the different people with one focus, the empire could be held together by the persona of the ruler. But this often presented difficulty for Christians. Even though they did not understand their theology, the Romans recognized that Jews had an aversion to worshipping other gods, but Christianity was placed outside this understanding after they broke away from Judaism. Christians often tried to argue they would pray for the health of the emperor and the empire. Christians, however, refused to pray to the ruler, even for his safety. For many Romans it seemed only as an exercise in semantics, but for Christians it violated the commandment of not worshipping other gods. In their daily lives Christians had to negotiate this difficult line between safety and beliefs. This act made Christians traitors and easy targets for persecutions.

The idea of the imperial cult should be seen as the continual evolution of Mediterranean ideology beginning with Alexander the Great. This concept of worshipping or glorifying the living ruler stood as anathema to Christianity. In the final struggle, Christianity, believing in the risen human-God Jesus, stood against the living current emperor, with only one religion being able to prevail.

TEMPLES AND DECLINE

In the ancient world temples were the focus for religion. Since the traditional religions served the welfare of the state, and not the individual, ritual and form became crucial. In antiquity the celebration of the gods centered on their temples and associated cults. In Rome temples were erected not only to the traditional Olympic gods, but for the numerous cults and foreign deities that were imported and worshipped. Emperors and wealthy pagan senators erected and refurbished temples. Although the construction of temples varied from region to region, in regions other than Rome, particularly during the 3rd-century crisis, there was often a decline in their construction and repair.

In Egypt, the state temples showed a clear decline during the 2nd and 3rd centuries, with new construction ceasing in the 2nd century. Many of the temples were converted into other structures during the late 3rd century. For example, the temple at Luxor became a military post, and at Panopolis a temple was converted into a residence for Diocletian when he arrived on a state visit. This decline does not necessarily mean that paganism was dying. Rather, during the 2nd and 3rd centuries the central government's construction of temples, especially the old pharaonic sites, ended due to the mounting financial burdens and other problems facing the empire. In other areas of the empire, however, evidence indicated that temple construction continued, but again, with the problems facing the empire, many of the temple sites were merely maintained, rather than embellished or new ones undertaken.

There is an equal lack of evidence in Egypt of continual pagan sacrifices. Although the evidence for all periods is at best scanty, 3rd- and 4th-century evidence indicated that the practice of pagan sacrifice declined. This decline again focused on the temples and reinforced the view that the temples were losing power and prestige, at least in Egypt. In other areas of the empire pagan sacrifices continued, and some Christian fathers urged their congregations to quit visiting the old pagan temples and sanctuaries. It is apparent that many regions retained and maintained popular shrines, while others were allowed to fall into disuse. The major overriding influence in both instances was local support and belief. Further, with the exception of the imperial cult, many emperors did not care about local cults and their temples since their existence in no way benefited them.

When Augustus reorganized the city of Rome into the different regions it is apparent that the city quarters *(vici)* were associated with neighborhood gods. Each *vicus* had a shrine. These shrines were probably from the original animistic deities, "spirits," originating from the city's foundation. This belief in the "spirits" was not confined to Rome, and in fact several Christian fathers complained about their congregation believing and worshipping these "spirits" even though they were supposed to be Christians.

In the late 4th century, after the establishment of Christianity, a struggle erupted in the city of Rome between the new and old religions. The center of this struggle centered around the Statue or Altar of Victory, which the first emperor Augustus had erected in the Senate House in 29 B.C.E. and which promoted the idea that the emperor received his power from the gods, a concept that was anathema to Christians. Constantius II, a Christian, ordered the statue removed in 357. Julian subsequently

Rome: Pantheon. James W. Ermatinger.

ordered it returned, and it stayed until 383 when Gratian ordered it removed again.

These two individuals, Ambrose and Symmachus, provide excellent examples of highly educated Roman patricians on opposite sides of the religious field.

Ambrose

Like Augustine and Jerome, Ambrose (ca. 340–397) ranks as one of the great Latin fathers of the Western church. Born the son of the Gallic Praetorian prefect, Ambrose received a thorough training in law and philosophy. He became governor of Liguria (Northern Italy) and in 374 was made the bishop of Milan by popular acclamation, even though he had not yet been formally baptized.

Ambrose fought two major foes, paganism and Arianism. Advisor to emperors Valentinian I, Gratian, and Theodosius, he used his position as bishop to urge war against both paganism and Arianism. In 382 he convinced Gratian to remove the Statue of Victory, a golden statue of Nike, the goddess of Victory, from the Senate House where Augustus had placed it. His relative, the pagan philosopher Symmachus, wrote a series of hymns (letters) trying to have the statue restored. Ambrose responded with his own letters and sermons, arguing for its permanent removal; he was victorious in 384. In 391 Ambrose convinced Theodosius to make a permanent end to paganism by closing all the pagan temples. Some of these temples were converted into churches, which saved from being destroyed.

Through his writings, especially *On Faith* and *On the Holy Spirit,* as well as through his sermons, Ambrose fought against Arianism and defended the Nicene Creed. Ambrose forced the emperor to remove several Arian bishops at the Council of Aquileia (Italy) in 381. When a Jewish synagogue burned down in northern Italy in 385, Ambrose and his followers occupied the site to prevent the Arian Empress Justina from constructing an Arian church in its place.

Ambrose completed Augustine's education and journey toward Christianity, a process that culminated in Augustine's baptism on Easter of 387. Although not trained as a theologian, Ambrose defined in Latin the arguments of Christianity by using Greek theology and Neo-Platonism, and he employed his Latin legal training to make Orthodox Catholic policy supreme in the West.

Ambrose also used the Roman bureaucracy, as well as his oratorical abilities, to further the power of the church. He held sway over emperors, even forcing Theodosius to seek absolution and do public penance for having massacred 7,000 citizens in Thessalonica in 390. Through his actions and writings Ambrose secured both the independence and dominance of the church over imperial control.

Symmachus

An outstanding orator and leader of the Senate, Symmachus (c. 340–402) was a pagan who beseeched the Christian emperors Valentinian and Gratian to uphold the pagan ideas of state, which included maintaining paganism as the state religion and honoring the position of Rome, a pagan city, over Constantinople, a Christian city. He held the governorship of Africa in 373, the urban prefecture in 384, and the consulship in 391. His writings are the major source for information about the jobs of leader of the Senate, judge for Rome and Southern Italy, and supervisor of Rome's grain and safety. His extensive letters provide details of the social life for Rome's upper classes. Although not wealthy by Roman standards, he did have vast holdings in Africa and paid 2,000 pounds of gold to help his son put on games for the enjoyment of the Roman mob, making him a member of Rome's aristocracy. His conflict with kinsmen Ambrose over the Statue of Victory provides not only an excellent sample of his eloquence, but also shows the conflict between two upper-class Romans over religion. Nevertheless, he lost his appeal to the emperor, and the statue was not returned to the Senate House.

This order culminated in the final debate between Symmachus, an ardent pagan and senator arguing for its return, since it was the basis of Roman rule, and his kinsman Ambrose, bishop of Milan (Italy), who successfully persuaded the emperor to prevent the statue's reestablishment. It returned briefly to the Senate House from 393 to 394 when Eugenius, a Christian in need of the pagan senator's support, restored it. In 394, after his victory over Eugenius, Theodosius ordered the statue removed for good, but even as late as 402, when Prudentius wrote his work *Against Symmachus,* an attack on the pagan Symmachus who wanted the statue returned, the controversy was still current. Ultimately the statue was melted down to pay the German Alaric his booty in 410 in order to save Rome from total destruction and plundering. The triumph over the Statue (Altar) of Victory marked Christianity's victory over paganism. The passages from Ambrose and Symmachus included here point to part of this final struggle.

LAST GASP OF PAGANISM

EPISTLE XVII. AMBROSE TO VALENTINIAN II

4. And they are complaining of their losses, who never spared our blood, who destroyed the very buildings of the churches. And they petition you to grant them privileges, who by the last Julian law denied us the common right of speaking and teaching, and those privileges whereby Christians also have often been deceived; for by those privileges they endeavoured to ensnare some, partly through inadvertence, partly in order to escape the burden of public requirements; and, because all are not found to be brave, even under Christian princes, many have lapsed.

5. Had these things not been abolished I could prove that they ought to be done away by your authority; but since they have been forbidden and prohibited by many princes throughout nearly the whole world, and were abolished at Rome by Gratian of august memory, the brother of your Clemency, in consideration of the true faith, and rendered void by a rescript; do not, I pray you, either pluck up what has been established in accordance with the faith, nor rescind your brother's precepts. In civil matters if he established anything, no one thinks that it ought to be treated lightly, while a precept about religion is trodden under foot.

9. If today any heathen Emperor should build an altar, which God forbid, to idols, and should compel Christians to come together thither, in order to

be amongst those who were sacrificing, so that the smoke and ashes from the altar, the sparks from the sacrilege, the smoke from the burning might choke the breath and throats of the faithful; and should give judgment in that court where members were compelled to vote after swearing at the altar of an idol (for they explain that an altar is so placed for this purpose, that every assembly should deliberate under its sanction, as they suppose, though the Senate is now made up with a majority of Christians), a Christian who was compelled with a choice such as this to come to the Senate, would consider it to be persecution, which often happens, for they are compelled to come together even by violence. Are these Christians, when you are Emperor, compelled to swear at a heathen altar? What is an oath, but a confession of the divine power of Him Whom you invoke as watcher over your good faith? When you are Emperor, this is sought and demanded, that you should command an altar to be built, and the cost of profane sacrifices to be granted.

THE MEMORIAL OF SYMMACHUS, PREFECT OF THE CITY TO VALENTINIAN

3. But it is our task to watch on behalf of your Graces. For to what is it more suitable that we defend the institutions of our ancestors, and the rights and destiny of our country, than to the glory of these times, which is all the greater when you understand that you may not do anything contrary to the custom of your ancestors? We demand then the restoration of that condition of religious affairs which was so long advantageous to the state. Let the rulers of each sect and of each opinion be counted up; a late one practised the ceremonies of his ancestors, a later did not put them away. If the religion of old times does not make a precedent, let the connivance of the last do so.

4. Who is so friendly with the barbarians as not to require an Altar of Victory? We will be careful henceforth, and avoid a show of such things. But at least let that honour be paid to the name which is refused to the goddess— your fame, which will last for ever, owes much and will owe still more to victory. Let those be averse to this power, whom it has never benefited. Do you refuse to desert a patronage which is friendly to your triumphs? That power is wished for by all, let no one deny that what he acknowledges is to be desired should also be venerated.

5. But even if the avoidance of such an omen were not sufficient, it would at least have been seemly to abstain from injuring the ornaments of the Senate House. Allow us, we beseech you, as old men to leave to posterity what we received as boys. The love of custom is great. Justly did the act of the divine Constantius last but for a short time. All precedents ought to be avoided by you, which you know were soon abolished. We are anxious for the permanence of your glory and your name, that the time to come may find nothing which needs correction.

10. We ask, then, for peace for the gods of our fathers and of our country. It is just that all worship should be considered as one. We look on the same stars, the sky is common, the same world surrounds us. What difference does it make by what pains each seeks the truth? We cannot attain to so great

a secret by one road; but this discussion is rather for persons at ease, we offer now prayers, not conflict.

14. And let no one think that I am defending the cause of religion only, for from deeds of this kind have arisen all the misfortunes of the Roman race. The law of our ancestors honoured the Vestal Virgins and the ministers of the gods with a moderate maintenance and just privileges. This grant remained unassailed till the time of the degenerate money-changers, who turned the fund for the support of sacred chastity into hire for common porters. A general famine followed upon this, and a poor harvest disappointed the hopes of all the provinces. This was not the fault of the earth, we impute no evil influence to the stars. Mildew did not injure the crops, nor wild oats destroy the corn; the year failed through the sacrilege, for it was necessary that what was refused to religion should be denied to all.

EPISTLE XVIII. REPLY OF AMBROSE TO VALENTINIAN

1. Since the illustrious Symmachus, Prefect of the city, has sent petition to your Grace that the altar, which was taken away from the Senate House of the city of Rome, should be restored to its place; and you, O Emperor, although still young in years and experience, yet a veteran in the power of faith, did not approve the prayer of the heathen, I presented a request the moment I heard of it, in which, though I stated such things as it seemed necessary to suggest, I requested that a copy of the Memorial might be given to me.

3. The illustrious Prefect of the city has in his Memorial set forth three propositions which he considers of force: that Rome, as he says, asks for her rites again, that pay be given to her priests and Vestal Virgins, and that a general famine followed upon the refusal of the priests' stipends.

10. But, says he, let the altars be restored to the images, and their ornaments to the shrines. Let this demand be made of one who shares in their superstitions; a Christian Emperor has learnt to honour the altar of Christ alone. Why do they exact of pious hands and faithful lips the ministry to their sacrilege? Let the voice of our Emperor utter the Name of Christ alone, and speak of Him only, Whom he is conscious of, for, "the King's heart is in the hand of the Lord." Has any heathen Emperor raised an altar to Christ? While they demand the restoration of things which have been, by their own example they show us how great reverence Christian Emperors ought to pay to the religion which they follow, since heathen ones offered all to their superstitions.

11a. We began long since, and now they follow those whom they excluded. We glory in yielding our blood, an expense moves them. We consider these things in the place of victories, they think them loss. Never did they confer on us a greater benefit than when they ordered Christians to be beaten and proscribed and slain. Religion made a reward of that which unbelief thought to be a punishment. See their greatness of soul! We have increased through loss, through want, through punishment; they do not believe that their rites can continue without contributions.

30. If the old rites pleased, why did Rome also take up foreign ones? I pass over the ground hidden by costly building, and shepherds' cottages glittering

with degenerate gold. Why, that I may reply to the very matter which they complain of, have they eagerly received the images of captured cities, and conquered gods, and the foreign rites of alien superstition? Whence is the pattern for Cybele washing her chariots in a stream counterfeiting the Almo? Whence were the Phrygian bards, and the deities of unjust Carthage always hateful to the Romans? And her whom the Africans worship as Celestis, the Persians as Nitra, and the greater number as Venus, according to a difference of name, not a variety of deities. So they believed that Victory was a goddess, which is certainly a gift, not a power; is granted and does not rule, results from the aid of legions not the power of religions. Is that goddess then great whom the number of soldiers claims, or the event of battle gives?

31. They ask to have her altar erected in the Senate House of the city of Rome, that is where the majority who meet together are Christians! There are altars in all the temples, and an altar also in the temple of Victories. Since they take pleasure in numbers they celebrate their sacrifices everywhere. To claim a sacrifice on this one altar, what is it but to insult the Faith? Is it to be borne that a heathen should sacrifice and a Christian be present? Let them imbibe, he says, let them imbibe, even against their will, the smoke with their eyes, the music with their ears, the ashes with their throats, the incense with their nostrils, and let the dust stirred up from our hearths cover their faces though they detest it. Are not the baths, the colonnades, the streets filled with images sufficient for them? Shall there not be a common lot in that common assembly? The faithful portion of the senate will be bound by the voices of those that call upon the gods, by the oaths of those that swear by them. If they oppose they will seem to exhibit their falsehood, if they acquiesce, to acknowledge what is sacrilege.

39. I have answered those who provoked me as though I had not been provoked, for my object was to refute the Memorial, not to expose superstition. But let their very memorial make you, O Emperor, more careful. For after narrating of former princes, that the earlier of them practised the ceremonies of their fathers, and the later did not abolish them; and saying in addition that, if the religious practice of the older did not make a precedent, the connivance of the later ones did; it plainly showed what you owe, both to your faith, viz., that you should not follow the example of heathen rites, and to your affection, that you should not abolish the decrees of your brother. For if for their own side alone they have praised the connivance of those princes, who, though Christians, yet in no way abolished the heathen decrees, how much more ought you to defer to brotherly love, so that you, who ought to overlook some things even if you did not approve them in order not to detract from your brother's statutes, should now maintain what you judge to be in agreement both with your own faith, and the bond of brotherhood.

Ambrose, Letter 17; Memorial of Symmachus; Ambrose, Letter 18 Sym Ambrose, in *A Select Library of the Nicene and Post-Nicene Fathers of the Christian Church*, ed. Philip Schaff and Henry Wace, 2nd series, Vols. 1–14 (New York: The Christian Literature Company, 1890–1900), Vol. 10 (1896), trans. H. De Romestin, pp. 414–422.

Eros as Horus; Harpocrates. The Walters Art Museum, Baltimore.

END OF PAGANISM

Christianity struggled with all of these varied religions throughout its early history. With the victory of Constantine over Maxentius, Christianity now had official protection. Within a short time Christianity became the favored religion, and within less than a century, Christianity was the official religion of the state. This recognition did not mean that everyone was a Christian; however, it did mean that Christianity, once an obscure offshoot of Judaism, was now the most important religion in the Mediterranean. Paganism, however, endured. The rural regions in particular still clung to the old ideas, especially the animistic beliefs. Paganism would endure until well into the late medieval period in Europe.

4

ROME'S INITIAL CONTACT WITH CHRISTIANS

Rome's reaction to Christianity, viewed as an Eastern religion but initially tolerated and protected, was not based upon an isolated and singular incident. Rather, Rome had experienced Eastern religions, including Christianity's parent religion Judaism, for nearly 200 years, viewing most with suspicion. Rome, however, did not and cared not to understand the religious difference between Judaism and Christianity. For Christians the differences went beyond religiosity and in turn affected the social and economic conditions of Christian society. This chapter attempts to explore the various reactions to Christianity by Roman elites, Jews, and other members of ancient society. Finally, this chapter showed how Christians moved from an insignificant protected sect to a persecuted and ultimately prominent sect.

ROME'S INTERACTION WITH EASTERN CULTS

During Jesus' and Augustus' time Rome practiced polytheism, the belief in many gods. Although generally tolerant of other religions, Rome expected the same consideration and respect from other groups, and when it was not forthcoming responded forcefully against them. New Eastern religions had arrived in Italy as early as the 3rd century B.C.E. At first Rome viewed these religions with suspicion, since their rituals tended to be personal, orgiastic, and Semitic, which republican Rome equated with its greatest and current enemy, North African Carthage, a colony of Palestinian Tyre. Although Rome accepted the Syrian religion Cybele during the Punic Wars (260–200 B.C.E.), the Senate stipulated that Roman citizens could not officiate at the cult's ceremonies. After the war with the Carthaginian Hannibal (218–204 B.C.E.) a Bacchanalian conspiracy erupted in 187 B.C.E. in which leading Romans, especially women, were accused of, and executed for, immoral and conspiratorial actions. The authorities associated this Eastern religion with emotions bent on destroying the social fabric of the state. Due to the conservative nature of the Senate, any challenge to traditional ideas was equated with conspiracy.

Rome came into contact with Judaism during the 2nd and 1st centuries B.C.E. through their negotiations and support of the Maccabean rulers against Syria and later with Herod the Great, who ruled Judea during Julius Caesar's reign. This early contact and support did not mean that Rome endorsed the monotheistic religion, but rather that it viewed Judea's strategic and political position against Syria and the East as paramount. Despite supporting Judea politically, Rome viewed Judaism with the same suspicion it held for the other Eastern religions. Judea's strategic position between Syria and Egypt forced Rome to become directly involved in the kingdom after Herod's death in 4 B.C.E. and his son Archaelaus' subsequent banishment in 6 C.E. When leading Jewish authorities complained of Archaelaus' behavior, Augustus, who knew of Herod's legacy of cruelty, officially annexed Judea as a province. In so doing Rome came into direct association with Judaism and had to govern this strategic Jewish region.

This association and relationship tested both Rome and its Jewish subjects. Rome portrayed the Jews as obstinate and arrogant for not permitting Gentiles admittance into its temple and for their intolerance toward polytheism; the Jews viewed the Roman Gentiles as occupiers bent on destroying their religion. Political, social, economic, and religious problems constantly arose during the next century, culminating in the Jewish rebellion of 66 C.E. and the temple's destruction four years later. The Romans systematically looted and destroyed the city, with Herod's temple burned. This action obliterated not only Judaism's most sacred structure, but dashed any hopes of a restored Jewish monarchy, since Rome would never allow a subject people who had rebelled and forced the Romans to expend a great amount of energy to be ruled by their own leader either as an independent or even dependent state. After Vespasian razed their temple in 70 C.E., Jews no longer paid a temple tax to Jewish authorities, but were instead made to pay a "Jewish tax" to Rome. Domitian in the 80s and 90s continued repression by hunting down and killing descendents of David, the ancestral Jewish king. The Bar Kochbar rebellion of 131–134, begun when Hadrian established the Roman colony Aelia Capitolina in Jerusalem with a temple to Jupiter on the old Jewish temple site, culminated with the destruction of Jerusalem and the near extermination of the Jewish population in Palestine. It was within this complex context that Christianity existed and was identified by the Romans.

Arch of Titus. James W. Ermatinger.

Christianity, as seen in chapter 1, began as a Jewish sect, spreading first among the Jews of Judea, then to the Jews of the *Diaspora,* and, finally, to the Gentiles. From the Roman perspective the Christians were a sect of Jews, like the Pharisees, Sadducees, and Essenes. The Acts of the Apostles recorded the first interaction between Christians and Roman officials when Paul met Sergius Paulus, proconsul of Cyprus, who apparently converted to Christianity. Paulus then recommended that Paul and his friends proceed to Antioch Pisidia, where Paul began his missionary activities. Paul's next contact with Roman officials occurred in Greece when the proconsul Gallio refused to arrest Paul despite the urging of the Jewish authorities. The third and most important contact occurred when the Roman procurator Felix in Judea arrested and held Paul at the urging of Jewish authorities. Felix clearly saw Paul as a Jew. When the new procurator arrived and it appeared that the Jewish authorities would prevail and have Paul put on trial, Paul appealed to the Roman emperor, claiming to be a Roman citizen. By making his claim as a Roman citizen and appealing to the emperor for judgment, Paul put himself beyond the Jewish authorities. These initial interactions between the Christians and Romans clearly indicated that the Romans viewed Christians as an innocuous offshoot of Judaism. Paul was then sent to Rome, and fellow Christians met him when he arrived outside the city, showing that Christians had already arrived and established themselves in the capital. But the Roman state's initial view of Christianity was mainly favorable. The Roman authorities, as related in Acts, did not view the Christians as potential enemies, and in fact the Romans tended to protect the Christians against Jewish authorities and mobs, probably to prevent whole-scale riots and ensure that Rome maintained its monopoly on judicial proceedings.

JEW VERSUS GENTILE

The distinction between early Christianity and Judaism was not clear or precise, since both Jews and Gentiles composed the early church, with both claiming preeminence. The initial debate that led to a distancing of both groups arose over circumcision. Previously, a male Gentile converting to Judaism underwent circumcision, a painful act for adults, which signified the individual's acceptance of the covenant between God and his chosen people, the Jews. Many Gentiles, however, heard the early Christian missionaries, especially Peter and Paul, and desired to become members of this church. This desire to follow Christ necessitated a discussion on whether an individual had to first become a Jew and then a Christian, necessitating circumcision. At the council of Antioch Peter argued and prevailed against such an act, and Gentiles no longer had to convert to Judaism before becoming Christian. This decision, not accepted by all the early followers, created a division in early Christianity between Jewish Christians and Gentile Christians. The Jewish Christians, represented by James, one of the original 12 and leader of the Jewish Christians in Jerusalem, sought to have Christianity fulfill the ideas of the Old Testament and the concept of the Messiah for the Jews. In his view Christianity was for the Jews and fulfilled the ancient promise of a Messiah. Individuals who believed in Jesus as the Messiah therefore had to become Jewish.

This division between Jewish and Gentile Christians is best seen in the early Christian manual, the *Didache*, which discussed, among other things, the issue of dietary laws, fasting, and worship days. Although probably written by a Jewish Christian, the manual was clearly intended for the Gentile convert. Gentiles no longer followed the strict Jewish dietary laws; whereas Jews, and presumably Jewish Christians, fasted on Mondays and Thursdays, the Gentile Christians were encouraged to fast on Wednesdays and Fridays. Finally, Jews and Jewish Christians kept the Sabbath day (Saturday) holy, while the Gentile Christians kept Sunday holy, in commemoration of Christ's Resurrection. These differences produced changes in the daily life of Christians. Whereas Jewish Christians would continue to be seen as a subsect of Judaism, these changes in dietary laws, fasting, and worship days placed the Gentile Christians outside mainstream Jewish life and more into Greco-Roman life, where they could blend into Roman society. This assimilation, however, was not complete, for unlike pagan inhabitants, Christians refused to celebrate the pagan festivals, which often drew attention to them and may have led to persecutions.

Like members of all new religions, early Christians desired and needed to increase their numbers. This led to missionaries such as Peter and Paul, who went first to Jewish synagogues, where they attempted to convert Jews into the new religion. This was only natural, since Christianity began from Judaism, and the concept of a Messiah had been expected and desired. As time passed small communities including both Jewish Christians and Gentile Christians began to meet in each other's houses, since mainstream Judaism rejected them. This moved Christians further away from the Jewish synagogue, attracting more Gentiles, and increasing this distinction between Christianity and Judaism. In contrast to the Jews of the Diaspora, Christians did not meet in a set structure like the synagogue. Instead, early Christians met in these so-called house churches, where they reflected on the life of Jesus, celebrated the Eucharist—a commemoration of the Last Supper—and often finished with a meal. The remnants of these house churches are often hard to detect and are usually hypothesized from literary materials.

These house churches would be used until at least the end of the 2nd century. The institution of the house churches had advantages and disadvantages to the early Christians and their daily life. One advantage was that Christians were separated into small communities within a larger community, so any persecution would not eliminate all the members of the religion. Although one unit may be found out, tortured, and potentially executed, the other units would survive. Also, these separate units allowed for more local autonomy and dispersion of resources, for example, taking care of the poor, sick, and elderly. Locally performed services and rituals would be more intimate and perhaps more meaningful then those controlled from a centered organization. However, the disadvantages were also strong: If the Romans discovered one of these Christian house churches and its members, there would be little help from other house churches. But perhaps separatists' movements became the most serious problem. House churches, independent units, made it easier for heretical teachings and ideas to exist and disperse, since local control was more common. The bishops and other nominal leaders of the church often had little control over their subjects' worshipping habits and beliefs. If a forceful or charismatic leader emerged, this separatist movement might gain power and overshadow mainstream Christianity.

Almost immediately the Christians formulated their ideas of eternal salvation and the role of God. What separated the Christians from the Jews was the Christians' belief that Jesus was the Son of God, the Messiah. The Christians pointed to Jesus' resurrection to prove his divinity. This belief became the central theme of Christianity. Although monotheistic (believing in one God), Christians argued that this one God contained three God-Heads: the Father, Son (Jesus), and Holy Spirit. This concept of three Gods in one, the Trinity, became the second major Christian philosophy. Jesus as the Messiah clearly delineated Christianity from Judaism, and Christianity being monotheistic differentiated it from paganism. Socially, with Gentiles being accepted into the religion without converting to Judaism, Christians now did not form a distinct social-ethnic identifiable group like the Jews. Many congregations had both Jews and Gentiles who worshipped Christ. The congregations in the East developed along this line, whereas in the West a different pattern occurred.

It appears that in the city of Rome the early Christian community was again composed of Christian Jews and Gentiles. In 49 c.e. the emperor Claudius issued an edict expelling from Rome Jewish individuals who had caused some sort of civil disturbance. Suetonius, writing a century later, indicated that the disturbance had been caused by Chrestus, which some scholars argue to mean Christ or Christians. It is not clear what took place, but it is possible that tensions erupted between mainstream Jews and those who followed Christ as the Messiah. This tension may have produced some kind of disturbance in which Rome ousted the leaders and prominent backers of this subsect of Judaism. Claudius had earlier dealings with Jewish problems in Alexandria, Egypt.

In 38 c.e., under the emperor Gaius (Caligula), Claudius' nephew, Herod Agrippa I, heading for Judea to take over as king, stopped in Alexandria. The Jews, delighted that one of their own had arrived and was held in high favor by the emperor, decided to have a celebration. The Greek Alexandrians, remembering the historical and often bloody rivalry between Egypt and Judea, best seen with Cleopatra and Herod the Great, Agrippa's grandfather, and probably desiring to deflate the local Jews' pride and festivities, dressed the town idiot up in royal clothes and praised him and had a guard of make-believe soldiers escort him. This insult to Caligula's friend was dangerous, and to avoid charges of sedition, the crowd demanded that the governor, Flaccus, who had been an enemy of Caligula's mother, Agrippina, under Tiberius, acquiesced in the mob's demand to publish an edict ordering the emperor's image to be displayed in the synagogues. This resulted in a riot, with Alexandrians attacking Jews and sacking over 400 houses. The Jews protested to Flaccus, who disregarded their pleas. In the autumn of 38, after Flaccus had been arrested and banished for his earlier anti-Agrippina connection, both the Jews and Alexandrians sent embassies to Rome to argue their case. Soon after Caligula's assassination and Claudius becoming emperor in 38, the Jews in Alexandria, with help from Jews in other parts of Egypt and Syria, planned to attack the Alexandrians. The Jews rioted, and the bloodshed came close to civil war before the garrison restored order. Claudius then published an edict, preserved in a papyrus, where he ordered both sides to desist from violence and from antagonizing either group.

This edict probably occurred in 40 c.e., and Claudius may have remembered the trouble in Alexandria concerning the Jews when he issued his edict expelling certain Jewish leaders from Rome. Suetonius mentions it, saying of Claudius that "He banished from Rome all the Jews, who were continually

CLAUDIUS' DECREE CONCERNING JEWS IN ALEXANDRIA

As to the question which of you were responsible for the riot and feud (or rather, if the truth must be told, the war) against the Jews, I was unwilling to commit myself to a decided judgement, though your ambassadors, and particularly Dionysius son of Theon, pleaded your cause with much zeal in confrontation (with their opponents), and I must reserve for myself an unyielding indignation against whoever caused this renewed outbreak; but I tell you plainly that if you do not desist from this baneful and obstinate mutual hostility I shall perforce be compelled to show what a benevolent prince can be when turned to just indignation. Wherefore I conjure you yet once again that, on the one side, the Alexandrines show themselves forbearing and kindly towards the Jews who for many years have dwelt in the same city, and offer no outrage to them in the exercise of their traditional worship but permit them to observe their customs as in the time of Divus Augustus, which customs I also, after hearing both sides, have confirmed: and on the other side, I bid the Jews not to busy themselves about anything beyond what they have held hitherto, and not henceforth, as if you and they lived in two cities, to send two embassies—a thing such as never occurred before now—nor to strive in gymnasiarchic or cosmetic games but to profit by what they possess, and enjoy in a city not their own an abundance of all good things; and not to introduce or invite Jews who sail down to Alexandria from Syria or Egypt, thus compelling me to conceive the greater suspicion; otherwise I will by all means take vengeance on them as fomenting a general plague for the whole world. If, desisting on both sides from these proceedings, you are willing to live with mutual forbearance and kindliness, I on my side will continue to display the time-honoured solicitude for the interests of the city, with which my family has a traditional friendship.

H. Idris Bell, ed., *Jews and Christians in Egypt* (London: British Museum, 1924), pp. 28–29.

making disturbances at the instigation of one Chrestus" (Suetonius, *Claudius* 25). A similar idea is presented in Cassius Dio, "As for the Jews, who had again increased so greatly that by reason of their multitude it would have been hard without raising a tumult to bar them from the city, he did not drive them out, but ordered them, while continuing their traditional mode of life, not to hold meetings" (Cassius Dio, *Roman History* 60.6.6). If this new edict took place in 42 C.E., as some have argued, rather than the traditional date of 49 C.E., then Claudius may have had the Alexandrian issue fresh in his mind and hoped to prevent a similar riot in Rome.

Claudius was known to be on good terms with the above-mentioned Herod Agrippa, who now executed James, the leader of the Jewish Christians in Jerusalem, in a persecution. It is possible that Claudius now extended that "persecution" of Christians to Rome by expelling the Jewish Christian leaders from the capital. When these individuals were exiled, the separation between the Jewish community, now without the Jewish Christians, and the Gentile Christians became more pronounced. The Gentile Christians had no need of the Jewish synagogues and their customs and turned more to the house churches. When the leaders of the Jewish Christians returned to Rome some years later, they faced a very different Christian community. The Gentile Christians had continued to develop their faith without the need or desire for Judaism. These Jewish Christians leaders could not bring back the old system; they either had to return to Judaism or move toward the idea that Christianity was no longer for the Jews but for the Gentiles.

Since the Gentile Christians did not have the same beliefs as the Christian Jews, they developed their own form of Christianity around the sayings of Jesus and his apostles outside the context of Judaism. Since they were not versed in the Old Testament and its ancient customs and laws, the Gentile Christians did not have the dietary law restrictions, the need to worship in the synagogue, or the tradition of Jewish fasting. This group now prospered and dominated the Christians in Rome.

Still, the Roman government viewed this new religion in the context of Eastern religions. When Christians broke with Judaism, Rome did not understand that Christianity viewed itself as fulfilling the ancient Jewish ideas of a Messiah. Rome instead viewed Christianity first as a sect of Judaism and, when Christians objected to this view, as an alien religion, or worse yet as atheistic, not believing in any gods. When Rome viewed Christianity as an alien religion, Christians were confronted with innuendoes and misconceptions spread by its enemies. Some Romans proclaimed that Jesus did his deeds, or miracles, through magic and sorcery. Since both were illegal and condemned, Rome could now punish Jesus' followers as magicians and sorcerers, further discrediting the religion. Rome had often lumped magicians, sorcerers, and easterners together. The emperor Tiberius had expelled astrologers and Jews from Rome, again tying religion and magic together. In the 2nd century Roman commentators continued this charge and added that the Christians were superstitious, usually ignorant, from the lower classes, and potentially disruptive. This reinforced in Roman society the notion that Christians were dangerous, since Rome had faced numerous rebellions in the provinces and in Italy only a century and half earlier with the great slave rebellions, particularly that of Spartacus. Pagan commentators accused Christians of cannibalism and of holding depraved parties. These charges came about from the Eucharist and its associated feast. The Christians commemorated Jesus' mission by the Eucharist, where they were invited to eat the body (bread) of Jesus and drink his blood (wine). How seriously the Romans believed this charge that Christians were depraved cannibals is unknown, but it was often repeated. The charge of depraved parties flourished because after the Eucharist individuals would have a feast, the *agape*, from the Greek word for "love feast," an idea that Christians said was a meal of fellowship promoting spiritual, not carnal, love. The Romans, however, viewed it as a ceremony and festival similar to the depraved Bacchanalia. Finally, Rome attacked the concept of Christian monotheism. Christianity believed in only one god, but Christians also stated that there existed God the Father, God the Son, and God the Holy Spirit. For the Romans this was not one god but rather three gods—this was *polytheistic*. These arguments reinforced the Roman view that the Christians were foreigners, superstitious, depraved, and atheists. When and how did these notions first occur?

Claudius' decree banishing certain members of Rome's Jewish community, including leading Jewish Christians, may be seen as the government's first notice of Christianity. Paul's interactions in the East also brought Christians in contact with the government. In these contexts, however, Rome placed the religion within Judaism. During the mid-60s C.E., however, a fire that broke out in the city of Rome brought Christianity to the forefront of Roman consciousness. It is unclear how or who started the fire, but most likely was an accident. Nevertheless, the fire destroyed most of Rome's center, displacing a large segment of the population. The emperor Nero, who was not present, returned and began to oversee the setting up of relief centers. Nero soon enacted legislation forbidding buildings from being over five stories tall, constructed of flimsy material, and overhanging into the street. He enacted these measures since the fire had spread so quickly by jumping from one side of the street to another due to building heights, flimsy construction, and overhangs. The emperor, however, now decided to confiscate most of downtown Rome, the section around the present day Coliseum, for his new residence. This action caused a series of protests, and it was soon rumored that Nero had started the fire so that he could build his new palace. Stories were soon told about how the emperor played his lyre with Rome burning, similar to the burning of Troy. These stories, untrue, soon circulated throughout Rome, causing hatred. Nero further aggravated the situation by constructing, in addition to his new palace, the *Domus Aureus* or Golden House, a private lake and an immense garden, all on land previously occupied by the populous. To deflect attention from his actions, Nero proclaimed that the fire had been started by a new insidious cult, the Christians, and ordered that Christianity be outlawed. The ensuing order made Christianity illegal and punishable by death. According to the Roman historian Tacitus, numerous Christians were captured and executed for the crime of being Christian, as seen in the accompanying Point in Time.

Needing a scapegoat, Nero had chosen the Christians, since they were on the fringes of society; Nero's wife Poppaea Sabina supported the Jews and may have known and hated Christians personally, suggesting to Nero that they would be good scapegoats. What is interesting is that the Christian religion is not attacked as such; rather, Tacitus' distorted view of Christianity, one shared by the majority of Romans, led to beliefs of

GREAT FIRE IN ROME DURING NERO'S REIGN, 64 C.E.

A disaster followed, whether accidental or treacherously contrived by the emperor, is uncertain, as authors have given both accounts, worse, however, and more dreadful than any which have ever happened to this city by the violence of fire. … However, to relieve the people, driven out homeless as they were, he threw open to them the Campus Martius and the public buildings of Agrippa, and even his own gardens, and raised temporary structures to receive the destitute multitude…. These acts, though popular, produced no effect, since a rumour had gone forth everywhere that, at the very time when the city was in flames, the emperor appeared on a private stage and sang of the destruction of Troy, comparing present misfortunes with the calamities of antiquity…. Nero meanwhile availed himself of his country's desolation, and erected a mansion in which the jewels and gold, long familiar objects, quite vulgarised by our extravagance, were not so marvellous as the fields and lakes, with woods on one side to resemble a wilderness, and, on the other, open spaces and extensive views….

Of Rome meanwhile, so much as was left unoccupied by his mansion, was not built up, as it had been after its burning by the Gauls, without any regularity or in any fashion, but with rows of streets according to measurement, with broad thoroughfares, with a restriction on the height of houses, with open spaces, and the further addition of colonnades, as a protection to the frontage of the blocks of tenements…. But all human efforts, all the lavish gifts of the emperor, and the propitiations of the gods, did not banish the sinister belief that the conflagration was the result of an order. Consequently, to get rid of the report, Nero fastened the guilt and inflicted the most exquisite tortures on a class hated for their abominations, called Christians by the populace. Christus, from whom the name had its origin, suffered the extreme penalty during the reign of Tiberius at the hands of one of our procurators, Pontius Pilatus, and a most mischievous superstition, thus checked for the moment, again broke out not only in Judaea, the first source of the evil, but even in Rome, where all things hideous and shameful from every part of the world find their centre and become popular. Accordingly, an arrest was first made of all who pleaded guilty; then, upon their information, an immense multitude was convicted, not so much of the crime of firing the city, as of hatred against mankind. Mockery of every sort was added to their deaths. Covered with the skins of beasts, they were torn by dogs and perished, or were nailed to crosses, or were doomed to the flames and burnt, to serve as a nightly illumination, when daylight had expired.

Tacitus, Annals Book XV, *Complete Works of Tacitus*, trans. Alfred John Church, William Jackson Brodribb, and Sara Bryant (New York: Random House, 1873).

misanthropy and that Christians worshipped an ass, held criminal rituals, and engaged in incest. Suetonius would later view the Christians as seditious: "Punishment was inflicted on the Christians, a class of men given to a new and mischievous superstition."[1] Nero's actions indicated that there must have been a sizable number of Christians known by the public, and he tried to make them an easy target of attacks; however, they were not numerous enough to fight back against the persecution. Nero made belief in Christianity criminal, based on the idea that it was an atheistic religion. Although this crime could have been applied to Judaism, the old connection with Palestine spanning over a century and Judaism's antiquity prevented it. Since Christians in Rome had moved away from the Jewish community, and perhaps fostered by Jewish antagonism, Rome declared Christianity anathema. It was at this time that Paul and Peter are executed. It is during this time that these two individuals, Nero and Paul, coexisted. Although it is impossible to determine if the two met, their lives did intersect with Nero's persecutions of Christians in the city of Rome.

Nero

Lucius Domitius Ahenobarbus, son of Gnaeus Domitius Ahenobarbus and Agrippina, daughter of Germanicus and Agrippina the Elder, grew up under the chaotic reigns of Caligula and Claudius. A great-great-grandson of Augustus, he could claim lineage to both Augustus and Livia through his mother Agrippina the Younger. Caligula banished his mother when Lucius was two, but she returned and later married Claudius, her uncle. Upon this marriage Claudius adopted Lucius, and the boy's name became Nero Claudius Drusus Germanicus. This adoption gave Nero precedence in the succession over Claudius' own son, Britannicus. Nero married Claudius' daughter Octavia and received his education from the philosopher Seneca the Younger. When Claudius died Nero, not yet 17, was proclaimed emperor.

During the early period of his rule his mother Agrippina took a dominant position, with advisors Seneca and Burrus, commander of the guard, engineering the deaths of political rivals. Nero allegedly murdered Britannicus and then transferred his mother to a separate residence, removing her from influence. During this time his rule improved public order, increased protection of provincials, and led to legal reforms. Nero himself applied his talents and hard work to practical judicial reforms. He seems to have disliked the taking of life, and he attempted to reform the tax system to prevent corruption. Although not successful, these undertakings indicate a picture of the emperor often lacking in contemporary literature.

Still, as time went on, Nero began to devote more time, energy, and money to public entertainment. He particularly enjoyed horse racing, poetry, music, acting, and singing. Agrippina disapproved of her son's activities, and when Nero learned that she was questioning his behavior, he had her executed. Most of the senators had not approved of her dominating the political life of Rome and therefore protested very little when she died for such a very minor offense.

After the deaths of Burrus and Seneca, Nero seems to have lost all self-restraint. He divorced his wife, Octavia, exiled her, and had her executed in 62. He then took as his new wife Poppaea Sabina, the wife of his friend Otho, a future emperor who would rule briefly. He also performed singing, poetry reading, and acting, much to the chagrin of the senators. The fire in Rome in 64 caused much damage, and although he was not present, many soon accused the emperor of setting the fire and supposedly playing his lyre and singing while Rome burned. Nero's reputation was not helped by his aggressive rebuilding of Rome, seizing parts of it for his private palace. During this time his rule became more repressive, with attacks on leading senatorial families and individuals related to him who might pose a threat to his rule. Traveling to Greece, where he participated in the Olympic Games, Nero used the time to liberate the Greeks from taxation and to collect works of art. During his absence, the situation in Rome deteriorated, and by the time of his forced early return, the provinces in Gaul, Spain, and Germany were near revolt. When word reached him that the legions were in rebellion on June 9, 68, Nero committed suicide.

During his chaotic rule Rome and the Christians became more directly involved with each other. During his rule the rebellion in Judea forced Christianity to recast itself not as a sect of Judaism but as a separate religion. The great fire in Rome also showed the problems this new religion would have; being on the edges of society and unprotected, they were liable for persecution. Nero's justification for the persecutions of the Christians would set the mark for the next 2 1/2 centuries.

Paul

Paul of Tarsus was born Saul, a Roman citizen in Tarsus Cilicia. He was the son of a Jew belonging to the tribe of Benjamin, and he knew Greek and Aramaic and studied under Gamaliel, the greatest Jewish teacher of the time. A Hellenized Jew, Saul allied himself with the Pharisees. In the beginning he opposed Christianity and even helped martyr Stephen. He approached the Jewish leaders, asking for permission to persecute the followers of Jesus in Damascus. Having received this commission, he set out toward Damascus where, according to his own account, he was struck blind by Jesus. Instructed to proceed to Damascus to find Ananias, he was cured of his blindness and then baptized as a follower of Jesus. He went to Arabia for three years and then returned to Damascus before going to Jerusalem.

At Jerusalem he met and was accepted by Barnabas and was ultimately accepted by the other followers of Christ, who initially doubted his sincerity. Traveling with Barnabas, Saul went to Cyprus, Barnabas' homeland, where he began his ministry. It is here that he seems to have taken the name Paul. The two then traveled into the interior of Asia Minor, where they established churches at Antioch in Pisidia, Iconium, Lystra, and Derbe. They returned to Jerusalem to discuss the admission of the Gentiles without converting to Judaism first, which they favored. After the apostles agreed to allow Gentiles to be admitted as followers of Christ without undergoing circumcision, Paul traveled to Antioch, where the matter of Gentiles entering the fold without converting to Judaism was fully decided. Paul and Barnabas separated, and Paul traveled with Timothy and Silas again through Asia Minor and Galatia and then to Greece. In Greece Paul established churches in Macedonia at Philippi, Thessalonica, and Berea. Meeting no success in Athens, Paul went to Corinth, where he established a successful church and met Aquila and Pricilla from Rome, who had been exiled by the decree of the emperor Claudius that exiled certain Jewish "troublemakers" (possibly Christians). He then traveled again to Ephesus in Asia Minor, where he composed his letters to the Corinthians, who were suffering from internal dissension.

After leaving Ephesus, Paul returned to Jerusalem, where he was imprisoned by the corrupt procurator Felix, who hoped to extort money from him and others. With the arrival of a new governor, Festus, Paul appealed to Caesar for a trial based on his Roman citizenship. After a harrowing sea voyage, including a shipwreck at Malta, Paul arrived in Italy and was held in Rome under house arrest, with a constant guard of Praetorian soldiers for two years. After a total of four or five years of imprisonment, Paul was released, possibly through a general amnesty granted by Nero. He may have traveled back to the East—there is only a late, uncorroborated, story of a travel to Spain—before returning to Rome. He was arrested again, probably in connection with the fire and the general persecutions and was executed.

Paul's greatest achievement was his ability to reach out to Gentiles and bring them into a religion based upon Judaism. His work in uniting Jews and Gentiles into a new religion broke new ground and promoted the growth of Christianity. Paul's other achievement was the creation of the new theology of Christianity through his epistles. In these letters he attempted to explain the theology, which had elements of Judaism as well as the peculiarities of the different regions where Christianity was taking root. These epistles also acted as guides for how individuals were to lead their lives as Christians.

Together with the apostles, Paul stands as one of the greatest missionaries for Christianity. His Roman citizenship, Jewish background, and Greek philosophical training joined the different strands of Mediterranean life to help create Christianity.

CHRISTIANITY AFTER NERO

The Christians were not safe with Nero's death, since Nero's decree outlawing Christianity remained. From the Roman perspective, Christians were outside of the law. During the reign of Trajan (98–117), the governor of Bithynia (northern Turkey), Pliny the Younger, wrote a letter to Trajan giving an account of how he had dealt with those accused of being Christian: He disregarded anonymous charges and offered those who were formally accused a chance to recant. He indicated that his efforts were successful, even though the number of Christians was quite large. Trajan's response to Pliny indicated that Nero's decree was still in force; being a Christian was illegal, as seen in the accompanying Point in Time.

Trajan's reign produced other acts against Christians. One of the early leaders of Antioch, Ignatius, was also executed during Trajan's reign. Given that Nero's original order outlawing Christianity continued, Christians had to continue meeting without government approval, in secret. Christians were continually subjected to threats forcing them to remain secretive, which in turn made them even more suspect. Many Christians, especially in the early years, followed Judaism; to the outside observer, the rituals for both religions were synonymous.

CHRISTIAN RITUALS

The outward signs that separated Christianity from Judaism included not only the absence of circumcision, but Christian rituals. Many of these rituals came from Jewish elements of Judaism, most noticeably the use of water and oil. One element of Christianity was baptism with water.

LETTER XCVIII

TRAJAN TO PLINY

You have adopted the right course, my dearest Secundus, in investigating the charges against the Christians who were brought before you. It is not possible to lay down any general rule for all such cases. Do not go out of your way to look for them. If indeed they should be brought before you, and the crime is proved, they must be punished; with the restriction, however, that where the party denies he is a Christian, and shall make it evident that he is not, by invoking our gods, let him (notwithstanding any former suspicion) be pardoned upon his repentance. Anonymous information ought not to be received in any sort of prosecution. It is introducing a very dangerous precedent, and is quite foreign to the spirit of our age.

Marcus Tullius Cicero, *Letters of Marcus Tullius Cicero, with his treatises on friendship and old age,* trans. E. S. Shuckburgh; *Letters of Gaius Plinius Caecilius Secundus,* trans. William Melmoth, rev. F.C.T. Bosanquet, with introductions and notes, Harvard Classics Vol. 9 (New York: P. F. Collier, 1909), letter 98.

John the Baptist had adopted the ritual of using water as a sign of washing away one's sins. John may have learned this ritual from the Jewish Essenes, who are thought to have used baptism as a sign of initiation into their sect. Christians adopted baptism as their initiation rite. Individuals had to prepare for baptism with a period of instruction leading to the initiation into the faith. For early missionaries preaching to Gentiles, baptism was proclaimed as the rite of initiation, showing the covenant between Christians and God, similar to the initiation of Jews with circumcision. Baptism offered an alternative to circumcision the Gentiles to believe in the God of the Jewish Old Testament and the Messiah, which was simpler and less painful and allowed missionaries the opportunity to convert large numbers at one time. Whole households could now be converted in one setting.

But baptism, occurring only once in one's life, was only one ritual employed by Christians. Another major ritual was the regular celebration of Jesus' Last Supper, developed from the Passover into the Eucharist. The ritual involved the use of bread and wine, representing Jesus' body and blood. Through this regular celebration, usually weekly, Christians were reminded of Jesus' divinity and his personage. The ceremony occurred on Sunday, the day that Jesus rose from the dead, and the fact that it occurred weekly, like the Jewish Sabbath, meant that Christians followed the Jewish week. Only baptized believers could participate in this ceremony. This ritual tied the Christians to their God and provided regular celebration for believers. A third ritual, anointing, involved oil. The use of oil was not unique to Christians: It was a traditional sign of anointing an individual to a priestly or kingly position. Christians used oil to anoint an individual as a sign of their full initiation within the church, at the ordination of a priest, or for someone who has died. The early signs and customs of Christianity had their roots in Judaism with water, bread, and oil. As time passed, Christians created a formalized ritual of their own including local calendars, buildings, and prayers.

NOTE

1. Suetonius, *Lives of the Twelve Caesars,* trans. J. C. Rolfe (London: Heinemann, 1913), Nero 16.2.

5

PRIVATE LIFE

How Christians lived their private lives is the subject of this chapter. The family and its size, house designs, home implements, food and drink, and clothes all impacted Christians and their private lives. Although often similar to their pagan counterparts, Christians purposely set themselves apart and altered their behavior to be in contrast to their non-Christian neighbors. The following discussion examines not only these private aspects but also how Christian leaders and church theologians attempted to guide and persuade their followers to live a life they believed to be Christ's intention.

LIVING IN ROME

To understand Christians' private lives, one can examine inhabitants living in ancient Rome, regardless of their religious practices. Since the early Christian writings are minimal, we often must rely on pagan writers and archaeological material to obtain a fuller understanding. However, it is not too far a leap to extract information about the different classes and regions in the city and to then make some general inferences about the private lives of Christians. Furthermore, information concerning the private life of Christians from a variety of sources, not simply from Rome or from the early period, can also help. The New Testament and other Christian writings indicate that the whole spectrum of social/economic class backgrounds was represented. The pagan author Pliny remarked that persons of all rank, sexes, and geographical locations belonged to Christianity.

The Acts of the Apostles indicated that wealthy individuals, such as the tent-makers Pricilla and Aquila with slaves and large houses, were Christians. Upper-class Romans who may have been attracted to the new cult, or were at least sympathetic, included Sergius Paulus, the proconsul of Cyprus, who converted to Christianity and urged Paul and his followers to proselytize in the interior of Asia Minor. Gallio, the proconsul of Achaea (Greece), protected Paul from the Jews. Although perhaps not a convert, Gallio did not act in a hostile manner toward the early Christians. In Ephesus, Paul had friends, perhaps even converts, who were town officials, the Asiarchs. It is possible that Pomponia Graecina, wife of Aulus Plautius, a general who commanded legions in Britain, may have been a Christian, since she was accused of believing in strange rites. In addition to these upper-class individuals, middle-class shop owners and government officials were known, such as Lydia at Philippi Greece, a seller of purple cloth, who was baptized along with her household. Finally, there were the poor and slaves, where Christianity, like most religions, received the majority of their converts. Although Christianity may have had its largest numbers from the lower classes, it was by no means only a lower-class religion.

TWO UPPER-CLASS CHRISTIAN INTELLECTUALS

Marcella

A friend of Jerome whose writings are our chief source for her life, Marcella was a noble woman from the Marcelli and possessed great wealth, which she inherited from her father. When Athanasius arrived in Rome in 340, her mother Albina was already widowed. Marcella learned from Athanasius the story of Anthony and the monasteries in the Thebaid in southern Egypt. It appears that Marcella's desire to live an ascetic life can be traced to her interaction with Athanasius. Although she married, her husband died after only seven months, and she refused to marry again. In 374 the Egyptian monk Peter arrived in Rome, and Marcella became the first in the city to take the monastic profession. She lived with her mother in their palatial estate on the Aventine, but did not live a life of either ostentatious behavior or immoderate asceticism. Jerome arrived in Rome in 382, and Marcella, almost to the point of pestering, sought him out. She gathered a circle of women companions who formed a rudimentary convent where they studied scriptures and prayed. She forced Jerome to provide evidence for his ideas and even questioned him on his severity and quarrels. Jerome wrote 15 treatises on scriptures for her and hoped, when he departed in 385, that she might go with him to Bethlehem. She remained in Rome, however, and when her mother died in 387 she retired to a small house outside of Rome with a young friend, Principia, and devoted the remainder of her life to good work. She used her education, training, and intellect to force Pope Anastasius

(400–403) to condemn Origen and his followers, with Jerome praising her role. When Alaric sacked the city of Rome in 410, the Goths assumed she was concealing her wealth and attacked her. Through her pleas she convinced the Goths to spare Principia, but she herself soon died in the arms of Principia. She left her wealth to the poor.

Jerome

Jerome (345–420), one of the four fathers of the Western church (the others being Augustine, Ambrose, and Gregory the Great), wrote extensively on biblical and historical scholarship. Born at Stridon, near Aquileia in Northern Italy, and a student of Latin literature and rhetoric education in Rome, Jerome lived in a monastic community and then traveled to Gaul and back to Aquileia before going to Antioch in 374. Here Jerome reported that Christ condemned him, saying, "You are a Ciceronian, not a Christian," in reference to his love of Latin literature. For the next three years Jerome lived in the deserts of Syria.

In 379 Jerome traveled to Constantinople, where he translated into Latin Eusebius' *World Chronicle*, extending its coverage to the year 378. Jerome then traveled to Rome in 383, where he became the secretary to Pope Damasus, who urged him to translate the Hebrew Old Testament and Greek New Testament into Latin. He now began this great task, which he completed during 390–405. This work, his most famous, became known as the Vulgate and became the Bible used in the West during the medieval ages.

While at Rome, Jerome became the spiritual advisor to Paula and her daughter Eustochium, supposedly a descendent of Rome's founder, Trojan War hero Aeneas, and of the great republican family the Scipios. Paula and Eustochium became Jerome's patronesses, traveling with him to the Holy Land in 385, where they settled in Bethlehem and established monasteries. Jerome continued his work on the Bible, wrote commentaries on the books of the Bible, and engaged in theological discussions. In his works he praised Origen, although he later condemned him, attacked Ambrose, and fought with his oldest friend, Rufinus. In addition to the commentaries, Jerome wrote a work on illustrious men.

Working on the book of Ezekiel in 410, Jerome lamented the fall of Rome. After this disaster many refugees fled to the East. One such refugee was Pelagius, a British-born monk, who argued that man was committed to sin, and responsible for his actions, which reduced the need for divine grace, contrary to the chirch's teachings. Jerome's opposition forced Pelagius to move to North Africa, where Pelagius was condemned. Jerome died in Bethlehem on September 30, 420.

As a rule, Christians engaged in most of the usual laboring professions. In fact, Christianity praised individuals who did manual labor. Like the Jews, Christians viewed labor as deriving from God, hence the ban on certain professions that dishonored humans and therefore God. But one's occupation ensured the family's survival, which in turn contributed to the state's prosperity. Augustine argued that labor was

God's commandment, so all healthy men had to provide for their own maintenance through their labors. Although most Christians before Constantine were from the lower classes, the church did not argue for a change in the social orders; rather, the employer owed a just wage, but he was still in charge.

Some occupations, however, were strictly forbidden, mainly those that impinged upon Christian morals such as prostitution or working as pimps, brothel owners and workers, and actors, since these professions sold their bodies for pleasure and had no regard for chastity. Those that demeaned human life such as gladiators, charioteers (although it was acceptable to watch the races), civic magistrates, and military personnel (since they violated the commandment not to kill) were forbidden. And those that participated in idolatry such as magicians, sorcerers, astrologers, soothsayers, and makers of idols, since they did not profess God's ultimate power, were likewise condemned. Some professions, however, that were originally "banned" were later accepted such as soldiers and treasurers for gladiators. Ultimately Christians could be slaves, soldiers, bureaucrats, merchants, professionals, and artisans, for in Christianity, with those few exceptions, no profession was seen as too demeaning for admittance into the religion.

SIZE OF THE EARLY CHRISTIAN FAMILY

As seen, most early Christians did not come from the elite due to two reasons. First, the number and percentage of the elite in the Roman world was small. Nearly 90 percent of the population engaged in agriculture and stockbreeding, which were lower-class occupations. Throughout the Roman Empire the amount of revenue from land far outpaced that from industry. The three major upper classes—senators, equestrians, and *decurions* (local town aristocrats)—never amounted to more than 5 percent of the total population. Therefore, the number of converts likely to come from this upper echelon of society remained quite small. The second reason early Christians did not come from the elite lay in the fact that the original Christians were converted Jews, and the Roman upper echelons did not accept these Christians due to the prevailing anti-Semitism and prejudices against this monotheistic religion.

Since most of the early Christians in Rome tended to be Jewish, it is most likely that they lived in the Trans Tiberim district (Region XIV), or modern Trastevere, where immigrants tended to flock. The area had numerous tenement houses, *insulae*, and many of the lower-class laborers probably worked on the docks along the Tiber River. The living conditions in the city were harsh, with many of the poor living in squalor. The normal lower-class Roman family and immigrants seems to have had an average of three children, any more would have made it too hard to supply enough food. Evidence from literature and inscriptions further indicates that Roman families with more than three children were rewarded with benefits, since Augustus attempted to increase the number of citizens. Although these measures were aimed at Roman citizens, in particular the nobility, it seems then that the average number of children for all segments of society living in the city was three. As in other societies, boys were desired while girls were seen as a burden, since they had to be provided with a dowry.

The institution of marriage differed between Christians and pagans. Although Christian writers, for example Clement, indicated that celibacy and chastity were to be preferred, if one had to marry, it was to beget children and produce a large family. Thus, for Christianity marriage was meant for procreation, which in turn enlarged the Christian community. Unlike pagans, however, Christians did believe that both parties in the marriage were equal before God. As such, there was a moral equality of the sexes, unlike in Roman ideology, where men had superiority. Christian men were required to be faithful to their wives. The church fathers condemned infidelity equally harshly regardless of the sex of the offender, unlike pagan Roman society, where a double standard existed favoring the man.

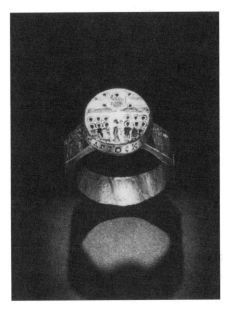

Marriage Ring with Scenes from the Life of Christ. The Walters Art Museum, Baltimore.

HOUSES

Throughout the Roman Empire archaeological excavations have provided evidence for houses that generally fall into the categories of villas, often large and for the wealthy, multistory structures for several families, and individual farmsteads and homes. The archaeological excavations in Ostia, Herculaneum, and Pompeii have revealed houses of various sizes. Throughout the Roman world small city houses occupied by normal working-class people existed, and in these small homes ordinary Christians lived and worked. These are not the great palaces or villas, but rather the ordinary homes similar to the modern ranch houses built in the United States in the 1960s and 70s. Evidence

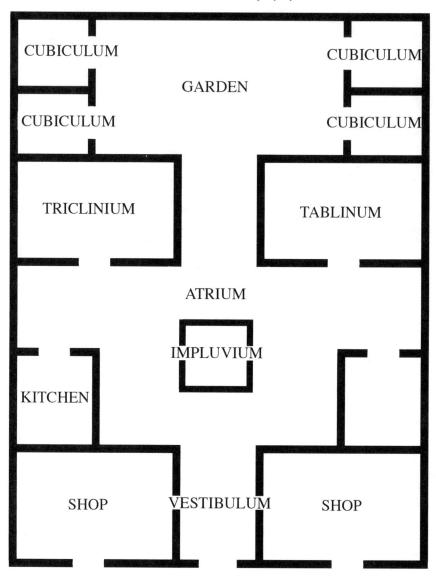

Plan of Atrium House. Courtesy of Greg Aldrete.

in Egypt indicated that houses were small with a floor space equal to a modern one-bedroom apartment, with three to six rooms, often with no real floor plan. Many did not have a second floor. Although families may have had about 6 people, it is clear that more than that lived in these small houses, usually 10–12 people, consisting of extended families, slaves, and servants living in houses with a courtyard, stable, and kitchen complex. But due to the small house size, individuals spent most their time outdoors, using the house for sleeping and perhaps for meals.[1] Throughout the Mediterranean world there existed housing types that promoted this type of communal living. Ancient society, much more than modern 21st-century living, had multiple generations living in one household. In addition to the social makeup of the houses involving multigenerations, slaves, free workers, and clients likewise lived under the same roof.

One interesting feature of Mediterranean homes, especially rural homesteads, was the open courtyard. In Palestine, houses typically had three large rooms laid out to form a U, with a courtyard accessible from all three rooms and a gate that could enclose the courtyard and protect the house. Two stories high, these houses provided room for families, livestock, and supplies. The Greek peristyle was similar, but had covered walkways surrounding the courtyard where rainwater was often collected in a basin. Traditional Roman houses were similar to the Greek style, although early homes were more self-contained around the *atrium* without the open courtyards. Around the 2nd century B.C.E., Romans modified their large palatial houses to include not only the traditional atrium-style house but the large imported Greek courtyard.

The central part of a traditional Italian Roman's life was the house. Unlike rural peasant homes in Italy, the Italian houses in cities, like Rome,

Pompeii: Wall Painting. James W. Ermatinger.

allowed individuals to not only sleep, live, and raise their families, but the house provided a place where the family could engage in trade, politics, and entertainment. The Romans built their houses around a central atrium, with an opening in the roof, the *compluvium,* allowing smoke to escape from the central hearth and let in light and rain water, collected into a basin, the *impluvium,* with rooms placed around the exterior of the atrium. The family occupied the rooms around the atrium: A vestibule or entry room in the front contained the household gods or *Lares,* and directly in the rear on the same axis as the vestibule was the *tablinium,* or receiving hall, where the master received visitors. On either side existed bedrooms, and perhaps a library and storerooms. Christian homes may or may not have continued the practice of the Lares, since their absence would have attracted attention and since not all members of a household were Christian. The Lares was also the family history; ancestors were honored and represented. Their continual representations under Christianity would be seen as honoring one's family lines, a worthy endeavor. The rooms around the atrium would have received some light from the compluvium, but would also have windows with shutters on the outer walls. Nevertheless, during the day the rooms had little light, and at night virtually none except for lamps. This description fits the middle-class houses. In more opulent or wealthy homes the tablinium overlooked an open courtyard surrounded by a peristyle or covered walkway supported by columns. The floors were decorated with mosaics composed of tesserae often forming stories of mythology and great deeds, such as the famous portrayal of Alexander the Great's victory over Darius, king of Persia, now preserved in Naples. The walls had painted frescoes and niches with statues. Moving beyond the tablinium, one entered the peristyle, with its columned porticoes and a large open space, which was usually a garden, often with a fountain. Around this open space other rooms—bedrooms, sitting rooms, another library, and storage rooms—allowed the family more privacy than the atrium, which was now reserved more for formal visitors and business, and was not living space. In the rear, the kitchen, central hall, and *triclinium,* or dining room, allowed for both formal and private interaction. The central hall could be used for parties, dining, and meetings. The kitchen tended to be located in the rear, often detached from the house, to prevent fires from spreading. The cooking hearth was a large box-like container with holes in the top for the fire and an inside area for charcoal or wood. Fumes and exhaust would be drafted up into an overhead hood and vented through flues to chimneys. Cooks would place pans and pots on these open holes; the stoves, however, were potentially dangerous, not only from fires but from noxious fumes. Located in the rear of the property, for obvious health reasons, were the latrines. Behind this back structure, through the kitchen or triclinium, was the small garden, with perhaps a pond, fruit trees, and statues providing the family with a space for solitude. Finally, a high wall protected the house's rear. While the first floor housed the family residences, the second floor, made of wood, provided living quarters for the servants and contained storerooms. The windows on the ground floor were virtual slits to protect the house from intruders, while on the second floor larger grated windows let in more light. The amount of light entering the house depended on the time of day, cloud cover, number of windows, and size of the compluvium. Of course, for illuminating after sundown artificial light was needed in the form of lamps and candles.

For the house, lamps were made of clay, glass, or metal, usually bronze, filled with oil and lit with wicks. The more wicks, the more light was given off, but with more wicks, more oil was consumed. This is reminiscent of the parable of the women in the New Testament who did not have enough oil to wait out the night. Although not common, lamps made of glass existed and were highly valued for their craftsmanship. The amount of light, however, was not great. Candles made from wax or tallow gave some light, but again, not a substantial amount. Still, in some houses dinner parties undoubtedly took place late in the night. Most Roman families then set their rising and retiring to the sun.

Since Roman houses did not have large fireplaces due to the mild winters, the Romans used braziers, usually metal containers filled with hot charcoal, to heat a small room, or part of one, to take the chill off. At night Romans typically wore heavy cloaks to bed, which, while bulky, were effective. For the

Pompeii: Mosaic, Dog. James W. Ermatinger.

Pompeii: Roman House. James W. Ermatinger.

Pompeii: Roman House. James W. Ermatinger.

lower classes, cold winter nights were kept at bay by wearing more clothes. For middle-class Romans bed cloaks and blankets provided more comfort, while for wealthy inhabitants braziers put beside their bed provided warmth. Like today, one's comfort depended on how much one could afford.

Wealthy Roman homes often had public shops and businesses connected with them. These businesses, frequently run by the owner's freedmen, were set up on the ground floor fronting the busy avenues, and without direct entrance into the home. In addition to rent, and perhaps a percentage of the sales, the owner now had a buffer from the street noises and a ready supply of watchmen and laborers for the home.

Roman houses differed from modern American houses in several important ways. First, Roman houses looked inward. Opulence was located inside the house, while the exterior remained simple. American houses, in contrast, look outward, publicly displaying their owner's position and wealth. Second, Roman houses had a public flow—vestibule, atrium, triclinium, and peristyle courtyard—all concealed within the house's walls, whereas many American homes exhibit only private rooms. Finally, Roman homes were utilitarian, with their public front rooms serving as shops and businesses, in contrast to American homes, which are primarily private.

For the early Christian family that inhabited these houses, a variety of social and economic classes existed. Furthermore, it is clear that not all members of a family converted to Christianity. This led to situations where some members of the household were Christian while others were pagan, and it would not be uncommon for a family with extended members and slaves to have a variety of religious beliefs under one roof. These houses, then, served as principle residences for the wealthy and powerful. During the 1st century some wealthy Christians allowed their homes to be used as "house churches" where other Christians could assemble, especially after the break with Judaism. Christians met in these houses, where they not only worshiped, but also socialized. Many of the worshipers were from the lower classes and did not have such sumptuous houses. Often such individuals were related to the owners as freedmen or slaves, but many were merely other Christians from the poorer classes. Their meeting place would have been in the reception room off the peristyle or in the traditional tablinium. In either instance the amount of space available was limited, meaning that these communities were small.

Many Christians who attended these house churches lived outside these houses with their families in the *insulae,* or tenement houses, whose location and size determined their rent. Like all large cities that attracted people from other regions, rents in Rome were determined not by size alone, but also by locations and artificial factors. Unlike modern apartments, where the penthouse or upper floors are most desirable, in ancient Rome living on the bottom floors with their stone walls was desired, since as one moved up, the building material became inferior and was usually wood, which had the potential for fire, and substandard building practices existed. Built five to six stories high, these insulae, too, were built around an interior courtyard, which often had a fountain. Although an individual could own a few rooms or even a floor, most residents rented. The apartments on the first floor had a living room, dining room, and bedroom, with enough space for servants. These were the largest apartments and brought in a large rent. Moving upstairs, the apartments in the insulae were usually subdivided into small one- to two-room apartments, some with balconies. Again, most were poorly lit, had few amenities, and were really more like boarding houses. Ultimately apartments on the top floor in the attics were dark, cramped, poorly constructed and ventilated, hot in the summer, cold in the winter, and usually housed the very poor. Individuals had no private bathrooms; rather, they either shared a common latrine on the first floor or made do with chamber pots. There were no kitchens, except for the owners' on the first floor, so individuals either had to cook in public, or more commonly would go out and buy their daily meals, which of course increased the family's cost of living. Again lamps were used for light and, if one could afford it, a brazier for heat.

As seen in chapter 2, Rome in the 1st century had an abundant supply of fresh water. Many of the wealthy homes accessed direct plumbing by tying into the water lines, either legally or illegally. Tenement houses usually did not have water, but instead relied on the numerous public and private fountains, often in the insulae's courtyard, for fresh water. Individuals would carry the water up the floors each time, probably several times a day, for drinking, cooking, washing, and other functions. While some houses had private baths in addition to latrines, the vast majority of Rome relied on the public and private commercial baths. In later Rome, some of the former wealthy homes were subdivided into apartments. This may have been due to hard times for the owners, the need for more housing, or both.

Juvenal, a Roman satirist in the 1st century c.e., gives a vivid portrait of Rome in his 3rd satire. According to Juvenal, rents are high, even for a dark upper-attic room. Most ill people perish in Rome for lack of sleep produced by undigested food. Also, no one can sleep in Rome except for the wealthy since the wagons, prohibited from entering Rome during the day, move noisily through the streets all night long. Wealthy individuals can traverse the crowded streets during the day since people make way for their litter, but the rest of Rome is hit by a pressing crowd. At night the perils of walking in the street are horrendous; for example a pot or unusable vessel might be pitched out to the streets below and hit an unsuspecting traveler. There are, of course, robbers and murderers eager to separate one from one's wealth. And, of course, one's room in the attic is supported by substandard construction, with the roof ready to collapse or catch on fire from a careless tenant and his lamp. With nothing to shelter one but the roof tiles, the room is hot, stuffy, and cramped. But as Juvenal said, why would someone subject themselves to live in Rome? The answer is easy: location, location, location. The heart of the empire and a large city is always more exciting than a small bucolic town

Plan of Insula (Apartment House). Courtesy of Alicia Aldrete.

Pompeii: Balcony. James W. Ermatinger.

with no excitement. That is why even today New York, with its exorbitant rent, is home to millions, while small Axtell, Nebraska, has barely 800 souls.

FURNITURE

Most Roman houses possessed less furniture than modern houses, which provided them more flexibility for the available space. A lower-class domicile would be sparsely furnished. With only two rooms in an insula, one would have a small table and two or three chairs. For eating there might be pottery plates and earthen mugs, again all fairly inexpensive, but durable and practical. The second room had for a bed a mattress, or *torus*, originally made of straw, hay, leaves, or similar material stuffed inside to make it as soft as possible. This bed would be covered with sheets or blankets called *toralia*.

In a "middle-class" apartment with several rooms, there were probably several beds, this time made of wood and having a mattress. Instead of pottery plates and mugs, there might be some silver plates and goblets, showing an increase in wealth. Middle-class families could also possess more lamps and candles, making their apartments appear more open. In addition, in winter they could have a brazier or two to provide heat.

Wealthy Christians, like their pagan counterparts, had in addition to superior dinnerware, cabinets for clothes, tables of metal and marble, and more luxurious chairs and couches in order to relax. Paintings, sculptures, frescoes, and mosaics would grace their houses, showing a visitor not only their status but their wealth. The family treasures would be not just money but such things as plates, books (papyri rolls), furniture, and other movable goods. A daughter's dowry often included plates, furniture, and clothes, indicating that these items were more than just utilitarian goods. Wealthy families would also have more light and heat. For a proper bed for the wealthy, a *lecti cubicuares,* one climbed into a raised platform, usually by a ladder or steps. The bed could be made of metal, wood, or ivory, and often had silver or gold feet, or *fulcra.* The mattress was placed upon strings or ropes. There were twin and double beds; the latter had terms designating the sides where people entered: the open side, called the *sponda,* and the closed other side, which had a board and was called the *pluteus,* and most likely these beds had two mattresses placed side by side to create a double bed. The mattresses of the wealthy were stuffed with wool or feathers and had pillows. These mattresses were covered with sheets, and there were blankets, often of rich material, especially the highly prized purple-colored spreads, some with embroidered gold material, placed on top. It is possible that there were hanging bed curtains, which kept out dust and drafts. The Christian Clement of Alexandria forbade expensive bedding, gold-sprinkled rugs, rich purple bed robes, and elaborate purple blankets, since the use of these materials leads to corruption of the soul. The purple cloth was highly prized since it was not only aesthetically pleasing but difficult to dye; hence its expense. Clement also forbade sleeping on soft

Banquet couch. The Walters Art Museum, Baltimore.

down, since it not only panders the body but is injurious. He clearly had the wealthy in mind when he made these pronouncements.

TIME

One of the key components in life for all individuals is the knowledge of the passage of time. While modern society has the use of sophisticated timepieces using atomic clocks, ancient society relied on the changes in the seasons for the calendar and the movement of the sun for time. Most Romans calculated daily time by the sun's rising and setting. They then divided the day into 12 hours and the evening into 12 hours. But since the amount of sun time changes, the hours were of different lengths; in the summer the daylight hours had more minutes per hour while in winter the daylight hours had fewer minutes. Most Romans then merely indicated time as an approximate position; noon was between the 6th and 7th hour during the day, meaning that in the summer the hours were longer and in the winter shorter; and midnight was between the 6th and 7th hour during the evening, shorter hours in the summer, longer in the winter. The Romans did have sundials, but again, they were not accurate or portable. Christians were therefore faced with the same situations as everyone else.

The reckoning of time also included the calendar. During the Roman Republic the calendar was based upon the lunar cycle, in which extra days were added to take into account the differences between the lunar and solar cycles. Near the end of the republic the calendar was out of sync, and Julius Caesar attempted to correct it. His solution was the implementation of a solar calendar, the Julian calendar, which, while revised by Pope Gregory in the 16th century, is still the basis of the modern calendar. Originally the Romans did not use the concept of weeks based on seven days. Instead, their calendar used the months centered around three days, the *kalends,* the first day of the month, the *nones,* the 5th or the 7th, and the *ides,* the 13th or 15th, with the month being reckoned backwards from these days; for example, the last day of January would be the day before the kalends of February.

More important in keeping track of time on the larger scale would be the reckoning of time between market days, usually held every 9th day in the countryside. The Christians would use the solar calendar developed by Julius Caesar, but they used the seven-day week calendar of the Jews, having weekly celebration of their religion. The difference between the Jewish and Christian week centered on the Sabbath: For the Jews it was on Saturday; for the Christians, Sunday. This adoption by the Christians of Sunday lay in part because of a conscious effort to distance them from Judaism, but also because Sunday was the day on which they believed Jesus to have risen from the dead. The Christian week, however, became a mixture of astrological, Jewish, and Christian aspects. Although the week was Jewish, the names of the days came from the pagan astrological names, which the Christians modified to suit their needs, such as Sunday coming from dies Solis or day of the sun but also interpreted as son for Son of God (Jesus). The impact of the Christian week is still seen today.

In addition to this normal reckoning of time, Christians had their own liturgical calendars listing the feasts for the days of the month observed by a particular church or community in local regions. Christian writers attested that local communities kept lists of martyrs, and bishops celebrated their feasts on a particular day. Since each church had its own calendar, differences occurred between communities, even when nearby. The oldest surviving calendars were the Calendar of Carthage and the Deposition of Martyrs and Bishops in Rome of 354 c.e..

NOURISHMENT

While Christians may remember Jesus' statement that "man does not live on bread alone," it was nevertheless crucial for human survival to constantly have nourishment.

The Roman emperors realized that two types of nourishments were needed for their survival and to keep the inhabitants satisfied and peaceful: bread and circus. Christians living in Rome and other major cities had a variety of foodstuffs to choose from. What determined an individual's meal was status, wealth (or lack thereof), and family. If the Christian was from the upper class, more opportunities to dine out and have elaborate meals existed. If he was poor his meal would be sparse. And, if the Christian had a family, a sufficient amount for all members of the family was needed.

Pitcher, Bronze. Saint Louis Art Museum.

Christians living in the countryside had a different lifestyle, neither harder nor easier. Again all three determinants played crucial roles. A wealthy owner could supply his family with enough foodstuffs to provide a well-balanced diet. A poor family had to struggle in the countryside as well as in the city. As seen in the accompanying Point in Time, the Roman writer Celsus in his work *On Medicine* gives types of food that were good and bad for the stomach. Although by modern standards Celsus' advice might seem harsh or even distasteful, many of his ideas had some basis for maintaining a somewhat healthy constitution. Most of his advice was geared for the wealthy Roman and not the urban or rural poor.

Christian writers drew distinctions between themselves and their pagan counterparts, for example, in the accompanying letter from Basil to Gregory, where he gave the following suggestions: less culinary and more

Cup (Skyphos), Glass. Saint Louis Art Museum.

morality. Basil's advice was to make the Christians realize the importance of God in society's life.

MEALS

Most Romans generally had three meals: breakfast *(ientaculum)*, lunch *(prandium)*, and dinner *(cena)*. Breakfast generally consisted of bread, with perhaps some olives and or cheese. Lunch, like in modern Italy, was a quick affair, with bread, fruit, and cheese. Most of these breaks were taken at the small shops or from street vendors. Dinner was not only the main meal, but was the most important, often supplying leftovers for the following day's breakfast or lunch. The meal might consist of bread, vegetables dipped in olive oil, cheese, and, if fortunate, some kind of meat, although

Cup (Skyphos), Glass. Saint Louis Art Museum.

for the poor this might be irregular. For the rural inhabitants food tended to be simple and usually consisted of vegetables, some bread, legumes, cheese, fruits, and occasionally meat. Although the ancient writers praised the simplicity of the country diet, they had in mind the wealthy estate owner, not the poor tenant farmer, peasant, or slave. For the inhabitants of Rome, however, securing food could be both a pleasure and a challenge. There were immense varieties of shops and restaurants to provide an almost endless supply of food and drink. The urban poor, however, probably did not have as much or as healthy a diet as their rural counterparts. Hence, the challenge lay not for the wealthy, but for the average urban laborer, who sometimes had to rely on the government-sponsored programs, especially the distribution of grain that became the chief source of food for the urban masses.

The emperors continued to provide free and cheap grain to the urban poor, because they could not risk an outright riot or rebellion if the grain ended. Indeed, some of the worst situations in Rome, under the emperors Augustus, Tiberius, Claudius, and the year of the Four Emperors (69 C.E.), resulted when a grain shortage or even the fear of one provoked the masses to riot. Together with the games (see below), these two institutions helped mollify the urban mob. In addition, there were benefits to this

Plate, Bronze and Silver. Saint Louis Art Museum.

grain program. The supply and transport of grain allowed for employment. Grain, in the form of wheat and or barley, was distributed to citizens
in Rome, mainly the poor. The individual would then have to turn the
grain into bread at one of the numerous bakeries. If the individual could
not pay for this transaction in money, the bakers would take a percentage of the grain and sell it to others. The bakeries provided employment
for numerous citizens. Other cities such as Alexandria, Constantinople,
and even distant outlying cities such as Oxyrhynchus in Egypt had grain-
distribution programs. The bread and circus impacted Christians as well.
If they were citizens, and it is probable that some were, they were entitled
to the free grain distribution. In addition, some Christians, if not many,
went to the circus and games for enjoyment.

Since most poor Christians living in insula could not prepare their own
meals, numerous taverns, or *thermopolii*, prospered in the cities. In the city
of Pompeii, a medium-sized town of about 20,000 inhabitants, over 200
taverns and small eateries have been excavated, meaning that for a city
like Rome the number would have been 50 times greater.

Like most of the non-Jewish Romans, Christians fell into the different
social structures that had a gradation of food and drink depending on
their status. At the lowest level, the urban poor usually had a breakfast
of porridge, if they were lucky, or a loaf of bread baked of at one of the

A PAGAN ROMAN DOCTOR'S ADVICE FOR A CALM STOMACH

24 But best suited to the stomach are: whatever is harsh, even what is sour, and that which has been sprinkled moderately with salt; so also unleavened bread, and spelt or rice or pearl barley which has been soaked; birds and game of all kinds, and both of these whether roasted or boiled; among domesticated animals, beef; of other meat the lean rather than the fat; the trotters, chaps, ears, and the sterile womb of a pig; among pot-herbs, endive, lettuce, parsnip, cooked gourd, skirret; among orchard fruit, the cherry, mulberry, service fruit, the mealy pear from Crustumeria, or the Mevian; also keeping-pears, Tarentine or Signian, the round or Scandian apple or that of Ameria or the quince or pomegranate, raisins preserved in jars; soft egg, dates, pine kernels, white olives preserved in strong brine, or the same steeped in vinegar, or black olives which have been well ripened on the tree, or which have been preserved in raisin wine, or in boiled-down must; dry wine is allowable even although it may have become harsh, also that doctored with resin; hard-fibred fish of the intermediate class, oysters, scallops, the shellfish murex and purpura, snails; food and drink either very cold or very hot; wormwood.

25 But on the other hand materials alien to the stomach are: all things tepid, all things salted, all things stewed, all things over-sweetened, all things fatty, broth, leavened bread, and likewise that made from either millet or barley, pot-herb roots, and pot-herbs eaten with oil or fish sauce, honey, mead, must boiled down, raisin wine, milk, cheese of all kinds, fresh grapes, figs both green and dry, pulse of all sorts, and whatever causes flatulence; likewise thyme, catmint, savory, hyssop, cress, sorrel, charlock, walnuts. But it can be understood from the above that what has good juice does not necessarily agree with the stomach, and that whatever agrees with the stomach has not necessarily good juice.

A. Cornelius Celsus, *De Medicina (On Medicine)* 2, Loeb Classical Library (London: Heinemann, 1935), pp. 24–25; cf: http://penelope.uchicago.edu/Thayer/E/Roman/Texts/Celsus/home.html.

numerous bakeries. The cheapest loaves were made of coarse grain *(panis sordidus)*, while a bit better quality *(panis secundus)* was available for the upper poor class, and finally, if one could afford it, the *siligineus*, very white and sweet bread. The loaves were flat and about two inches thick, weighing about a pound. In the afternoon, lunch was probably the same, with perhaps some vegetables grown in the neighboring regions of Rome. Finally, dinner might be salted fish or, if one could afford it, poultry. The average Roman, especially the poor, ate little beef, since there was no way to preserve it. Only when there was a festival would a Roman have some beef. Pork was widely eaten, however, especially among the middle class. Pigs were driven into the city and then slaughtered and the meat distributed.

A CHRISTIAN BISHOP'S ADVICE FOR MEALS

So too as to food; for a man in good health bread will suffice, and water will quench thirst; such dishes of vegetables may be added as conduce to strengthening the body for the discharge of its functions. One ought not to eat with any exhibition of savage gluttony, but in everything that concerns our pleasures to maintain moderation, quiet, and self-control; and, all through, not to let the mind forget to think of God, but to make even the nature of our food, and the constitution of the body that takes it, a ground and means for offering Him the glory, bethinking us how the various kinds of food, suitable to the needs of our bodies, are due to the provision of the great Steward of the Universe. Before meal let grace be said, in recognition alike of the gifts which God gives now, and which He keeps in store for time to come. Say grace after meal in gratitude for gifts given and petition for gifts promised. Let there be one fixed hour for taking food, always the same in regular course, that of all the four and twenty of the day and night barely this one may be spent upon the body.

Basil, Epistle 2, in *A Select Library of the Post-Nicene Fathers of the Christian Church,* ed. Philip Schaff and Henry Wace, 2nd series, trans. into English with prolegomena and explanatory notes. (New York: The Christian Literature Company, 1895), Vol. 8, *Basil: Letters and Select Works,* p. 112.

Romans, rich and poor, drank wine with their meals. Wine, usually diluted with water, was the main beverage. Even the poorest Roman could afford a jug of *posca,* vinegar mixed with enough water to make it drinkable. The final commodity, also grown in Italy, was the olive. The olive could be eaten, and, when pressed, the oil used in lamps, as soap, for cooking oil, and in dips. A versatile commodity, the olive was second only to grain, and ahead of wine, for ancient society's survival. In addition, Romans liked to have sauces for their food and breads. A common sauce, *garum,* was used by most inhabitants. Garum was a salty fish sauce that the Romans inherited from the Greeks. During the Roman Empire, Spain provided the best supply of garum.

For the upper class, the variety of foods available was immense. In addition to grain, oil, and wine, meats such as wild boar, venison, and hare, and birds such as pheasant, quail, peacocks, goose, and chicken were served. The Romans especially liked fresh fish, a standard commodity, and other seafood, such as urchins, oysters, and octopus. While most Christians, like most Romans, could not enjoy these delicacies, some upper-class Christians undoubtedly enjoyed the sumptuous banquets.

These banquets were more than just culinary events; they were social and political occasions. The party of the wealthy Roman Christian must have looked similar to that of a wealthy pagan Roman. The number of guest was socially fixed at nine, with three guests per couch. If you wished

Ostia: Taverna (Food Shop). James W. Ermatinger.

to have more guests you needed more dining rooms (triclinium). Unlike in Greece, where women were sequestered, Roman women were invited to dine with the men. These parties served as social functions, showing how well one could entertain, and political as well, as determined by what type of guest you had sitting at your table. It is most likely, though, that Christians avoided the licentious behavior found at many Roman meals, especially the wild drinking. These elaborate meals probably also allowed Christians to meet and have their commemorative feast, the Eucharist. Christians were expected not to become drunk, with wine at least, but rather to become filled with the Holy Spirit. Likewise, in eating, Christians were not to be gluttonous. Clement of Alexandria also urged restraint in meals, arguing that pagans were given over to luxury and gluttony. Christians, meanwhile, should eat a plain diet of olives, milk, cheeses, fruit, and if meat, it should be boiled rather than roasted. In addition, Christians were not to carouse about seeking worldly pleasures. Clement also urged Christians to refrain from a variety of food and to drink wine sparingly. At banquets, individuals should be modest. In the same way, gold and silver drinking cups and expensive dinner plates should be avoided, since these led to envy and, thus, greed. Banquets were to be for God, and not for worldly pleasure. This advice clearly indicated that Christians celebrated like their pagan counterparts, and obviously some celebrated too much.

Complementing Clement's view was Juvenal, who wrote in the 1st century. His 5th satire presented the problems of the lower-class citizenry, who were forced to grovel at their master's feet as clients. The institution

Measure (Modiolus), Terracotta. Saint Louis Art Museum.

of the client harkened back to the republic when powerful individuals protected the weak and poor in return for political support. The patron (powerful individual) would give aid and protection to his client (the weaker individual) who in return would give his patron political help: votes, campaigning, and even illegal acts such as intimidation. The institution had now degenerated into pandering the powerful. In return, the client received an occasional meal and some money. The meal was not elaborate. The client's wine, drunk from a cracked goblet, was awful, while the great man had the best types from gold and jeweled cups. The master received his lobster with asparagus, while the client got a tiny plate of shrimp with half an egg. While the master had mullet and lamprey, the client received an eel, a relative of a water snake, or a pike from the foul Tiber River. The master received delicacies untold, while the client had dubious toadstools. Juvenal clearly made fun of the relationship of

The Rubens Vase. The Walters Art Museum, Baltimore.

the client and master, but it existed, and the occasional meal or banquet was seen as a reward. Christians must have been drawn into this realm as well. Clement clearly condemned the wealthy ostentations, but he acknowledged that they existed.

Romans also enjoyed eating out. At the local shops or *taverna*, a wide variety of foodstuffs were available: hot sausages, bread, dates, olives, cheese, and wine. These shops catered to all classes, providing a quick lunch or snack. The Romans also ate at the baths and games, which provided fast food.

The author of the Epistle to Diognetus declared that Christians were not different from their non-Christian neighbors in dress and food; however, there were some exceptions. Christians were not to eat the blood of animals, meaning they were to abstain from the meat of pagan sacrifice, and were to restrain from all luxury, including food and clothing.

CLOTHES

The proper Roman citizen would wear a toga, the traditional form of dress. Made of wool, shaped and wrapped around the body, the toga symbolized a Roman citizen's status. In addition to this garment, worn in public, the Roman, whether citizen or not, would wear a tunic. These garments could be layered to provide warmth in winter, whereas in summer the tunic was often the only garment worn around the house. Made of two pieces of cloth sewn together with holes for arms, the tunic was the normal clothing of the 1st century C.E. For outerwear, the lower-class Roman wore a *paenula*, a cape without sleeves but having a hood, made from coarse wool. This was common for not only lower classes, but also for slaves. Lower-class Christian citizens would have a toga, tunic, and paenula; if not a citizen they would have the latter two garments. Roman women would have a tunic, and over that a *stola*, similar to a man's toga, again a symbol of citizenship and normally put on after marriage. For going outside, the Roman matron would wear a *palla*, a large shawl. These clothes would usually be made of wool, but the very wealthy used silk. Around the house Romans wore sandals made of leather, while outside they wore the *calceus*, a type of shoe with straps, rather than laces. An example of the Christians philosophy for clothing, similar to their view of food, can be seen in the accompanying Point in Time letter sent by Basil to Gregory Nazianzus.

In addition to these standard accoutrements individuals would also have jewelry, rings, brooches, hair pins and other items. The Christian must have been like their pagan counterparts, with wealthy individuals setting

---

A CHRISTIAN BISHOP'S ADVICE FOR CLOTHING

From the humble and submissive spirit comes an eye sorrowful and down-cast, appearance neglected, hair rough, dress dirty; so that the appearance which mourners take pains to present may appear our natural condition. The tunic should be fastened to the body by a girdle, the belt not going above the flank, like a woman's, nor left slack, so that the tunic flows loose, like an idler's ... The one end of dress is that it should be a sufficient covering alike in winter and summer. As to colour, avoid brightness; in material, the soft and delicate. To aim at bright colours in dress is like women's beautifying when they colour cheeks and hair with hues other than their own. The tunic ought to be thick enough not to want other help to keep the wearer warm. The shoes should be cheap but serviceable. In a word, what one has to regard in dress is the necessary.

Basil, Epistle, in *A Select Library of the Post-Nicene Fathers of the Christian Church*, ed. Philip Schaff and Henry Wace, 2nd series, trans. into English with prolegomena and explanatory notes. (New York: The Christian Literature Company, 1895), Vol. 8, *Basil: Letters and Select Works*, p. 111.

the fashion trends. Along with jewelry, perfumes and hair styles showed social and economic status. Again, like their modern counterparts, Roman inhabitants dressed to be seen by all. However, Christian women were not to display ostentatious hair, jewelry, and dress, which might arouse envy or jealousy. Cyprian went so far as to say that ostentatious dress was the sign of a prostitute. In addition, Christian men should not shave. This would have fit in well with the 2nd- and 3rd-century Roman perspective as well. Christians attempted to set themselves apart from their pagan counterparts through dress and behavior. The fact that many Christian writers had to preach against behaving like pagans indicate the difficulty Christian leaders faced. For example, as witnessed in the accompanying Point in Time, Gregory of Nazianzus in his VIII oration about his sister points to the idealized Christian.

When Christianity was legalized, the church struggled to control the luxurious clothing and eating habits of the recent pagan upper classes who converted to Christianity. The result was that the church never eradicated

---

A CHRISTIAN PRAISE FOR AN IDEALIZED WOMAN'S DRESS

10. Here, if you will, is another point of her excellence: one of which neither she nor any truly modest and decorous woman thinks anything: but which we have been made to think much of, by those who are too fond of ornament and display, and refuse to listen to instruction on such matters. She was never adorned with gold wrought into artistic forms of surpassing beauty, nor flaxen tresses, fully or partially displayed, nor spiral curls, nor dishonouring designs of men who construct erections on the honourable head, nor costly folds of flowing and transparent robes, nor graces of brilliant stones, which color the neighbouring air, and cast a glow upon the form; nor the arts and witcheries of the painter, nor that cheap beauty of the infernal creator who works against the Divine, hiding with his treacherous pigments the creation of God, and putting it to shame with his honour, and setting before eager eyes the imitation of an harlot instead of the form of God, so that this bastard beauty may steal away that image which should be kept for God and for the world to come. But though she was aware of the many and various external ornaments of women, yet none of them was more precious to her than her own character, and the brilliancy stored up within. One red tint was dear to her, the blush of modesty; one white one, the sign of temperance: but pigments and pencillings, and living pictures, and flowing lines of beauty, she left to women of the stage and of the streets, and to all who think it a shame and a reproach to be ashamed.

Gregory Nazianzen, Oration 8, in *A Select Library of the Post-Nicene Fathers of the Christian Church,* ed. Philip Schaff and Henry Wace, 2nd series, trans. into English with prolegomena and explanatory notes, Vols. I-VII (New York: The Christian Literature Company, 1895), Vol. VII, *Select Orations of Saint Gregory Nazianzen, Sometime Archbishop of Constantinople,* trans. Charles Gordon Browne and James Edward Swallow, pp. 240–241.

human vices and pleasures but consistently argued for its adherents to practice restraint.

Clement of Alexandria indicated that wearing gold and using soft garments need not be absolutely avoided, but the individual must be honorable and above reproach to the pagans. Christians should wear plain garments of white color, unadorned but clean. Women should not pierce their ears (nor presumably should men) and may wear rings, but they must be restrained. Men may wear rings, but Clement says that when they wear signet rings, the signet should be a dove, fish, ship running in a fair wind, musical lyre, or a ship's anchor. If a man wore one showing fishing, it recalled the apostles and the children drawn up out of the water. Of course, it was forbidden to have idols or the face of idols, or the sword or bow, since Christians followed peace. Drinking cups were very forbidden, because Christians must be sober.

Head of Domitia. Saint Louis Art Museum.

Clement also said that men should be bald unless they had crisp, curly hair, and they should have a beard. This was in keeping with the vogue of the 2nd and 3rd centuries. Women should have their hair neatly put up with a brooch at the neck and not have coquettish braiding or courtesan-like hair. Christians should definitely not have artificial or dyed hair and should not wear makeup, since these are signs of prostitutes.

Further, individuals should avoid ostentatious sandals and not be bedazzled by gems. The charge that women should be reserved in their behavior was echoed in pagan writers as well. In his 6th satire on women, Juvenal presented a virtual cacophony of women's vices and why a man should not become involved. For the ancient Roman, as well as Christians, moral behavior, especially in regard to women, was important, and how women looked reflected upon their morality.

MORAL BEHAVIOR

The early church was concerned with its flock's moral behavior. Clement urged laughter to be restrained and asserted that individuals should have no indecent talk. He further extorted that Christians should not listen, look, or talk about obscene things. In the same vein women should not wink or kiss, since these were signs of adultery. At the other end, when men and women come to church they should not have a pompous walk, respect silence, and have a pure body and heart. Clement also attested that women should be completely veiled. It was expected of course that Christians pray, follow the social and hierarchical order, affirm their beliefs, abstain from lusts, and do not worship idols. These ideas were easier said than done, for many Christians faced continual tests both within and outside the Christian community. Church leaders stressed the importance of abstaining from the lusts of the body. What soon developed was the idea that the Christian behavior was regulated with a series of don'ts rather than cans. This, in turn, began a process of deciding who made the rules and how they were interpreted and enforced. To become a Christian one had to agree to Christianity's rules, even if it meant giving up one's profession. However, the church also discovered that people were human and frail. During the persecutions individuals often resorted to *apostasy*, denying their faith. The church fathers had to decide first whether to accept these individuals who denied their faith back into the religion. Some writers vehemently opposed their reconciliation and acceptance back into the fold. Viewing themselves as purists, they wanted nothing to do with them. Others, especially family and friends of the apostates, wanted little or no barriers to their return. Ultimately the church settled on a middle course, forgiveness but with punishments. Church leaders now had to develop a system to punish apostates after they had forgiven these fallen souls. The church also had to deal with the conversion of new members, especially the leaders in the town and communities who traditionally were expected to perform the pagan sacrifices and pay for the religious banquets, games, and the theatre, all of which Christians renounced. As Christianity became more established, and when it became tolerated and ultimately legalized and favored, either religious practice or society had to change; usually both evolved to survive.

An example of how the church attempted to deal with society while showing it could change was the Council of Elvira, held in Spain in the early 4th century, probably before Christianity was legalized. The council had to deal with a wide variety of issues concerning individual morals and how Christians interacted with others (see next chapter). The canons were issued in response to common behavioral troubles. These canons clearly indicated that problems existed and that they had become public knowledge. The first canon stated that anyone of mature age of the Christian faith who sacrificed at a pagan temple cannot receive the Eucharist, even at the end of life. From this canon it is clear that some Christians had sacrificed to pagan gods, although it is unclear if this act was related to apostasy during the persecutions of Diocletian or some other event such as a town celebration. What is even more interesting are canons 2 through 4 regarding *flamens,* pagan priests who were also local magistrates. Canon 2 stated the flamens who had sacrificed were not to receive communion if their sacrifice involved murder—the reference to murder probably meant gladiatorial games—whereas canon 3 suggested that flamens who have not sacrificed but had sponsored games could receive communion at the end of their lives, but only after penance. The reference here to games probably meant circus games or theatrical exhibits and not gladiatorial games. Canon 4 stated that flamens who were catechumens and who had refrained from sacrifice, could be admitted after three years. These canons clearly indicate that some Christians and would-be Christians were pagan priests actively involved in the pagan cults. Although the church was unhappy with Christians being flamens, it did not stop flamens from being Christians, merely making the process of conversion harder. These canons also indicated that Christianity had become accepted by the upper class, since they were the individuals who became flamens. These individuals, however, were not quite willing to abandon Roman society completely. A similar canon (56) ordered a magistrate, *duumvir,* to keep away from the church during his one-year term. Again, the canon showed the attempt to negotiate Christianity with Roman society and politics, since the duumvir was the town's chief councilor. And canon 55 allows a priest who simply wears the wreath and does not offer sacrifice or incense to idols to receive communion after two years, indicating that it was acceptable to be a pagan priest in name only while being a Christian. Individuals were not allowed to go to the temples and watch sacrifices, since they would be guilty of the same crime (canon 59). Finally, the council ordered that idols should be kept out of the home unless there was a fear of violence from slaves, in which case the home owners must keep themselves pure (canon 41). Clearly a Christian home might have both Christians and pagans, and the home might have the traditional pagan Lares.

A series of canons related to killing, seemingly only affecting women. Canon 5 said that if a woman beat her slave so that the slave died within three days and if it was uncertain if the death was intended or merely an accident, she could receive communion after seven years if intentional, five years if accidental. The canon does not mention men and does not condemn the institution of slavery. Canon 6 stated that if one killed by magic, therefore being done through idolatry, no communion at all may be received.

A significant number of canons deal with desertion in a marriage. If a woman leaves her husband without cause and marries, no communion (canon 8); if a baptized woman leaves her husband due to his adultery and marries again it is not recognized as a marriage and she can only receive communion when her first husband dies or if she becomes extremely ill (canon 9). And if a woman is deserted by her catechumen husband and she marries another man, she may be baptized. If a man leaves an innocent woman and marries a Christian woman who knew he had a wife whom he left without cause, communion may be given to her at death (canon 10). Clearly there was a problem with Christians divorcing one another and attempting to remarry within the church. These canons take great pains to separate the innocent from the guilty. Associated with this was canon 17, in which parents may not receive communion if they give their daughter in marriage to a pagan priest. Women were also forbidden to spend the night in cemeteries, since they secretly commit evil deeds, that is, meet men (canon 35). Clearly mixed marriages between Christians and non-Christians were also a problem, as indicated in canon 15, which also stated that there were more Christian girls than boys.

The Council of Elvira clearly pointed to the problems of everyday Christians and how they were dealt with in the early 4th century. Their private lives had now become public, with issues about remarriage coming to the forefront. In addition, problems between the sexes were clearly shown, with a greater burden placed on women than men. The canons paint a picture in which wealthy, powerful Romans desired to continue their political, social, and economic policies, which often came into conflict with Christian ideology and morality.

The fact that the early church fathers so often addressed the immoral behavior in Rome and elsewhere indicate that society was not always pure. Writing in the 4th century, the pagan Ammianus Marcellinus spoke about Rome and its people during the Christian period 353–369; in part Ammianus was attacking the Christian mob as well as all inhabitants of Rome.

A LATE ROMAN VIEW OF THE URBAN MOB

But of the lower and most indigent class of populace some spend the whole night in the wine-shops. Some lie concealed in the shady arcades of the theatres, or else they play at dice so eagerly as to quarrel over them; snuffing up their nostrils and making unseemly noises by drawing back their breath into their noses; or (and this is their favourite pursuit of all others) from sunrise to evening they stay gaping through sunshine or rain, examining in the most careful manner the most sterling good or bad qualities of the charioteers and horses.

And it is very wonderful to see an innumerable multitude of people with great eagerness of mind intent upon the event of the contests in the chariot race. These pursuits, and others of like character, prevent anything worth mentioning or important from being done at Rome.... And let us come to the idle and lazy common people, among whom some, who have not even got shoes, boast of high-sounding names: calling themselves Cimessores, Statarii, Semicupae, Serapina, or Cicinibricus, or Glutariorus, Trulla, Lucanicus, Pordaca, or Salsula, with numbers of other similar appellations. These men spend their whole lives in drinking, and gambling, and brothels, and pleasures, and public spectacles; and to them the circus Maximus is their temple, their home, their public assembly; in fact, their whole hope and desire.

Ammianus Marcellinus, *Roman History*, translated by C. D. Yonge(London: George Bell and Sons, 1894), pp. 491–492.

Although this description was from a pagan writing about the troubles in Rome, he nevertheless attempted to show that the Roman public was a mob of lazy, gaming, pleasure-seekers, a charge similar to the complaints raised by church fathers.

NOTE

1. Deborah Hobson, "House and Household in Roman Egypt," *YCS* 28 (1985): 211–229.

6

PUBLIC LIFE

It is easy to forget that most Christians, like their pagan neighbors, lived normal everyday lives in the Roman Empire. While not being able to publicly profess their religion until Constantine, most Christians held existing occupations not out of the ordinary: farmers, bankers, merchants, soldiers, and bureaucrats, while remaining disdainful of other common professions. Christians frequented the same establishments: taverns, baths, games, and markets as seen in the Point in Time, concerning the circus. Christians also attempted to assimilate within Roman society, which often caused significant problems. How church fathers reacted to this assimilation can be seen in the canons or rules of behavior from pre-Constantinian Spain. This chapter attempts to present the private daily life of Christians and how they interacted with both state and church leaders.

PUBLIC LIFE

In the 2nd century the Christian writer Tertullian defended his fellow Christians, saying that they existed everywhere: "They (pagans) cry aloud that the state is besieged: that (even) in the country-districts, in the (walled) villages, in the islands, you will find Christians"(chap 1 apology). Further, Christians engaged in most occupations, provided they were honorable:

We reject no fruit of his works; though it is true we refrain from the excessive or wrong use of them. Consequently we cannot dwell together in the world, without the market-place, without the shambles, without your baths, shops, factories, taverns, fairs and other places of resort. We also sail with you and serve in the army and we till the ground and engage in trade as you do, we join our crafts, we lend our services to the public for your profit. How we can seem unprofitable to your business affairs, when we live with you and by you, I do not know. But if I do not frequent your rites, nevertheless even on your holiday I am a human being. I do not bathe at dawn on the days of the Saturnalia, lest I should lose both night and day; nevertheless I bathe at a proper and healthful hour, which will keep me warm and ruddy; I can be stiff and sallow enough after my last bath when dead. I do not recline at table in public at the Liberalia, as is the custom of those who contend with the beasts when partaking of the last meal of their lives; yet I dine anywhere on your supplies. I do not buy a garland for my head. What difference does it make to you, how I employ flowers which are none the less purchased? I think they are more pleasing when free and unbound and trailing everywhere. But even if we have them combined into a garland, we know a garland by the nose; let those who have perfumed locks see to it. We do not meet together at the public shows: if nevertheless I want what is advertised at those meetings, I will take them more freely from their own places. We absolutely refrain from buying incense; if the Arabias complain, let the Sabaeans know that their wares are used in greater quantity and at greater cost for the burial of Christians than for the fumigating of gods. "Exactly," you say, "the revenues of the temples are daily failing; how few people now cast in pieces of money!" Yes, for we are not able to bring help both to men and to your gods when they beg, nor do we think that we ought to share with others than those who ask. So, let Jupiter himself hold out his hand and receive his share, while meantime our pity spends more street by street than your religion does temple by temple. But your other revenues will give thanks to the Christians, who pay down what they owe, in accordance with the belief by which we abstain from appropriating what is another's, so that, if the question is raised how much is lost to the revenues through the dishonesty and lying of your returns, a calculation can easily be made, as a complaint of one sort is balanced by the gain coming from all other calculations.[1]

As seen, Christians in the city of Rome engaged with their fellow pagan inhabitants in daily life. These activities focused on their careers, political and personal interaction with government officials, and leisure. An examination of jobs in the city of Rome shows a wide variety of occupations. For example, there were carpenters, stoneworkers, contractors, painters, and other artisans. Christians would have learned these trades as apprentices or more likely as slaves in the households of a free worker, especially wealthy Romans. Rome was a bustling city always reinventing itself with new construction by the current emperor. Public works would have been the steadiest employment form, but steady work did not always remain. In addition to the construction industry, lower-class urban Romans engaged in the manufacturing of goods. Information from Egyptian papyri and inscriptions throughout the Roman Empire indicated that some of the common professions included manufacturing in metalwork, jewelry, and clothing. The latter employed the most in trades, such as weavers, spinners, dyers, fullers, cobblers, and leather makers. Since many of these occupations were done in the home, women often took a leading role in their manufacturing. Home production always existed, lasting until the modern industrial revolution.

Records from Egypt indicate that women not only manufactured clothes, but they also took a leading role in management. Women negotiated contracts for the leasing of space, looms, supplies, and most importantly for workers. These contracts were very explicit as to production, taxes, rents, and time that workers were to provide. For example, a papyrus (P.Oxy. 275 from 66 C.E.) has an agreement where Tryphon, son of Dionysus, apprenticed his son Thoonis to a weaver, Ptolemaeus, for one year. Tryphon's family members were also weavers, but apparently they wanted their son to work outside the home business. Tryphon paid the expenses for his son Thoonis to be an apprentice and would also feed and clothe him and pay all the taxes. Although Thoonis' expenses were paid by his father, the master weaver, Ptolemaeus, was to pay Tryphon an allowance of 5 *drachmae* for food per month and 12 drachmae at the end of the year-long contract for clothing. Thoonis would serve for a year, making up any days he missed. Ptolemaeus agreed to apprentice him to his best abilities. Tryphon also could not take his son away until the completion of the period, and if Thoonis does not make up any days missed, a penalty of 1 drachma per day would be paid.

Another important trade included the public millers and bakers, which provided the essential services of turning wheat into flour and then into bread. Archaeological and literary evidence from Rome shows that each of the 14 regions had numerous bakers and mills in addition to the large commercial mills on the Janiculum. These trades provided one of the most crucial occupations for Rome, since the production of food was always needed. The baker also acted as a miller and distributor of bread since most people did not have facilities for grinding wheat into flour and then baking flour into break. Although some large bakeries with state contracts existed, most were small neighborhood bakers in the *vici*. Large houses probably had their own bakers and millers on site.

Domestic workers were also a major source of employment, the most common being nurses, attendants—for rooms, tables, and personal needs—teachers, gardeners, and cooks. Many of the individuals working in the construction business were slaves or from the lower class. Christians, both slaves and free workers, would have been engaged in these activities as well. Although some, like teachers and cooks, required education or training, most of the other trades focused on an individual's ability to interact within the home. Bridging the public and private sphere would be those in services such as barbers, entertainers, doctors, midwives, and nurses interacting with the public, but often in a private setting. Since these individuals would be hired on an individual contract basis, they were self-employed. With the possible exception of entertainers, some of whom would be prostitutes, Christians could reasonably be expected to have engaged in most of these occupations. Another line of occupations that crossed between the public and private was that of those engaged in transportation, including drivers, boatmen, and baggage handlers. Again, these individuals could be employed by the state or by individuals.

The occupations that were public included merchants, such as food dealers, restaurant owners and tavern workers, slave dealers, cloth and leather merchants, and perfume sellers. These individuals would primarily sell their wares from the small shops and market stalls in the various fora throughout Rome. Christians would be involved in such activities, even as slave dealers, since Christianity did not prohibit mercantile activities or slavery. Finally, Christians could have engaged in financial and administrative work, plying their trade as scribes, financiers, administrators, and government officials. Christians well placed in these services would be seen as valuable agents for the new religion, since they potentially had the ear of powerful politicians and even worked in the emperor's household. In addition they could act as agents, keeping an eye and ear open for information that might be damaging to their movement.

These occupations, mainly at the lower socioeconomic level, remained constant within the history of Christianity. Christians, however, did engage in other activities, some of which were held traditionally by upper-class individuals. In the New Testament, Paul has friends who were tent-makers and merchants of some means. There was also the possibility that some upper-class individuals were Christians, for example, Flavius Clemens, who was executed, and his wife Flavia Domitilla, the emperor's niece, who was banished. In the early 4th century, before Christianity was legalized, the council of Elvira in Spain imposed penalties for Christians who continued to be pagan priests and government officials who had to officiate at sacrifices (see chapter 5). It was known that in North Africa Christianity tended to spread among the lower classes, while the upper class tended to resist, even after Christianity was legalized.

Nevertheless, by the end of the empire, Christianity had permeated all elements of society. Two important public individuals were Augustine and Cassiodorus, both from the aristocracy. Each affected the Roman state in different ways, Augustine as a church leader and Cassiodorus as a Christian working in the government.

Augustine

Born in Thagaste in Numidia (modern Algeria), Augustine (354–430) was the son of Patricius, a town official and a small landowner, and Monica, a Christian. He studied rhetoric at Carthage before traveling to Rome and ending up in Milan, where he befriended Ambrose.

After reading Cicero's *Hortenius* (now lost) at age 18, which inspired him to seek wisdom, Augustine studied Manichaeism at Carthage. This Gnostic sect, however, proved intellectually and spiritually unsatisfactory, and Augustine abandoned it in favor of skepticism. Augustine secured a position in Milan and, after hearing

Ambrose's sermons, he abandoned skepticism in favor of Christianity and Neo-Platonism.

Augustine returned to Thagaste where he withdrew from public life, living as a hermit from 388–391 in a villa that resembled a monastery. He gave up public office and a marriage to his common-law wife of 15 years. The people of Hippo forcibly ordained him a priest, against his will, in 391, and he accepted his fate. He spent this early time learning the scriptures and writing against the Manichees. He also preached in church at the request of his bishop, even though this was not the African custom. In 395 Augustine was consecrated an assistant bishop, and, in 397, bishop, after which he studied theology. After becoming a bishop Augustine entered into a second career as a forceful preacher, promoting Catholic unity in Africa. Augustine preached and advocated unity, even forceful coercion, against Donatism in order to reunite Christendom. Augustine preached against Pelagius and his definition of free will. He died August 28, 430, of old age while the Vandals besieged Hippo.

Augustine's two greatest works were the *Confessions* and *City of God*. The *Confessions*, written in 397–400, was an autobiography, discussing his life down to 387. The work also shows the influence Neo-Platonism had on his life and his conversion to Christianity. His second work, *City of God*, 413–426, produced a theological rebuttal to the charge that Christianity caused the sack of Rome in 410. Instead, Augustine promoted the idea of the Eternal City, the next world, where the believers and nonbelievers would be separated. Augustine wrote 93 works in 232 volumes and well over a hundred sermons and letters. With Jerome, Ambrose, and Gregory I, Augustine is hailed as one of the four fathers of the Catholic Church. His prominence is seen in medieval philosophy, influencing thinkers such as Thomas Aquinas. Augustine attempted to resolve the issue of reason and faith. His conclusion was based on the idea that both were required in order to be a Christian. One needed to have reason to understand and have faith, and one needed faith to conduct reason. Having developed these ideas Augustine began to explore the relationship between God and man, argued against predestination, and developed the theology of redemption and grace.

Cassiodorus

A senator and chief minister to the Ostrogoths during the 5th century, Cassiodorus was born in 469–70 c.e. to a noble and wealthy family. He had an excellent education, based not only in the reading of scripture, but also in the classical schools of rhetoric, grammar, music, and math. He was initially employed by Odoacer and later by Theodoric, where he rose through the ranks of the new Germanic kingdom. He was a confident of Theodoric, writing the king's public communications. His skill lay in his diplomacy between the old Roman ideas and the new German conquerors. He desired to fuse the Catholic religion and ideology of the Italians with the Arianism of Theodoric, to continue to promote good relations with the Eastern (Byzantine) empire, and perhaps to resurrect Rome as the center in the West. With Theodoric advancing in age and becoming more violent, Cassiodorus retired to his Calabrian estate, thereby saving himself, unlike his contemporaries, Boethius and Symmachus. After Theodoric's death Cassiodorus became advisor to Theodoric's daughter Amalasuntha and her young son Athalraic. Cassiodorus continued to serve them and promoted peace with Justinian. After Athalraic's death and the murder of Amalasuntha, Cassiodorus served Theodatus, the new ruler. With the victory of Belisarius, Justinian's general, and the defeat of the Ostrogoths, Cassiodorus, now 70 years old, withdrew and founded the monastery of Viviers at Mount Moscius. He endowed the monastery with his extensive library and urged his followers to study classical and sacred literature. He composed works even until his 90s. His writings show the classical influence of Cicero and provide insight into the late Roman rule of a Catholic subject under the Arian king Theodoric.

BANKING

The prosperity of the city of Rome required a vibrant banking class that could provide economic capital and saving opportunities for both rich and poor. The powerful bankers represented by the equestrian class made loans to emperors and nobles. The usual legal interest was 12 percent per year, although for hazardous missions such as transporting grain and other commodities by sea, interest could rise to 50 percent, the extra percentage being more of an insurance premium than loan interest. Christian businessmen needed such services as well. Canon 20 of the Council of Elvira decreed that usury was not allowed, since the church prohibited this act, but since the council had to issue an injunction, it is clear that some individuals engaged in it. By usury the council probably meant charging interest above the normal percentage.

Although there was no stock market, credit cards, or debit cards, there did exist some "modern" fiduciary concepts including savings accounts, checks, money changing, commodity brokers, safe deposit boxes, and loan sharks. These services were available to rich and poor, pagan and Christian alike.

Bankers provided rich merchants the necessary capital for long-distance trade, the most profitable enterprise, and upon a merchants' return they deposited their profits in strong boxes in the temple of Saturn or other temples for safekeeping. These temples acted as banks. Bankers also provided mortgages for wealthy Romans to purchase *insulae*, warehouses, businesses, and homes. In fact, research indicates that wealthy Romans, with all of their estates and businesses, were always taking loans for ready cash. These Romans would mortgage their estates until their investments came through. Wealthy Christians could have taken advantage of these services, and probably did.

A second type of banker dealt with the lower classes. Important bankers would not have directly concerned themselves with the poor; instead they would have had their freedmen operate these banks. In addition to these subsidiary bankers, others would have lent money, stored valuables, and changed non-Roman coinage into Roman currency. Jews were often stereotyped as moneylenders, but they were not the only moneylenders in Rome. Christians would have been in such a group, lending money to fellow Christians of similar economic/social standing, thus avoiding the charge of usury.

These lower bankers provided the necessary economic livelihood for lower classes. In addition to the normal activities of loans, savings, and money changing, they provided loans to individuals who were poor credit risks, charging high interest. In other words, they acted as loan sharks. These individuals would exact exorbitant interest rates, and those who could not pay would lose their collateral. These "bankers" were not the most reputable individuals.

MILITARY

Christians undoubtedly came into contact with the military, especially since it was the major avenue for social advancement in the Roman world. A citizen would join the army and serve 20 years before retiring and receiving a pension. Noncommissioned officers were technically not allowed to marry until their discharge, but their inevitable nonmarriage unions were given special status. After discharge they could marry, and their offspring born before discharge from the army were recognized as Roman citizens and as their heirs. Commissioned officers could marry, since they joined the military as part of their political training and not as professional soldiers, often leaving the army to take a post in the government. Noncitizens could join the auxiliaries, serving 25 years before being discharged, with their children becoming Roman citizens who could then enter the military as citizen legionaries, not auxiliaries. The roman army then gave all inhabitants of the empire, even noncitizens, the opportunity to increase their social standing.

In Rome, a special class of soldiers existed, the Praetorian Guard. Created by Augustus and dispersed throughout Italy, including Rome, the Praetorian's power grew when the emperor Tiberius brought them all together in Rome and built the *castra* Praetorian (Praetorian camp) to house them. The Praetorians originally protected the emperor, but soon became a political force for themselves. After Nero's suicide, the Praetorians made and unmade the emperors Galba, Otho, and Vitellius. Their power again was seen after Domitian's assassination when they forced the emperor Nerva, promoted by the Senate, to adopt Trajan, and again during the civil wars after Commodus' assassination.

In addition to the Praetorians keeping order in Rome, there existed the *vigiles*, or watchmen. Their job was to maintain public order and be on the watch for fires. Acting as firemen, they would sound the alarms and help battle the numerous fires in the city.

The military then became a mechanism for the advancement of civilians. In addition to their pay, soldiers would "shake down" civilians, as witnessed in papyri where estate owners often recorded in their account ledgers payments to soldiers, and in the New Testament when John the Baptist advised soldiers if they follow him not to charge more than they were entitled. These activities only increased during the chaotic times, providing little comfort and security for inhabitants. Upon retirement the soldier received income and even land sufficient for him to become a middle-class citizen, provided he did not squander it in the taverns and inns.

The military seems to have gone in and out of acceptance in Christianity. Soldiers certainly converted, such as the centurion Cornelius mentioned in Acts of the Apostles. But Christian philosophy argued for nonviolence. Jesus had taught that if one was struck one should offer the other cheek, a rule that soldiers would have found hard to follow, especially on the battlefield. Some early Christian writers condemned any type of violence, even in self-defense. Nevertheless, soldiers desired to convert. Soldiers were everywhere and came from all parts of the empire and from all social classes and could potentially provide the new religion with some political backing. For these reasons, the church vacillated between accepting soldiers, and therefore military service, war, and violence, and prohibiting the inclusion of soldiers in the church. Ultimately in the 3rd century soldiers were included, although the debate over their admission did not end. Before the last great persecutions by Diocletian, some soldiers in Africa refused to perform military service because they were Christians. Their persecutors noticed that soldiers were serving in the military already, indicating that the church had moved away from the idea of just turning the other cheek and converting soldiers.

TAVERNS

Travelers and those just wanting a drink would come to the local taverns and inns, and Rome had a host of them. Most outside the city had room for carts and horses/mules, for a fee. The sleeping quarters were small, but close to the dining and drinking facilities, where the fare was simple, consisting of wine, bread, cheese, and perhaps some meat. One could also get entertainment, a woman for the night, if one was willing to pay. These inns were rife with petty criminals waiting for a patron to become distracted or drunk in order to rob them. Christians would have been on both sides, some victims and other perpetrators of crime. Even the landlord could have been a Christian, since Christianity did not prevent this type of mercantile occupations.

Inside the city the inns or bars were more for eating and drinking. Standing at the tables, one could get hot soup, a piece of meat, bread, or cheese, and wine or beer. These establishments provided locals as well as travelers with food, drink, and entertainment. In addition to eating out, Christians would have also used the numerous baths in the city.

BATHS

In 20 B.C.E. Marcus Agrippa, Augustus' right-hand man, erected public baths for the populace. Before, baths were private business affairs, but imperial patronage now grew and continued throughout the imperial

Ostia: Bakery. James W. Ermatinger.

period, supplementing and ultimately surpassing the support for private baths. Entrance into either type was relatively cheap, a *quadrans*, the smallest coin, and often was free. Baths either existed solely for a single sex (especially private baths) or had times set aside during the day for a particular gender. Some baths did have separate quarters for the sexes, and during Nero's reign there were also mixed baths, although this was considered scandalous. Before bathing, individuals often played ball, exercised, strolled, or merely watched others exercise. One entered the baths and either had a slave or client watch over one's clothes; if one did not have a slave one could pay the attendant or leave them on a hook and take a risk. For the masses without much of any worth, it was probably safe to assume they just took a risk, and perhaps even came out ahead by stealing another's clothing. After disrobing, one passed through a series of rooms: the *frigidarium,* or cold bath, *tepidarium,* a warm bath, and the *calidarium,* or hot room where individuals sat and perspired. The heat came from hot air forced through the rooms under the floors by a hypocaust, a pipelike system that drew the hot air from a fire by means of air pressure. After a good bath visitors then scraped themselves with a strigil (scraper) or, if they could afford one, had their slave scrape them to remove the dirt and grime from their body. They often then took a plunge in the cold bath again to seal the pores before getting dressed.

After a bath the bather would often have something to eat, for the baths were not only places for hygiene but also had social meeting places, much like modern health clubs, with restaurants and even shops. The fare may be simple or extravagant, allowing friends to retire to read and talk. Of course this eventually led to other social interactions, often culminating in illicit affairs, gambling, and other vices. It was this aspect of the baths, mentioned by numerous writers, that provoked Christian responses against them. Clement of Alexandria viewed baths for women and for the wealthy as not conducive to morality. He condemned baths for both sexes, since in them bathers they strip before each other without modesty. He indicated that baths were for cleanliness, warmth, health, and pleasure. Of course Christians should not use the baths for the latter, while women should only use them for cleanliness and health. Clement as such urged the use of baths only for the "medicinal" purposes of cleanliness and health, not for the leisure time. An example of the Christian belief that women should avoid baths with men was presented in a 3rd-century constitution, seen in the accompanying Point in Time.

EXERCISE AND THE GAMES

Clement, however, urged young Christian boys to use the gymnasium to build their strength, even if baths, seen as a potential problem, were nearby. Clement wanted young men to exercise, since it was good and healthy. Even women should be allowed to play and exercise, but not to wrestle or to race like the boys.

The baths provided hygienic and social functions, but the urban mob needed additional entertainment. The emperors had discovered that in order to keep their hold on power they had to ensure for the distraction and wellbeing of the urban mob; they did so by means of the bread and

---

THAT A WOMAN MUST NOT BATHE WITH MEN

IX. Avoid also that disorderly practice of bathing in the same place with men; for many are the nets of the evil one. And let not a Christian woman bathe with an hermaphrodite; for if she is to veil her face, and conceal it with modesty from strange men, how can she bear to enter naked into the bath together with men? But if the bath be appropriated to women, let her bathe orderly, modestly, and moderately. But let her not bathe without occasion, nor much, nor often, nor in the middle of the day, nor, if possible, every day; and let the tenth hour of the day be the set time for such seasonable bathing. For it is convenient that thou, who art a Christian woman, shouldst ever constantly avoid a curiosity which has many eyes.

Constitutions of the Holy Apostles, in *The Ante-Nicene Fathers' Translations of the Writings of the Fathers Down to* A.D. *325*, Vol. VII, ed. Alexander Roberts and James Donaldson, American reprint of the Edinburgh edition revised and chronologically arranged, with brief prefaces and occasional notes by A. Cleveland Coxe (Grand Rapids, MI: Wm. Eerdmans, 1886), p. 395.

circus. The distribution of grain, discussed above, was crucial for the urban mob's survival; the games were crucial for their distraction. The circus, with the attendant gladiatorial games, provided the emperor a means to distract the urban poor. Instead of having the poor complain about their loss of political power or their inability to break into the real social power elite, the emperors promoted the games, where the mob could cheer for their favorite teams. The urban poor became more interested in their favorite chariot team or gladiator than in pursuing political power. During a typical year in Rome there were over 100 days devoted to the games, not that an individual could or would go to all of them. These "athletes" took on a cult status, as witnessed by inscriptions where athletes were praised and had their victories counted. Although not divided, as in our weekend, there would often be 5–10 consecutive days of games; the total number of days for entertainment equaled the modern equivalent of our weekends, or 100 days a year.

Clement of Alexandria and other Christian writers, however, criticized their fellow Christians for going to the theatre and stadium "seats of pestilence," which they considered wicked. Clement said that even attending the games was cursed. But by the time of Constantine there were 177 days of *ludi,* or games, each year in Rome. These games or competition were held in the theatres and amphitheatres, and 66 days, or about 5 per month, of circus racing was held in the great Circus Maximus. The

Intaglio Circus with Chariot Race. The Walters Art Museum, Baltimore.

average number of races per each of the 66 days was 24, or a total of 1,584 races per year. The circus games marked the climax of the old pagan festivities and the imperial games. Since the Christian emperors supported the races, Clement's condemnation probably did not make an impact upon Christians. In the provinces the local provincials were compelled to provide games, with town officials giving money for celebrations in order to help their political careers. In Rome, nobles seeking the office of *quaestor* had to fund games; but for the great circus races the imperial treasury usually covered the expenses.

The games were represented in art from the 4th century on the mosaics from the villa Piazza Armerina in Sicily, which show hunts and races with financial rewards for the victories. The records also indicated that the old pagan festivals with their games survived into the Christian era. Gladiatorial shows, more repugnant than the circus, disappeared around 400 C.E., while the beast hunts continued until 500 C.E. Nevertheless, the fact that both continued after the adoption of Christianity indicates how popular these games were. This popularity was due to society's need for distraction from daily problems, the institutionalizing of violence, and absence of other "sports." The church fathers had difficulty with the public and the games. For example, the council of Elvira indicated that if a charioteer or pantomime wanted to believe, they first had to renounce their profession and then could be admitted to the church, provided they did not return to their former profession (canon 62). And in 314, after Christianity was

Pompeii: Amphitheatre. James W. Ermatinger.

accepted, the council of Arles said that the charioteer could belong to the faithful, but as long as they drove in the races they were barred from communion. The strolling players, as long as they acted, were also barred from communion (canon 4). And Salvian later complained that Christians preferred going to the games and theatres rather than church (see below).

The games continued after Christianity was legalized. The two documents seen in the accompanying Point in Time come from the end of the Roman Empire and show how the games continued and were criticized by the later Christian writers. The first is a description of the circus from Cassiodorus, while the second comes from the 5th-century Christian Salvian, who bemoaned the empty churches and the crowded theatres.

OCCUPATIONS

Public interaction among Christians also occurred in their jobs. Christians worked so they would not be a burden to the church and its members, and also to help those unable to work, especially widows, who probably did not have the family and resources needed to survive. Indeed, in the early church, the preeminence of helping widows was striking, and their position in the church was seen as an example for all society. While certain jobs were forbidden to Christians, other professions were encouraged or at least allowed. Since most of the population engaged in manual labor, it was only natural that most Christians were also laborers. Christian writers

Ostia: Mosaic Showing Hunt. James W. Ermatinger.

Ostia: Theatre. James W. Ermatinger.

stressed the importance of agricultural laborers and their connection with the soil. Manual laborers included agricultural workers, herdsmen, construction workers, drivers, and general workers.

Because 90 percent of the population was involved in agriculture and therefore rural, one might assume that 90 percent of Christians came from this class. This assumption, however, is inaccurate for a couple of interrelated reasons. First, the vast majority of the empire did not convert immediately, so examining the percentage of the population's class to converts does not produce a sound number. Second, in the early period, Christianity drew heavily from the urban environment, since the early church recognized that the urban middle class—merchants, tradesmen, and artisans—were crucial for the church's prosperity and growth.

Later church writers stressed the importance that sons learn their fathers' trade to provide not only for themselves, but for the church as well. Again, this would have fit in well with the late Roman government view where the state attempted to mandate that sons follow their fathers' trade. Examples of important trades in the city were the bakers, fullers, and potters. In addition to bankers (discussed previously) another important group of tradespeople were the fullers and the associated jobs of laundress, cleaner, and dyer. Fullers not only cleaned garments but they finished them, sewing when needed, and worked in large shops where they received special water-gathering privileges. The fullers also had dyers who sold rare dyes from the East. Associated with the fullers were also the cobblers, who provided both common and specialized shoes for the populace. The clothing

THE CIRCUS

LETTER OF KING THEODORIC TO FAUSTUS, PRAETORIAN PREFECT

Constancy in actors is not a very common virtue, therefore with all the more pleasure do we record the faithful allegiance of Thomas the Charioteer, who came long ago from the East hither, and who, having become champion charioteer, has chosen to attach himself to "the seat of our Empire;" and we therefore decide that he shall be rewarded by a monthly allowance. He embraced what was then the losing side in the chariot races and carried it to victory—victory which he won so often that envious rivals declared that he conquered by means of witchcraft.

The sight of a chariot-race drives out morality and invites the most trifling contentions; it is the emptier of honorable conduct, the ever-flowing spring of squabbles: a thing which Antiquity commenced as a matter of religion, but which a quarrelsome posterity has turned into a sport.

For Aenomaus is said first to have exhibited this sport at Elis, a city of Asia, and afterwards Romulus, at the time of the rape of the Sabines, displayed it in rural fashion to Italy, no buildings for the purpose being yet founded. Long after, Augustus, the lord of the world, raising his works to the same high level as his power, built a fabric marvelous even to Romans, which stretched far into the Vallis Murcia. This immense mass, firmly girt round with hills, enclosed a space which was fitted to be the theatre of great events.

Twelve Ostia [gates] at the entrance represent the twelve signs of the Zodiac. These are suddenly and equally opened by ropes let down by the Hermulae [little pilasters]. The four colors worn by the four parties of charioteers denote the seasons: green for verdant spring, blue for cloudy winter, red for flaming summer, white for frosty autumn. Thus, throughout the spectacle we see a determination to represent the works of Nature. The Biga [two-horse chariot] is made in imitation of the moon, the Quadriga [four-horse chariot] of the sun. The circus horses, by means of which the servants of the Circus announce the heats that are to be run, imitate the herald-swiftness of the morning star. Thus it came to pass that while they deemed they were worshipping the stars, they profaned their religion by parodying it in their games.

A white line is drawn not far from the ostia to each Podium [balcony], that the contest may begin when the quadrigae pass it, lest they should interrupt the view of the spectators by their attempts to get each before the other. There are always seven circuits round the goals [Metae] to one heat, in analogy with the days of the week. The goals themselves have, like the decani of the Zodiac, each three pinnacles, round which the swift quadrigae circle like the sun. The wheels indicate the boundaries of East and West. The channel which surrounds the Circus presents us with an image of the glassy sea, whence come the dolphins which swim hither through the waters. The lofty obelisks lift their height towards heaven; but the upper one is dedicated to the sun, the lower one to the moon: and upon them the sacred rites of the ancients are indicated with Chaldee signs for letters.

The Spina [central wall or backbone] represents the lot of the unhappy captives, inasmuch as the generals of the Romans, marching over the backs of their enemies, reaped that joy which was the reward of their labors. The Mappa [napkin], which is still seen to give the signal at the games, came into fashion on this wise. Once when Nero was loitering over his dinner, and the populace, as usual, was impatient for the spectacle to begin, he ordered the napkin which he had used for wiping his fingers to be thrown out of window, as a signal that he gave the required permission. Hence it became a custom that the display of a napkin gave a certain promise of future circenses.

The Circus is so called from "circuitus:" circenses is, as it were, circuenses, because in the rude ages of antiquity, before an elaborate building had been prepared for the purpose, the races were exhibited on the green grass, and the multitude were protected by the river on one side and the swords [enses] of the soldiers on the other.

We observe, too, that the rule of this contest is that it be decided in twenty-four heats, an equal number to that of the hours of day and night. Nor let it be accounted meaningless that the number of circuits round the goals is expressed by the putting up of eggs, since that emblem, pregnant as it is with many superstitions, indicates that something is about to be born from thence. And in truth we may well understand that the most fickle and inconstant characters, well typified by the birds who have laid those eggs, will spring from attendance on these spectacles. It were long to describe in detail all the other points of the Roman Circus, since each appears to arise from some special cause. This only will we remark upon as preeminently strange, that in these beyond all other spectacles men's minds are hurried into excitement without any regard to a fitting sobriety of character. The Green charioteer flashes by: part of the people is in despair. The Blue gets a lead: a larger part of the City is in misery. They cheer frantically when they have gained nothing; they are cut to the heart when they have received no loss; and they plunge with as much eagerness into these empty contests as if the whole welfare of the imperiled fatherland were at stake.

No wonder that such a departure from all sensible dispositions should be attributed to a superstitious origin. We are compelled to support this institution by the necessity of humoring the majority of the people, who are passionately fond of it; for it is always the few who are led by reason, while the many crave excitement and oblivion of their cares. Therefore, as we too must sometimes share the folly of our people, we will freely provide for the expenses of the Circus, however little our judgment approves of this institution.

Thomas Hodgkin, *The Letters of Cassiodorus* (London: Henry Frowde, 1886), pp. 226–229, letter 51.

SALVIAN'S DESCRIPTION OF EMPTY CHURCHES AND FULL THEATRES

7. What is there like this among the Barbarians, where are there any Circus Games among them, where are their Theatres, where is the abomination of

all kind of impurities, that is, the destruction of our hopes and salvation? And although they, as Pagans, did make use of all these, yet their error would be much less culpable in the sight of God; because, although there would be uncleanness in the seeing of them, yet there would be no breach of a sacred obligation. But as to us, what can we answer for our selves? ... If at any time it chances, which it often does, that on the same day, there is a Church-Festival, and public Plays, I desire to ask of every Man's conscience, which of the two places has the greater congregation of Christians in it, the seats of the public Play or the court of God, and whether they love the words of the Gospel more, or those of the players, the words of Life, or the words of Death; the words of Christ, or the words of a mimical actor? For on every day of these deadly sports, if there happen to be any feasts of the Church, they who call themselves Christians do not only not come to Church, but if by chance, not having heard of any such thing, they have come, as soon as ever they hear there are plays, they presently leave the Church. The Church of God is despised, that they may haste to the Playhouse: The Church is emptied, the circus filled. We leave Christ on the Altar, that we may feed our eyes that run a whoring after the unclean sights, with the fornication of those filthy pastimes.

Salvian of Marseilles, *A Treatise of God's Government and of the Justice of His Present Dispensations in This World*, trans. Thomas Wagstaffe (London: Printed for S. Keble, 1700), pp. 171–173.

industry would take on even more importance, since the Roman military would later convert some of its monetary taxes into taxes in kind, one of which was the supply of clothes for the military. The final major craft was the potter, who manufactured plates and cups in Rome for local consumption. Higher-end pottery goods came from Arretium, outside Rome. The production and distribution of goods, regardless of the type, were local, produced in small shops for use in the local neighborhood.

While Christianity may not have been exclusively an urban phenomenon, it is certain that a large number of its converts were urban-ites. Nevertheless, it can be assumed that a majority of the followers were from the lower classes, which would have included both rural and urban manual laborers. Within the city, manual laborers included household slaves and workers, construction workers, and general workers, all from the lower classes. Their life was hard, and Christianity appealed to them by saying that no matter what their life on earth was like, a strong faith in Christianity would earn them a happy afterlife. In addition to these lower-class workers and of course slaves, bureaucrats, a part of the middle class, converted as well. In the Gospels and early writings, tax collectors, city officials, managers of estates, and even treasurers of gladiatorial games (but not gladiators) were mentioned as occupations to which Christians could belong, all representatives of the lower middle class. They enjoyed

some power and potential for climbing the economic ladder into the ranks
of the merchants, the solid middle and upper middle class, such as Paul's
friends Priscia and Aquila, tent-makers, who owned slaves and houses
in several cities and were connected enough to help and encourage Paul.
They, along with purple sellers and bankers, were crucial to the development of early Christianity. They provided the early Christians with
meeting places, clients who might convert, and connections with other
merchants both locally and beyond, and they potentially had connections
with imperial representatives. These individuals, more than anyone else,
promoted the spread of Christianity. While more educated individuals
and artists like lawyers, physicians, record keepers, and metal, wood, and
leather workers might have wealth and respectability, the merchants had
the contacts. As such, the early cross section of a Christian community
did not exactly look like the political, social, and economic cross section
of the Roman Empire, which was weighted heavily on the agricultural/
manual laborers side and less on the mercantile and upper class. Instead,
the early church's social and economic makeup had a majority from the
lower classes, including slaves, but the mercantile and upper class may
have been in greater percentages than in the general public. This makeup
would have given Christianity the finances and connections necessary to
spread, create a central administration, and ultimately survive.

In essence, the Christians performed jobs and trades like other religious groups in Roman society. Although some professions (gladiators,
prostitutes, and makers of idols) were not allowed, many professions
were practiced and promoted. For the early writers of Christianity manual
labor was seen as blessed; however modern observers may have difficulty
reconciling Christian ideals and their attitudes toward slavery.

SLAVERY

Christianity did not advocate the elimination of slavery, which in antiquity was common and expected. One became a slave through a variety of
means: capture in war, being born to a slave, having been abandoned by
parents and raised as a slave, or being a criminal. Although there was a legal
separation between slavery and freedom, conditions separating the poor
and slaves were not that far apart. Slaves had some legal protection, especially by the time of the empire. They could not be executed at the whim of
their master, who had to provide a reason for wanting a slave dead. Slaves
could also buy their freedom, and many were granted freedom. Often the
reason for this freedom was so the master did not have to take care of slaves
in their old age, a practice the emperor Augustus forbade, since it led to an
increase in urban poor who might resort to criminal activities to survive.
Nevertheless, when a slave was freed, so were his or her future children.

Christianity accepted this philosophy, and many Christian writers
mentioned slaves, not in a negative fashion, but rather as a matter of

fact. Slaves performed numerous tasks that needed to be done in an age without machines. For instance, slaves provided the necessary labor for agriculture, building, and domestic chores. Their labor was an integral part of the economy. Slaves working in the fields had the least amount of protection and chance for freedom and were at best viewed as beasts of burden. Working on estates, they were subjected to beatings and forced to toil year round. Comparable to field workers were those engaged in construction. These individuals did the dangerous tasks of working on roads, bridges, and buildings, with their lives often in danger from accidents. The domestic slaves had the most opportunity for manumission (freedom). They could be employed in the kitchens, cleaning, looking after children, and in other associated tasks. Their safety was not usually compromised, but they were more apt to be under the watchful eye of their masters. The group of slaves most abused and with the shortest life expectancy was the criminal assigned to the games or the mines. Christianity did not argue for the elimination of slavery, but rather exhorted masters to be fair and for slaves to remember that in heaven there was no slavery.

The occupations that Christians performed brought them into contact with other Romans who did not share the same beliefs. The interaction between their fellow citizens could be amiable or occasionally violent.

NOTE

1. Tertullian, *Tertulliani Apologeticus*, text of Oehler annotated with an introduction by J.E.B. Mayor and a translation by A. Souter (Cambridge: Cambridge University Press, 1917), chapter 42.

7

INTERACTION WITH PAGANISM

The following discussion attempts to place Christianity within the context of the Roman state, with its reaction to this new and strange religion producing a culture of fear and persecutions. This chapter explores how the Roman state went through a series of justifications for its violence: destroying atheism, attempting to bring the fallen back into the fold, and denouncing the religion on philosophical grounds. Christians, meanwhile, reacted to this violence not with armed conflict or even resistance. While some Christians sought to proclaim their faith by openly declaring their adherence to Christianity and suffer martyrdom, most attempted to merely survive, and some even committed apostasy, denying their faith.

Interactions between people, especially involving religions, ethnic groups, or politics, often lead to violence and bloodshed, destroying not only property, but lives. In the ancient world countless examples exist where different groups attacked each other, destroying property and harming individuals. Sometimes, when troubles occurred, people fled with their possessions. But often refugees realized they could not take all of their possessions, and they attempted to hide them in order to flee more quickly or avoid attacks. But when the owner fails to recover their temporarily hidden goods or treasures, the material becomes what archaeologist term a hoard and provides modern researchers material and information about the person and their society who left them behind. Archaeologists who uncover these hoards together with historians attempt to piece together the information and weave it together with other information to create an account of the time.

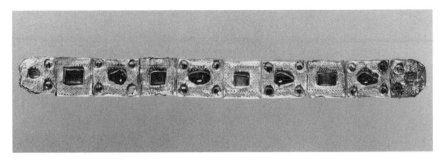

Diadem. The Walters Art Museum, Baltimore.

ROME AND THE CHRISTIANS

The year 303 C.E. witnessed the Roman government's last persecutions of the Christian Church; within a decade the persecutions not only had ended, but Christianity had become the favored religion. For nearly three centuries Christianity had existed in the Roman state as an illegal cult. While persecutions did not occur all the time, the legal system allowed any Roman official to begin proceedings against Christians. This legal situation against Christianity affected the daily lives of Christians. They were not able to publicly proclaim their religious beliefs without some fear. While in some periods there was peace, that time could quickly end and a new series of persecutions could break out. The Roman persecutions or even fear of persecutions produced constant fear and trepidation among Christians. This fear of discovery and possible punishment affected their daily lives, often making them secretive, which further exacerbated the situation.

The common perception that Rome sent Christians to the Coliseum every day under the empire needs to be dispelled. Most persecutions were not empire-wide, but were localized in distinct cities or provinces. Usually the repressions occurred when another group complained, either publicly or anonymously, about the presence or behavior of the Christian community. Like other minority groups throughout history, the attacks often did not relate to the stated cause, here religion, but to other reasons, such as fear or greed. Only after complaints were lodged did Roman officials begin an investigation, often reluctantly. Individuals identified as Christians were given the chance to recant by sacrificing to the pagan gods and cursing Christ's name. These acts struck at the center of Christianity. It is clear that some Christians recanted and sacrificed to the Roman gods, since Christian writers, such as the 2nd-century Cyprian, wrote theological works addressing the situation of those who had recanted and then wanted to return to Christianity. Called lapsed Christians, since they had lapsed into paganism by sacrificing to the gods, they were denied Christian sacraments for years until they had done penance and could be trusted again.

ARCHAEOLOGY AND THE PERSECUTIONS

In mid-eastern Britain, on the road between Lincoln and York in the north and London in the south, a small Roman town, Durobrivae, existed. The city flourished, with a tightly packed administrative center protected by walls, and with the inhabitants working in the countryside. In the mid-1970s an archaeological discovery here produced a hoard containing 1 gold and 27 silver objects, all of which were Christian in nature. The objects were carefully concealed, suggesting a deliberate attempt to hide them and not an accidental loss. The owner then intended to return and reclaim them, but failed for some reason. The bowls, jugs, cups, plates, and other materials contained the chi-rho symbol, usually associated with Christians, and the objects dated from the late 3rd/early 4th centuries C.E. Some have inscriptions, which led scholars to believe they were votive offerings to God. For example one has "O Lord, I, Publianus, relying on you, honour (or 'adorn') your holy sanctuary (or 'sacred place')" or a plaque with the inscription "Ancilla furnished a votive offering which she promised."[1] These sayings were similar to pagan votive offerings that have been discovered throughout the ancient world. A possible interpretation was that the treasure material was used by Christians for some part of their service, baptism (hence the jug and bowls), Communion (the plates, bowls, and cups), or *refrigeria*, the ceremonial meal for the dead. The plaques and some bowls have holes and hangers indicating that they were meant to be hung, probably on the walls of a building. But why were they buried? It is tempting to see the persecutions at work. The last persecutions raged throughout the Roman Empire during the early 4th century, and Britain was not spared. Churches were destroyed, as witnessed from literary sources and inscriptions, such as from Ferentium, in Italy, where the basilica was rebuilt after being destroyed by the savage persecutions. Records indicated that sacred objects were removed from Christian churches and destroyed, and it is possible that these objects were removed and concealed by Christians to prevent their seizure or destruction. But the hoard also showed that Christians had valuable goods used in their religious services.

An example of this local persecution is seen in the actions taken by Pliny the Younger when he was governor of Bithynia in modern Northern Turkey in the early 2nd century C.E. His letter to the emperor Trajan clearly reflects the problems faced by an individual who had little or no experience with Christians and was attempting to be fair but law abiding.

Pliny's letter makes clear that he had some success in combating Christians and restoring paganism and informed the emperor that the pagan temples were once again full and animals were being sacrificed; of course, this may have been a ruse to ingratiate himself with the emperor and to show that he was toeing the party line. But given the references in other sources, including Christian, that recent converts often abandoned Christianity at the first sign of trouble, Pliny's remark may have been accurate.

PLINY'S LETTER CONCERNING CHRISTIANS

To the Emperor Trajan

IT is a rule, Sir, which I inviolably observe, to refer myself to you in all my doubts; for who is more capable of guiding my uncertainty or informing my ignorance? Having never been present at any trials of the Christians, I am unacquainted with the method and limits to be observed either in examining or punishing them. Whether any difference is to be made on account of age, or no distinction allowed between the youngest and the adult; whether repentance admits to a pardon, or if a man has been once a Christian it avails him nothing to recant; whether the mere profession of Christianity, albeit without crimes, or only the crimes associated therewith are punishable in all these points I am greatly doubtful.

In the meanwhile, the method I have observed towards those who have been denounced to me as Christians is this: I interrogated them whether they were Christians; if they confessed it I repeated the question twice again, adding the threat of capital punishment; if they still persevered, I ordered them to be executed. For whatever the nature of their creed might be, I could at least feel no doubt that contumacy and inflexible obstinacy deserved chastisement. There were others also possessed with the same infatuation, but being citizens of Rome, I directed them to be carried thither.

These accusations spread (as is usually the case) from the mere fact of the matter being investigated and several forms of the mischief came to light. A placard was put up, without any signature, accusing a large number of persons by name. Those who denied they were, or had ever been, Christians, who repeated after me an invocation to the Gods, and offered adoration, with wine and frankincense, to your image, which I had ordered to be brought for that purpose, together with those of the Gods, and who finally cursed Christ— none of which acts, it is said, those who are really Christians can be forced into performing—these I thought it proper to discharge. Others who were named by that informer at first confessed themselves Christians, and then denied it; true, they had been of that persuasion but they had quitted it, some three years, others many years, and a few as much as twenty-five years ago. They all worshipped your statue and the images of the Gods, and cursed Christ.

They affirmed, however, the whole of their guilt, or their error, was, that they were in the habit of meeting on a certain fixed day before it was light, when they sang in alternate verses a hymn to Christ, as to a god, and bound themselves by a solemn oath, not to any wicked deeds, but never to commit any fraud, theft or adultery, never to falsify their word, nor deny a trust when they should be called upon to deliver it up; after which it was their custom to separate, and then reassemble to partake of food—but food of an ordinary and innocent kind. Even this practice, however, they had abandoned after the publication of my edict, by which, according to your orders, I had forbidden political associations. I judged it so much the more necessary to extract the real truth, with the assistance of torture, from two female slaves, who were styled deaconesses: but I could discover nothing more than depraved and excessive superstition.

I therefore adjourned the proceedings, and betook myself at once to your counsel. For the matter seemed to me well worth referring to you, especially considering the numbers endangered. Persons of all ranks and ages, and of both sexes are, and will be, involved in the prosecution. For this contagious superstition is not confined to the cities only, but has spread through the villages and rural districts; it seems possible, however, to check and cure it. 'Tis certain at least that the temples, which had been almost deserted, begin now to be frequented; and the sacred festivals, after a long intermission, are again revived; while there is a general demand for sacrificial animals, which for some time past have met with but few purchasers. From hence it is easy to imagine what multitudes may be reclaimed from this error, if a door be left open to repentance.

Pliny, *Letters* 10.96. Pliny the Younger, *Letters,* trans. William Melmoth and rev. Winifred Margaret Lambart Hutchinson, Loeb Classical Library (London: W. Heinemann, 1915).

If an individual did not sacrifice and curse the name of Christ, the Roman official might employ some form of torture. Torture provided some helpful outcomes for the Romans. First, the individual might recant and sacrifice to the Roman gods. Second, torture showed that the Roman state had immense power over individuals. Finally, torture appeased those groups who were opposed to Christians, providing some satisfaction to the hostile crowd.

Rome supposedly carried out nine persecutions before the great persecution of 303 C.E. For the most part, however, these were not really persecutions, but were the enforcement of traditional secular policy decisions. Before Diocletian there existed only two true persecutions, those under Decius and Valerian. The so-called persecutions of Nero, Domitian, Trajan, Hadrian, Marcus Aurelius, and Septimius Severus were either mob reactions or local responses, often urged by select elements of society, such as the Jews or pagan priests, and can hardly be seen as true persecutions. These acts tended to produce few martyrs, in comparison to the later persecutions of Decius, Valerian, and Diocletian. Although, as seen before, Pliny wrote to Trajan, and it was clear that being a Christian was punishable, there was no real hunt by the central government to eliminate Christians. Decius' persecution was the first real attempt to eliminate Christianity throughout the empire. During this persecution Dionysius of Alexandria mentioned that men and women, young and old, soldiers and civilians, and members of all classes and ages were martyred. The emperor planned that everyone at a prescribed time would offer sacrifice to the Roman gods. Those not doing so would be asked point blank to submit; if not, they would be arrested, and if they persisted in refusing to offer sacrifice, they were punished. The results were amazing for both sides. For the Romans, thousands of Christians lapsed and offered sacrifice to Rome's traditional gods or ran away, allowing Rome to claim victory over the Christians and their God. For the Christians, thousands refused to offer sacrifice and were tortured and killed, producing examples to be emulated. It is hard to know what would have happened if Decius had not been killed by the Goths, but clearly his death was providential for the Christians. Valerian's persecution operated in the same way, but targeted church leaders. Again, for the Christians the results were mixed; many preferred martyrdom to apostasy, while a significant number preferred to offer sacrifice rather than die. The church was saved by Valerian's providential capture and execution by the Persian king Sapor. In both instances the church claimed that God had punished the Roman emperors for their hostility.

After both persecutions, the church faced a serious problem: what to do with the lapsed Christians who now wanted to return. During the 250s Cyprian in North Africa wrote extensively about how to deal with the lapsed. Numerous letters and treatises throughout this period indicate that those who lapsed were serious about returning to the church, while local communities were divided in their feelings and responses. Cyprian instructed the church to treat apostates harshly by making them wait to return to the fold and ordered that local Christians should instead hold up the martyrs, especially from their local community, as symbols and examples.

A more difficult question was what to do with the lapsed clergy and bishops, and the issue of whether the sacraments that they had performed were legal or not. This last problem would surface periodically during the next 200 years, producing two camps: the purists, who argued that lapsed Christians could never reenter the church, and that the sacraments preformed by lapsed clergy had no value; and the reformists, who argued that an individual could reenter the church after a period of penance. More importantly, the validity of the sacraments was still maintained, although it would only be St. Augustine who would promote and articulate the Catholic view that the state of grace of the priest does not affect the validity of the sacrament.

After Decius' and Valerian's persecutions in the 240s and 250s, Roman emperors and pretenders fought among themselves while foreign invaders breached the frontiers. The Christians were not seen as a central problem to the emperors, who worried more about the survival of Rome and themselves. This period produced a religious peace between Christians and pagans. During this peace the church continued to grow. This peace also led to the church perfecting its organization, which created a central hierarchy at the regional level, later called dioceses, and local communities, or parishes. The increase in converts from the 3rd century produced a well-functioning system for the catechumen. The liturgical calendar made Lent the preparatory time for baptism and reconciliation, culminating in

Easter's celebration with baptism and the Eucharist. This period produced a strong system within the church that allowed the church to survive the later persecution.

Before Diocletian's final and most terrible persecution in 303, isolated instances during his reign occurred in which Christians were singled out for abuse. In Africa in 295 a certain Maximilian met the requirements for being recruited into the military but declined to be conscripted, saying he was a Christian.[2] When told that he was to serve or die, Maximilian continued to deny his military responsibility and instead vehemently stated that he would die rather than serve, since he was a Christian. The recruiting officer informed him that there were Christians already serving in the military. Maximilian replied that this was fine for them but not for him. The prosecution stated to Maximilian "Serve. If you despise the military service you will perish miserably." After he still refused to serve he was sentenced to death because "Whereas Maximilian has disloyally refused the military oath, he is sentenced to die by the sword." He was then executed. The importance of this act was not that the person was a Christian, as proven by the fact that the prosecutor knew of Christians serving in the Roman army; rather what was important was that Maximilian was a citizen who refused to do his duty to serve his nation in the military. This so-called persecution should not be seen as a persecution based on religion, but rather on the recruit's lack of patriotism. Maximilian was therefore a conscientious objector, and as is the case in modern states, the government did not recognize his defense or action. He was thus punished, as he would in a modern society.

A second incident occurred in Africa, probably a few years later. Here a Christian already in the military was at a celebration for the emperor's birthday. While there, the Christian centurion Marcellus rejected the pagan rites and threw down his soldier's belt in front of the legionary standards, stating: "From now I cease to serve your emperors and I despise the worship of your gods of wood and stone, for they are deaf and dumb images." He was arrested and asked, "What was your intention in violating military discipline by taking off your belt and throwing it down with your staff?" Again, the soldier's Christianity was not addressed. Marcellus claimed that it was not fitting that a Christian, who fights for Christ his lord, should fight for the armies of this world. Marcellus, like Maximilian, was sentenced to death, not for being a Christian but for displaying poor military discipline. The fact that Marcellus, as a Christian, was already serving in the army reinforced the prosecution's statement about Christians in the army in Maximilian's case. Again, looking at this case, the government's case was based upon rules of order, not one's religion. This would be similar to a modern soldier being insubordinate or desecrating his nation's flag because of a religious belief—both unacceptable. Both of these cases point to the fact that being a Christian was not the mitigating factor in their treatment; rather, lack of military service and poor discipline were. These so-called persecutions did not stem from a religious, but, rather, a military policy.

It is possible that a different message may have been preached to some African Christians against military service that was contrary to the current mainstream Christian message of working with the government. This new strain was pacifist and antiestablishment, resulting in the deaths of Maximilian and Marcellus, who tried to translate their military philosophy in inappropriate ways. From the Roman state's point of view the acts were confusing, since Christians served in the military, but suddenly others claimed that to do so was unchristian.

The Romans employed a standard formula during the persecutions. First the local officials or emperor's agent arrested the accused. Sometimes they interrogated the accused immediately, but usually they put them into jail to let fear take hold. If not in prison, the accused could be put under house arrest guarded by a soldier, public officer, or even another citizen. The public jail *(custodia publica)* was not punitive but was merely a holding place where the accused waited to be charged. The sexes were not segregated, which promoted such abuses as rape. Although the jail time was to be limited, in Diocletian's persecution it became a means of punishment and torture.

While in prison one might suffer from the stocks, the irons, and, of course, hunger and thirst. The stocks were meant not only to prevent movement but even to cause strains and rupture. Most prisoners were not put into the dark holes or bowels of the prison, but rather lived in the public prison, where they could receive communications, via bribes, and guest who brought them food and clothing.

After some time in jail, the accused was tried, usually at first by the local magistrate, who could not give capital punishment but could torture. After this initial investigation the local official took the accused, along with the records, to the provincial governor, where the real trial now took place. The judge or governor, seated on an elevated chair and surrounded by soldiers, officials, clerks, and reporters, looked down on the accused from a position of power. The provincial governor could order torture, although this was rarely used on citizens before the 3rd century. The judges usually offered a way out: Sacrifice to the emperor and gods of Rome and one could go free. If the accused refused, the sentence was passed. Torture was technically illegal if a full confession was made, but eventually torture became a type of punishment instead of a means to gather information.

By the time of Diocletian the persecutors used torture not to elicit a confession or even to obtain sacrifice, but, rather, to make a statement to the Christians. By using torture and the threat of pain, the Romans hoped that many Christians would convert back to paganism. Some of the forms of torture included the traditional whipping and beatings. But the Romans were also inventive. For example, there was the rack, in which the accused was stretched so that his or her arms and legs popped out of their sockets. Another favorite torture was to place the individual on the rack and then to use the comb, similar to a hair comb except that the teeth were razor sharp metal spikes, which were scraped down the side of the accused, ripping the flesh. Women, who were of course raped and abused, were thrown into the arena to face the wild beasts wearing a bikini outfit made of briar bushes. Finally, individuals were confined to the mines where they suffered deprivations. All of these acts were not only to punish the accused, but to make a statement to the numerous other Christians not arrested to give up Christianity.

After judgment, the guilty could be sentenced to a variety of forms of punishment, ranging from least to most severe: banishment, transportation to distant or inhospitable lands, penal servitude, or death. Many early Christians suffered banishment. Neither deprived of rights nor property, they were merely forced to leave an area, like Priscia leaving Rome, and there was the hope of returning after things calmed down. Transportation, to distant or inhospitable lands such as for Flavia Domitilla, was more severe and was seen as capital punishment, since the accused were treated as convicts being sent to inhospitable islands usually without any hope of returning and where many died due to the harsh environment. Even worse was penal servitude, such as those mentioned by Eusebius in the last great persecutions, and some were sent to the quarries and mines where they were scourged and branded on the forehead and bound by rings on their feet to prevent runaways, working in harsh conditions where they ultimately died. Finally one could be executed: by the cross, most cruel, for slaves and vile evildoers; by stake and beasts for criminals without Roman citizenship rights; and least degrading, beheading for citizens, where the individual knelt down and was decapitated by a sword, such as Paul.

Later emperors, like Diocletian, used other means such as boiling oil, pitch or tar, red-hot iron stools, being roasted on a grill, and burning one slowly. Being thrown to the beasts was a show for public holidays; typically the victims were placed on a raised platform at the mercy of the beast. Also in Diocletian's persecution drowning was used, being tied and thrown into the sea or being thrown into the river with a millstone around the neck. Other prisoners were enclosed in a skin with other animals—snakes, monkeys, or dogs—and thrown into the water. These savage acts were not only to punish the accused but to provide entertainment for the public.

In 303, when Diocletian began the last great persecutions of Christians, most were punished for not sacrificing to the Roman gods. For example, in January 304, Julius the Veteran refused to sacrifice. The judge tried to bribe him to sacrifice, but Julius refused and was beheaded. Irenaeus of Sirmium refused to sacrifice in the same way; he was tortured and beaten but still refused to sacrifice and was then beheaded. After Crispina of Tebessa refused to sacrifice, the judge tried to humiliate her by having her head shaved; however she still refused to sacrifice, and she was beheaded.

Agape, Irene, and Chione of Saloniki, along with four other women, fled into the mountains to avoid sacrificing. After they were caught, Agape, Irene, and Chione refused to sacrifice and were then burned. The other four were put into prison; one was pregnant, even though her husband had died seven months earlier. The judge asked how she became pregnant. She answered that it was by the will of God; clearly from the question and answer, she was not yet seven months along.

There were other notable instances, such as Felix, a bishop in North Africa. The emperors issued an edict for the sacred scriptures to be surrendered. There was the almost comical scene where government officials attempted to persuade Bishop Felix to hand over the gospels. Felix refused, and the officials then asked for just any old book, which again Felix refused. Finally Felix admitted to having the books, but refused to give them up; he was then beheaded. In France the bishop Quirinus was arrested and a millstone tied around his neck, and he thrown into a river. Many of the Christians wanted to save Quirinus when he didn't initially sink, but he prayed to God to take his life as an example and then sank and drowned. A final example was Euplus of Catania, who shouted to the judges outside the courtroom "I want to die; I am a Christian." After being arrested he arrived in court with the Gospels and goaded the judges to torture him. He refused to sacrifice, was raked with a steel comb and beaten, and, after again refusing to sacrifice, was executed.

These stories show that many Christians had a fervent desire to be martyred and can be divided into three classes: those who refused to cooperate, like Felix; those who refused to sacrifice after being accused; and those who actively wish to be martyred, like Euplus. Their fervor incited many Christians to remain loyal to their religious beliefs, but some, like Euplus, were not idolized. Christians viewed his form of martyrdom as inappropriate.

ROME'S RESPONSE

A central question in all of the discussions arises: Why did the Romans persecute? Was it because they desired to see the gods of Rome supreme? The answer seems in part due to Christian beliefs that do not accept any other religion or gods. For Christians one was either a Christian or the enemy—there was no compromise. This exclusiveness remained at the heart of the disagreement. For Romans, exclusiveness to the point of denying the other gods' existence was arrogant. For example, when one immigrated to a new place or city, one "converted" to that region's gods while retaining one's own gods. One accepted these gods as an act of goodwill and religious piety, but Christians refused to honor this sentiment. The Romans believed that this Christian arrogance undermined the state.

The Romans also worried about Christian secretiveness, but this was not directed at Christians alone. Throughout their rule, the Romans constantly disdained secret organizations, even volunteer firemen. Roman logic went like this: If you allow a group to gather and meet, what will they do when they meet? They will talk. And what will they talk about? The government, of course, and their remarks will not be positive. If this group was therefore allowed to meet and talk, they might propose changes or advocate the government's overthrow. Therefore, to prevent rebellion, the Romans went to the root cause—group meetings—and declared these meetings illegal. The Romans had a societal paranoia that someone was always trying to supplant them, even their own citizens. In addition, Diocletian desired to see everything conform. The chaos of the 3rd century convinced Diocletian that the military and its ordered life was the key to Rome's survival. Anything that went against this conformity was attacked. Another reason for the persecutions seems to have been a general distrust of the East. Rome's traditional enemy, Persia, was accused of exporting to Rome strange religions, such as Manichaeism, to which Christianity was strangely similar. Also causing distrust was the fact that, years previously, a Roman army was defeated by the Persians. Diocletian may have felt that his Eastern Roman army was infected with Christians and Persian sympathizers, which caused the army's defeat. Another reason for Diocletian's persecution was the general plea for help by the traditional pagan shrines, which had fallen into disrepair and disuse during the 3rd century as a result of the general political chaos. Diocletian restored shrines and temples. In addition, when Diocletian asked the oracles why the empire had suffered, they blamed the Christians. The final and strongest reason for the persecutions was the constant attack against the Christians by Diocletian's colleague, Galerius, whose mother had raised him to hate Christians. Individuals on both sides of the religious rift responded in different ways, as seen in the accompanying Biographies.

MARTYR AND PERSECUTOR

Perpetua (Early 3rd Century)

Vibia Perpetua, a martyr who was well born, had a father, mother, and two brothers, one of whom was a catechumen, when she was killed. She was married, with a son, when arrested. Her father, a pagan, attempted to have her recant, but she refused to do so. She and her fellow martyrs were baptized after their arrest and before their transference to the public prisons. While in prison she had a vision indicating her future passion, where a ladder guarded by a dragon reached to heaven. She and her companion Saturus came to a large garden where a shepherd fed his flock while thousands in white robes stood around. The shepherd gave her a piece of cheese. This dream probably meant that Christ, the shepherd, had given her faith and had fed her belief, making her strong.

Their trial came and the procurator condemned all of them to the beasts. After being condemned Perpetua saw a second vision where her brother, who had died much earlier, was in punishment, but after her prayers he was transferred to a place of peace. The story clearly showed that there were prayers for the dead in the early church. The day before her death Perpetua had a third vision, where she triumphed over an Egyptian, identified as the devil, and was awarded with a golden branch. She was attacked by a cow and tossed without pain, but was then executed by the sword. The date of her martyrdom is unclear, but it was probably in 202 when Septimius Severus published an edict against fresh converts such as Perpetua.

Diocletian

Diocletian (ca. 244–313) was born about 244 in Salona, Dalmatia, near modern Split (Croatia) and rose through the army ranks to become head of the protectors (officer corps) for the emperor Carus when Carus invaded Persia in 283–84. Carus' son Numerian became emperor upon his father's death. Upon the army's return, Numerian's murder was revealed and is traditionally blamed on his father-in-law Aper, the Praetorian prefect. Numerian's dead body was discovered, and the troops hailed Diocletian emperor in 284. Diocletian may, in fact, have had a hand in the murders of Carus and Numerian. In 285, Diocletian defeated Carinus, Carus' other son, at the Margus River and thus became sole emperor of the Roman Empire. Diocletian appointed his friend and fellow general Maximian his co-emperor, or Augusti, in 286. For the next seven years these two men waged war throughout the empire: against the rebelling local peasants of Gaul, the Bagaudae, the Germans on the Rhine, Carausius, a usurper in Britain, the Carpi on the Danube, the Saracens in Arabia, and the Persians, with success.

Needing more generals, Diocletian created the Tetrarchy, or rule of four, in 293. Here each Augusti received an assistant termed Caesar; Diocletian chose Galerius, and Maximian selected Constantius. These generals waged war throughout the empire. Constantius defeated Carausius in Britain; Maximian campaigned in North Africa; Diocletian waged war on the Danube against the Sarmatians and Carpi and later put down a second rebellion in Egypt in 297; while Galerius suppressed a rebellion in Egypt in 293, waged war on the Danube, and finally defeated the Persians in 298, producing a lasting peace.

Diocletian carried out numerous political and economic reforms during his reign. He accelerated and completed the process of dividing large provinces into smaller ones, including Italy. He closed the local mints, replacing them with a standardized mint system. He reformed the coinage, issuing large numbers of gold coins, called the *solidus*, a pure silver coin called the *argenteus*, and a large bronze coin, termed a *nummus*, which had the standard reverse type "Genio Populi Romani" or "Genius of the Roman People." In addition, Diocletian instituted a standardized tax reform and the most controversial reform, the price edict, or edict on maximum prices on goods and wages. Diocletian also carried out legal reforms and created a hierarchy for the imperial court.

Beginning in 303 with the last of the great persecutions, Diocletian attempted to eliminate Christianity. At first his persecutions were confined to intimidation of Christians and the destruction of churches and sacred books. Ultimately Diocletian issued orders that everyone in the empire perform sacrifice on pain of death. The persecutions were strongest in the East and North Africa.

Diocletian decided to retire in 305, after 21 years of rule, probably because he had accomplished all of the reforms he thought necessary. This retirement implemented his final reform, a plan of succession based upon merit and not birth in hopes of ensuring the empire's strong and peaceful rule. As such he forced his colleague Maximian to retire as well; the new Augusti, Constantius and Galerius, adopted Severus and Maximin Daia as Caesars, even though Maximian and Constantius had grown sons Maxentius and Constantine. Diocletian retired to his fortress palace at Split. After Galerius' death in 311, Diocletian's wife Prisca and daughter Valeria were unable or unwilling to join him in Split; Licinius executed them in 313. Diocletian, unable to save them, and distraught over his statues torn down with Maximian's attempted coup, either died or committed suicide in 313. He was declared a god, the last emperor to have such an act accorded to him.

MARTYRDOM

Christians prepared for the persecutions in some cases by promoting their own martyrdom, where the martyr received rewards for their acts. These rewards included immortality, forgiveness of sins, securing a special place, that is, heaven and privilege, defeating the powers of paganism, helping companions, judging the persecutors in heaven, and being with Christ. Martyrdom in fact became an important part in the struggle with paganism, since it was an outward sign that Christians could perform to show their commitment.

Diocletian's initial persecution, in addition to bringing about turmoil and pain for individuals, destroyed the church's buildings. Diocletian, however, was initially reluctant to kill anyone. Part of the reason may have been Diocletian's hope to avoid a bloodbath, or he may have underestimated the convictions of the Christians. Diocletian rather seemed more interested in the physical manifestations of the church; hence his edicts on the demolishing of the churches and the surrender of books. This was the traditional way one society would destroy another's religion, since so much of paganism was attached to physical buildings and sites. Since the beginning of Mediterranean civilization, societies held cult statues and their temples in great reverence. The Sumerians, in 3000 B.C.E., argued that if they defeated the enemy and captured the cult figure or statue and brought it back to their city, they could force the captives to "behave" or else their sacred figure would be destroyed. This destruction would end the life of the captives' god. For the Greeks the destruction of the temples, such as Xerxes' destruction of Athens in 480 B.C., meant that the gods had abandoned them. To have them return, the Greeks would have to not only rebuild the temple but receive divine instructions from the oracles as to what should be done. The Romans likewise believed that the cult statues and temples held sacred power. When Rome conquered a foreign tribe they would often absorb the local religion by renaming the deity, keeping the local name and adding a Roman name. To destroy an enemy shrine or temple meant the destruction of that god or goddess. The Babylonians and Romans had destroyed the Jewish temples, producing a state of despair among the Jews. Similarly, Diocletian in attacking the Christian churches was merely following the traditional idea of destroying an enemy religion by destroying its structure.

What made Diocletian's persecution so terrible was its magnitude. It was not a local or brief event, as were the earlier persecutions of Nero, Antoninus, or even Decius; rather it was empire-wide and lasted as long as a decade in some places. Although only about 140 deaths were specifically mentioned in the sources during the 10-year persecution, there must have been many more. Although the numbers given by later Christian writers were highly inflated, the impact was tremendous. But what was probably the greatest blow to the church was the number of Christians who sacrificed to the gods of Rome, committing apostasy, which would rip the church apart for the next two centuries, especially in Africa. In addition, this persecution had a philosophical champion in the form of Porphyry, a Neo-Platonist philosopher who ridiculed several ideas of the Christian Church: 1) Peter and Paul's fight over circumcision showed that the apostles, whom early Christians placed immense authority, were not reliable; 2) Paul showed great impudence and disrespect for those who knew Jesus personally; and 3) the disciples were not united. Porphyry therefore attacked the Christians in a way that was appealing to the educated—through rhetoric. Diocletian may have even asked Porphyry to write a work justifying the persecutions. With Diocletian's retirement in 305, his successors Galerius and Maximian Daia carried out an even more brutal suppression. Finally in 311 Galerius, dying of a painful disease, which he blamed on the Christian God, issued the Edict of Toleration, which allowed Christian to worship without fear. This was a complete reversal and victory for the Christians.

Why did the persecutions fail? They failed in part because the pagans believed that by attacking the physical structures of the religion, they could destroy that religion. The emperors failed to understand that the real structure of the church was its hierarchy, the bishops, who were often safe from persecution. If Diocletian had recognized the true power and influence of these bishops, he would have seen that killing them would have dealt a severe blow to the structure of the church. The persecutions also failed because the church was geographically spread out throughout the empire. Although one area might have been severely attacked, other regions had relative peace. Finally, the government could not offer an alternative to the salvation message taught by Christianity, which pagans attested and even admired.

Rome's interaction with the Christians was based in part on fear. The Romans distrusted the Christians, accusing them of being from the lower classes, menial, ignorant, and above all superstitious, a view constantly refuted by Christian writers. This attitude showing the Roman bias and indicating the type of occupations and the fact that women were seen as the major missionaries inside the home is from Celsus:

We see, indeed, in private houses workers in wool and leather, and fullers and persons of the most uninstructed and rustic character, not venturing to utter a word in the presence of their elders and wiser masters; but when they get hold of the children privately, and certain women as ignorant as themselves, they pour forth wonderful statements to the effect that they ought not to give heed to their father and to their teachers, but should obey them; that the former are foolish and stupid, and neither know nor can perform anything that is really good being preoccupied with empty trifles; that they alone know how men ought to live, and that, if the children obey them, they will both be happy themselves, and will make their home happy also. ... but that if they (children) wish [to avail themselves of their aid] they must leave their father and instructors, and go with the women and their playfellows to the women's apartments, or to the leather-shop, or to the fuller's shop, that they main attain to perfection;—and by words like these they gain them over.[3]

Although this highly charged passage attacks Christianity as a religion of stupid and foolish women, it nevertheless shows how many pagans viewed it. The passage also contains some interesting pieces of information that show how Christians were seen as missionaries in their daily life. First, the occupations mentioned were respectable trades: fullers and wool and leather workers as well as rustic laborers. This coincided with the traditional occupations that the church fathers argued were worthy. Second, these occupations were located in the home, a phenomenon well recognized as a typical Mediterranean process. Third, the value of women in the preaching of the new religion was attested. Finally, the passage indicated that the targets for new converts were the children, most likely, of the wealthy family's household. Although refuted by Christians, Celsus' account continued to be believed by pagans, especially those already biased against them.

Rome's interaction with Christians was often violent. But for the most part it was this fear of violence that kept the Christians secretive and scared. Christians never knew if the Roman government was going to initiate another reprisal or if they were going to be safe. This fear of attack influenced the Christians in their daily life, making them especially secretive, which in turn exacerbated the situation even more. Their secrecy became a target of reprisal. This vicious cycle engulfed both Christians and pagans, further affecting their daily life. This fear also affected their religious life and how Christians worshipped.

NOTES

1. K. S. Painter, *The Water Newton Early Christian Silver* (London: British Museum 1977), p. 15.

2. The following accounts are taken from Herbert Musurillo, *The Acts of the Christian Martyrs; Introductions, Texts and Translations* (Oxford: Clarendon Press, 1972).

3. Origen, *Contra Celsum* 3.55, in *Documents Illustrative of the History of the Church*, Vol. I to A.D. 313, ed. B. J. Kidd, translation of Christian Literature Series VI select passages (London: Macmillen, 1920), p. 108.

8

RELIGIOUS LIFE

Christianity grew out of Judaism, and in order to understand the religious life of Christians in their day-to-day setting, it is crucial to understand the growth and development of the early Christians and their practices. This understanding comes from examining the development of important Christian feasts and recognizing how some were related to Judaism and paganism, such as Easter and Christmas. After Constantine's conversion in 312 C.E., the growth in Christianity often led to some individuals who were not sincere, and some church fathers complained of lax Christians who still clung to their former ways. Christians' religious life, however, was always grounded in the family, with the interaction between spouses, parents, children, and the church structure coming into play. These interactions occurred not only through traditional pagan institutions and practices such as schooling but also through the direct intervention of the church leaders who attempted to control certain practices within Christian society. This attempt to guide and control often produced divisions in the church, such as the Donatists and the Arians.

Early Christian religious life traditionally focused on the small community within a particular district, or the house church, following Cyprian's advice to care for the poor, widows, and sick. In addition, since Christianity originally descended from Judaism, the synagogue retained its importance in the early church. In the Acts of Apostles, Peter, Paul, and undoubtedly other missionaries visited and preached in the synagogues when they first arrived in a community. If they found converts among the Jewish residents, these new Christians became organized into their own sect like in Palestine, becoming Jewish/Christians. If they were not welcomed by the Jewish congregation, the missionaries then preached to the Gentiles, finding converts. Early Christianity was organized in a similar way to a voluntary association, like the other associations in the Roman Empire, such as burial clubs. These associations ensured that a member received a proper burial and was remembered in the club's votives. Although Christianity was more than a burial club, to the Romans its organization and actions might have seemed like a burial association, since Christians had communal burial plots and meals of remembrance. Finally, Christianity was a philosophical school, trying to explain the afterlife and one's position in the cosmos. During the 3rd and 4th centuries Christian philosophy borrowed heavily from Plato, appealing to the educated Roman.

SYNAGOGUES AND HOUSE CHURCHES

The early Christians in Rome had contact with the Jewish synagogues. When Peter arrived in the city in the 40s, he naturally would have used his Jewish ancestry and tradition to begin his missionary activity in Rome. During this time there were probably five synagogues in Rome; one, the synagogue of the Hebrews, had existed since the late republic, while two others were established during the reign of Augustus, honoring him and his son-in-law Marcus Agrippa. A fourth synagogue honored Herod the Great and was probably also built during Augustus' time. A fifth synagogue may have honored a tribune in Syria, Volumnius, and a patron of the Jews. These synagogues were located across the Tiber region in Region XIV, which is modern Trastevere. Although no archaeological remains exist of the synagogues in Rome, in nearby Ostia, Rome's port, a 1st-century synagogue has been discovered and excavated. This building was originally built as a synagogue, as opposed to other sites, even those in Rome, which seem to have originally been private houses and then turned into synagogues. At present, no evidence exists for a contemporary Christian structure originally intended to be a church; instead, the early Christians used the house churches, similar to the other early Jewish synagogues. Early Christians presumably used these synagogues, at least during the initial stages of missionary activities. Undoubtedly tensions arose in the synagogues between the Jewish congregation and those who followed Christ. It is possible that Claudius' edict developed from a conflict within one or more of the Roman synagogues between the Jewish-Christians and Jews.

The rise of the house churches had a profound impact upon Christianity and its religious life. Instead of worshiping in the Jewish temple or synagogue, Christianity centered its worship on the family at a private residence. The house churches became centers of conversion, allowing the new religion to spread throughout the city. Since different house churches existed in the same city, different opinions among the early Christians arose, creating party strife, as mentioned in some of Paul's letters. These house churches contained a cross section of Christian society, which allowed new leaders to be trained after the Apostolic Age.

In Rome Paul mentioned three house churches; for example, Aquila and Priscilla lent their dwellings for services (Romans 16.5, 14, 15). The meetings took place at night on late Saturday and early Sunday. In Acts of the Apostles (20.15) services occurred in an upper room, styled caenaculum, on the third floor and lit by many lamps. The oldest churches in Rome, S. Prisca on the Aventine, S. Cecilia in Trastevere, and San Clemente, were all originally private homes. But by the 4th century separate churches had been built. The pagan philosopher Porphyry writing in 270 indicated that Christians imitated pagans with the construction of temples by building great buildings to meet and pray.

At Duro-Europas in Syria a house dating from the 250s had clearly been made into a religious building, a church, and no longer functioned as a private residence. It was probably not the first church there, given its frontier location. The Christian Justin writing in Rome in the 150s still makes reference to the house churches. It is probable that the change from house churches to churches occurred at the beginning of the 3rd century. Most likely the shift occurred at a place where Christians already met, a residential house used also for religious services. Conceivably when the owners died the house was given to the general Christian community and was renovated into a freestanding church. An example might be the *titulus Clementis*, later the Basilica of San Clemente in Rome. Originally a house for Bishop Clement in the 1st century, by the 3rd century it was a freestanding structure, and it was ultimately a basilica by the 5th. Even in Britain a villa has evidence of having a chapel, a reserved religious structure, dating from the 3rd and 4th centuries. By the time of the great persecutions the government already knew the locations of churches. In Cirta, North Africa, during the persecutions in 303, the government seized books from a church, probably a renovated house with a library, dining hall, and storerooms. At Nicomedia, in modern Turkey, a church existed since the emperor Diocletian ordered it destroyed.[1] And in Oxyrhynchus Egypt at least one church and perhaps two existed; one even had bronze doors.

Finally, the construction and design of the churches began as an offshoot of both private and public buildings. The churches took as their basis the New Testament description of the Last Supper, where the table became the altar. The actual development of the building, variously called basilica, ecclesia, and aula, came from Roman structures. After Constantine, the Latin term basilica became the usual word for church. These structures were rectangular, with three or five aisles and an apse opposite the main entrance. Above the supports and down the main aisle was a wall often decorated with mosaics and windows allowing light into the main area, the nave. The apse was usually semicircular; however, variations did exist. Often beneath the apse a crypt for burial or even a baptistery existed. Opposite the apse was the main entrance, usually going into the center aisles, and occasionally there were ancillary entrances for the side aisles. Between the aisles and apse was occasionally the transept, a small aisle running perpendicular to the main aisles, often giving the church a look of a cross. The transept's purpose is unclear, and it may have been to provide open space for services. The altar was inside the church, as opposed to the Roman pagan custom of having it outside. A custom arose where a piece of a relic from a saint or martyr was preserved under the altar, which consecrated the structure. These relics were not bones as found in later medieval churches, but rather mementoes, such as earth from their tomb or cloth. The altar had no clear position; some were located on the back wall of the apse while some were in front facing the center aisle. The clergy sat on ascending seats or benches according to their rank, with the most prominent position for the bishop who sat higher and in a more distinct chair, such as one made of ivory. The *ambo*, a raised tribune or circular platform two or three steps high, placed in the middle of or facing the congregation, was often employed for preaching. In the early church, baptism for the adults was done by immersion in the baptistery, not generally located inside the church itself, but outside; sometimes the baptistery was a separate attached room, other times a separate building. The baptistery's central part, where the baptismal pool was located, could be raised. The baptismal pool, a basin, came in various shapes—octagonal, cruciform, hexagonal, and so forth—and was about three feet deep, with water poured over the recipient, therefore making immersion symbolic.

Early Christianity developed its ideology distinct from Judaism. While Judaism preached that the Messiah would come, Christianity argued that he had already arrived. Christians were exhorted to always pray, since the time of Christ's return would not be made known and they should be ready. The early Christians believed in Christ's eminent return within their own lifetime, therefore individuals should pray constantly, but that was not practical since they needed to support their families. Since most early Christians were laborers, they often could only meet at night after a long work day; during the persecutions meeting at night was for protection. The original term for these night services, vigil, came from the Roman night watchmen, the *vigiles*.

In the early church, Wednesdays and Fridays were set aside for prayer. Both were days for fasting and meetings, the *synaxis*, with the Eucharist celebrated. These days were chosen for a couple of reasons. First, they were celebrated instead of the traditional Jewish days of Mondays and Thursdays. In addition, both days celebrated days of Christ's suffering, Wednesday the day Judas betrayed Jesus, and Friday the day Jesus died. They were mentioned as special days from the late 1st century in the *Didache* and by 2nd-century writers such as Hermas and Tertullian. Sunday became the most important day of the week, replacing the Jewish

Sabbath on Saturday, since Sunday was the day Christ rose from the dead. Using this day for the central weekly religious celebration made the cleavage between Judaism and Christianity complete. Saturday still retained some importance in Rome as a day of fasting and penance in preparation for Sunday's importance. The idea that the Christians met in the catacombs for their services is a popular misconception and may come from the custom of having a vigil for the dead in cemeteries or over tombs.

One of the earliest issues facing the young Christian church was the date for celebrating Easter. In the mid-2nd century in Asia, the feast remained on the Paschal, the 14th day of March's new moon, the Jewish date, while other Christians fixed it on the Sunday following the 14th day after the new moon. The former Jewish custom could be any day of the week, while the latter kept it on Sunday. In the West the latter custom prevailed. The Jewish festival of Pentecost, seven weeks later, became a Christian feast celebrating the Holy Spirit descending upon the apostles. Holy Week came into being as the days in Lent immediately before Easter to prepare oneself for Easter.

Although not as contentious as Easter, and still celebrated at different times in the modern era by different groups, the fixing of Christ's birthday, Christmas, also produced a heated debate. In the East the date was celebrated on January 6, while in the West December 25 was chosen, the same day as the Roman festival to the god Sol Invictus. Ultimately both days became feasts, with December 25 being Christmas, the day of Christ's birth, and January 6 the Epiphany, or the celebration of the Wise Men visiting the infant Jesus. This then made the date of Jesus' conception March 25, near the spring equinox (March 21), which also became an important feast day. The early feasts, existing by the 4th century, were Christmas, Epiphany, Lent or Holy Week, Easter, Low Sunday Eastertide, Ascension, and Pentecost, while all Wednesdays, Fridays, and Saturdays were days of fasting. The vigils for feasts days were at night.

These early meetings centered on the traditional services, which later became formalized into Christian beliefs. The early Christians had two important ceremonies: baptism/confirmation and the Eucharist. Baptism, representing the crossing over from dying, not believing to living, was meant to wash and cleanse an initiate of their sins and release demons from their souls. Baptism in which individuals were immersed in water and a seal in oil was made on the forehead was reserved for adults. Lent was for the initiate's preparation, with baptism occurring on Holy Saturday. Once the initiate was baptized, they received confirmation, the imposition of hands and the use of oil on their foreheads, although some had their whole body rubbed with oil. The Chrism, oil mixed with balsam, became the symbol for confirmation like water was for baptism. In the early church, confirmation was called the "imposition of hands" or "of the hand." Like baptism, the ceremony for comfirmation occurred on Holy Saturday after baptism. With the completion of these two sacraments, the final triad, the Eucharist, was then celebrated.

During Lent the initiates or catechumens prepared themselves for entrance by studying. By the end of the 2nd century catechumen's instruction period lasted three years. Due to Decius's persecutions, heretics, and the lapsed, the church subjected catechumens to an even longer time period for instruction and perseverance. After the emperor Constantine, two classes of catechumens existed, the long and the immediate. The individual would go "before the Learned" and be examined; to prevent a long period of waiting, some did not seek admittance until near death, although the fathers discouraged this. For immediate converts, the waiting period was 40 days, the period of Lent, and they were usually received on Easter Vigil. The catechumens could remain for the first part of the mass for the opening prayers, readings, and homily. Christians borrowed these components from the Jewish synagogues. After the homily the catechumens departed for further studying, and during the second part of the mass, only those baptized remained during the offertory or presentation of the gifts, prayers, and the anaphora or consecration. The early documents for consecration have the cup presented first, and then the bread. After the catechumen was baptized on Holy Saturday, they could enjoy the full benefits of being a Christian.

In addition to these sacraments, those of penance, holy order, marriage, and the anointing of sick existed. Baptism washed away sins, but what was to happen to an individual who sinned after their baptism? The early church promoted penance, where one avowed their faults in front of a priest. In contrast to the public sacrament of baptism, penance became private between the priest and the sinner, unless it involved some sort of public scandal, in which case there was to be some sort of public reparation. The selection of a priest, one who presided over the services, became a topic of utmost importance. Gathering on a Sunday for ordination or holy orders, the bishop alone performed the imposition of hands for the ordination of a priest. The individual who was to lead the community not only had to be acceptable to the community, hence one chosen by the community, but someone with the authority to speak. Individuals who became recognized for their piety, community service, and willingness to lead the community became paramount. The sacrament of holy orders involved the imposition of hands, witnessed Paul to Timothy (Timothy 1.4.14), while in the Acts of the Apostles and the *Didache* there was an election, prayer, and imposition of hands. In the 2nd century the church father Hippolytus was more explicit with the offices and duties of bishops and other ministers. By the time of Eusebius in the early 4th century, there existed a hierarchy, with bishops leading important and large communities. Like priests, bishops were also chosen by the whole community.

The sacrament of marriage in the early church differed from the Jewish practice, which allowed divorce and remarriage; Christianity argued for only one marriage, with the sacrament occurring in a mass. Tertullian in the 2nd century indicated it was a public ceremony with bishops, priests, deacons, and widows laying of the hands and all claiming the right to sanction any matrimony between two Christians, or to condemn it if it did not offer guarantees to Christianity, a reference to a Christian marrying a pagan. In art, relief sculptures show two clasped hands as a symbol of union.

The final sacrament, anointing of the sick, was again an early rite where prayers were offered for the sick and dead. Communion was reserved after mass for the faithful sick, who had it administered to them, even on days when there was no synaxis, or Eucharist.

These sacraments gave the early Christians a formalized ritual to support their evolving beliefs and further distanced them from Judaism. The elements used in these services were familiar to Judaism: water, wine, bread, and oil. Some elements were new: salt (for baptism and blessing holy water), fire (every hour was sacred), candles, incense, and ashes (for penitents). Blood, a traditional part of pagan sacrifices, was banished. In addition, prayers developed into the Acclamations, Anaphora (Eucharist), and general prayers. An example is preserved in a late 3rd-century papyri: "Almighty God, who didst create the heaven, the earth and the sea and all they contain, help me, have pity o me, cleanse me from my sings, save me in this world and in the next through our Lord and Savior Jesus Christ, through whom is glory and power would without end Amen."[2] This prayer, an example of the general collection, would also lead to the litany of saints and martyrs; the doxology or great prayer invoking the three persona of God: Father, Son, and Holy Spirit; and the creeds, which set out the doctrine of the church. The most famous of the latter was the Nicene Creed of 324, which set out that God the Father and God the Son were coeternal and that God the Son, Jesus Christ, was equally both God and human.

The conversion of individuals before the emperor Constantine took time and energy, especially since the religion was outlawed. With the conversion of Constantine there was a great surge of individuals who wished to convert to the newly accepted and favored religion. These conversions were both genuine and disingenuous, with some becoming Christians because it would help them in their political or social advancement. These individuals were often not sincere Christians. In addition some Christians continued to hold on to their pagan ways. These instances indicate that when Christianity became the official and favored religion it still competed with paganism.

Caesarius of Arles in the 5th century bemoaned that the resolve of many Christians who had converted after Constantine was tenuous. He accused Christians of still going to pagan shrines, making vows to trees, and praying to fountains; worse yet, some Christians were unwilling to destroy these shrines. Likewise Christians consulted seers, soothsayers, and fortune tellers. Evidence from Egyptian papyri indicated the same aspect with petitions for oracles. This phenomenon would continue well into the medieval period.

When Christianity had become legal, church leaders were able to express themselves in a public venue without fear of retribution. The event that made Christianity legal was not religious but political: the failure of the persecutions, the illness of Galerius, who promoted the persecutions, and the conversion of Constantine. The followers of Constantine would argue that his victory over the pagan Maxentius was due to God and Constantine's conversion. Constantine's conversion, a turning point in both Roman history and Christianity, formed the basis for future imperial and church history. His conversion became the source of legends in detailing the fight between Christianity (Constantine) and Paganism (Maxentius), as the accompanying Point in Time shows.

CONSTANTINE'S CONVERSION

CHAPTER XXVII. THAT AFTER REFLECTING ON THE DOWNFALL OF THOSE WHO HAD WORSHIPED IDOLS, HE MADE CHOICE OF CHRISTIANITY

Being convinced, however, that he needed some more powerful aid than his military forces could afford him, on account of the wicked and magical enchantments which were so diligently practiced by the tyrant, he sought Divine assistance, deeming the possession of arms and a numerous soldiery of secondary importance, but believing the co-operating power of Deity invincible and not to be shaken. He considered, therefore, on what God he might rely for protection and assistance. While engaged in this enquiry, the thought occurred to him, that, of the many emperors who had preceded him, those who had rested their hopes in a multitude of gods, and served them with sacrifices and offerings, had in the first place been deceived by flattering predictions, and oracles which promised them all prosperity, and at last had met with an unhappy end, while not one of their gods had stood by to warn them of the impending wrath of heaven; while one alone who had pursued an entirely opposite course, who had condemned their error, and honored the one Supreme God during his whole life, had found in him to be the Saviour and Protector of his empire, and the Giver of every good thing. Reflecting on this, and well weighing the fact that they who had trusted in many gods had also fallen by manifold forms of death, without leaving behind them either family or offspring, stock, name, or memorial among men: while the God of his father had given to him, on the other hand, manifestations of his power and very many tokens: and considering farther that those who had already taken arms against the tyrant, and had marched to the battle-field under the protection of a multitude of gods, had met with a dishonorable end for one of them had shamefully retreated from the contest without a blow, and the other, being slain in the midst of his own troops, became, as it were, the mere sport of death; reviewing, I say, all these considerations, he judged it to be folly indeed to join in the idle worship of those who were not gods, and, after such convincing evidence, to err from the truth; and therefore felt it incumbent on him to honor his father's God alone.

CHAPTER XXVIII. HOW, WHILE HE WAS PRAYING, GOD SENT HIM A VISION OF A CROSS OF LIGHT IN THE HEAVENS AT MID-DAY, WITH AN INSCRIPTION ADMONISHING HIM TO CONQUER BY THAT

Accordingly he called on him with earnest prayer and supplications that he would reveal to him who he was, and stretch forth his right hand to help him in his present difficulties. And while he was thus praying with fervent entreaty, a most marvelous sign appeared to him from heaven, the account of which it might have been hard to believe had it been related by any other person. But since the victorious emperor himself long afterwards declared it to the writer of this history, when he was honored with his acquaintance and society, and confirmed his statement by an oath, who could hesitate to accredit the relation, especially since the testimony of after-time has established its truth? He said that about noon, when the day was already beginning to decline, he saw with his own eyes the trophy of a cross of light in the heavens, above the sun, and bearing the inscription, Conquer by this. At this sight he himself was struck with amazement, and his whole army also, which followed him on this expedition, and witnessed the miracle.

CHAPTER XXIX. HOW THE CHRIST OF GOD APPEARED TO HIM IN HIS SLEEP, AND COMMANDED HIM TO USE IN HIS WARS A STANDARD MADE IN THE FORM OF THE CROSS

He said, moreover, that he doubted within himself what the import of this apparition could be. And while he continued to ponder and reason on its meaning, night suddenly came on; then in his sleep the Christ of God appeared to him with the same sign which he had seen in the heavens, and commanded him to make a likeness of that sign which he had seen in the heavens, and to use it as a safeguard in all engagements with his enemies.

CHAPTER XXX. THE MAKING OF THE STANDARD OF THE CROSS

At dawn of day he arose, and communicated the marvel to his friends: and then, calling together the workers in gold and precious stones, he sat in the midst of them, and described to them the figure of the sign he had seen, bidding them represent it in gold and precious stones. And this representation I myself have had an opportunity of seeing.

CHAPTER XXXI. A DESCRIPTION OF THE STANDARD OF THE CROSS, WHICH THE ROMANS NOW CALL THE LABARUM

Now it was made in the following manner. A long spear, overlaid with gold, formed the figure of the cross by means of a transverse bar laid over it. On the top of the whole was fixed a wreath of gold and precious stones; and within this, the symbol of the Saviour's name, two letters indicating the name of Christ by means of its initial characters, the letter P being intersected by X in its centre: and these letters the emperor was in the habit of wearing on his helmet at a later period. From the cross-bar of the spear was suspended a cloth, a royal piece, covered with a profuse embroidery of most brilliant precious stones; and which, being also richly interlaced with gold, presented an indescribable degree of beauty to the beholder. This banner was of a square form, and the upright staff, whose lower section was of great length, bore a golden half-length portrait of the pious emperor and his children on its upper part, beneath the trophy of the cross, and immediately above the embroidered banner.

The emperor constantly made use of this sign of salvation as a safeguard against every adverse and hostile power, and commanded that others similar to it should be carried at the head of all his armies.

Eusebius, *The Life of Constantine*, with a revised translation by Ernest Cushing Richardson, in *A Select Library of the Post-Nicene Fathers of the Christian Church*, ed. Philip Schaff and Henry Lace, 2nd Series, Vols. I-VII, trans. into English with prolegomena and explanatory notes, (New York: The Christian Literature Company, 1890), Vol. I, pp. 490–491.

FAMILY

The importance of family in the religious life of Christianity was fundamental. Unlike Judaism and Paganism, Christianity did not allow divorce. Romans allowed divorce in which the dowry was returned. Divorce became common during the Roman Empire, with either the husband initiating the complaint—such as when the wife left his house, he had dissatisfaction with the union, or when the wife stole property that he wanted back—or the wife filing the complaint, accusing the husband of misusing the dowry or spousal abuse. For Christians, since divorce was not recognized, any abuse or dispute could potentially lead to an unhappy life. In addition, Christians argued that marriage existed as a permanent bond lasting until death; for even after one member died, the other often did not remarry, especially if the wife survived. Several different types of marriage occurred in the Roman world. A true legal marriage (*matrimonium*) existed only when both individuals were Roman citizens; in this category there was marriage both with and without *manus*. Manus, the traditional republican patrician marriage, meant that the wife came under her husband and his family's control. By the early empire most marriages were without manus, meaning that the wife still remained under her father and his family's control. From a practical and economic status this marriage type protected the wife's family holdings, since the dowry normally returned to her family upon divorce. If both individuals were not citizens, Roman law did not recognize their union; this absence of recognition did not suggest a moral judgment, but rather a legal one. These unions did not satisfy the Roman requisite for legal standing, which meant the child's status evolved from the mother; so if the mother was non-Roman, the child was a noncitizen; if slave, the child was a slave. Fathers traditionally did not have any rights over their children born from these unions; while at the same time these unions usually prevented the children from receiving their father's inheritance. For Christianity this complicated legal system meant that if both members were not Roman citizens, the child was "illegitimate" under Roman law, and the mother solely responsible.

In Christianity marriage existed for procreation. This made sense since the religion needed more followers. Although pagans allowed contraception and abortion, Christianity viewed both with disdain. Contraception or anything that impeded pregnancy was frowned upon and disavowed, since couples married for children, not love. Likewise, the church fathers in their early writings, the *Didache* and the Epistle of Barnabas, taught that abortion was murder, a failure in the commandment to love your neighbor. All of the Christian fathers were against abortion.

Excavations uncovering Egyptian papyri have produced examples of pagan marriage contracts, usually with a stipulation of a dowry, which upon divorce was to be repaid to the woman, although sometimes the marriage contract had codicils for providing children with income. In addition women promised to be obedient, and men not to abuse their wives. These contracts were meant to protect not only the woman and her family, but the man and their children, if they had any. Not all marriages had a contract, but usually a dowry was still present, but with none of the contractual arraignments for duties of a married couple. A papyrus (P. Oxy 903) from the early 4th century, however, has a Christian wife submitting petitions to the courts for legal help, since her husband had hidden the keys (to their house or strongbox?) and did not trust her, even though he trusted his slaves with them. A marriage contract had then been made in front of the bishops that the husband would not hide the keys, but he broke the oath. She then went to the church building, and upon returning home he locked the doors, saying, "Why did you go to the church buildings?" which was probably a place of refuge. The papyrus showed some interesting points. First, Christians made contracts; second, the papyrus indicated that a form of abuse occurred and that the wife attempted to seek resolution through the church. Finally, the church was seen a place of refuge. Although the resolution is missing, it probably did not allow for a divorce, but rather attempted to force the husband to abide by his former oaths.

Evidence shows that the ages at which Roman and Jewish women and men married were similar. Women married as early as 12, although in practice it was probably around 15, while men tended to marry later, often as late as 30. This became a problem for the Romans, with the emperor Augustus attempting to increase the number of Roman citizens at the upper levels, and he tried to force men to marry early. The results, however, were not successful. One reason for the men's delay may have been to ensure their capability to provide for the family. Many of these older gentlemen would have established themselves in their trade and business. For Christians the situation was probably similar, with women marrying young and men later.

The Christian family structure probably mirrored the Roman family. At the social top, wealthy individuals had a larger extended family living with them. This would not only include the husband, wife, and children, but slaves, some freedmen, and perhaps unmarried brothers and sisters. For the lower classes, however, the family unit was much smaller: husband, wife, two or three children, and perhaps a slave.

In pagan Rome, relationships between the husbands and wives varied among the social classes. For the powerful, marriages were arranged to promote and protect the families' status and holdings. The couple was not usually consulted about the marriage, but instead marriages were used to form alliances between families. Upper-class Christians likewise functioned in the same manner. At the lower socioeconomic levels alliances could still be made, for example, between merchants and business owners. At the lowest level families may not have had formal alliances, but the marriages instead provided a system to ensure that the couple could survive. It was more likely that "love" entered into the picture at this level than at the upper levels. In all instances the overriding principle was the need to continue the family line through children. Christian families again would have followed their pagan and Jewish counterparts in this factor. Still, in the family the man ruled.

An interesting papyrus from 186 C.E. from Oxyrhynchus (P.Oxy. 237) detailed a dispute between a married woman and her father. The dispute originally centered on the father's business troubles and how, after his daughter helped him financially, and his obvious failure, he unsuccessfully tried to seize her dowry and estate. Failing this, he attempted to seize his daughter outright, probably to get control of her dowry by using the power of manus. She objected, however, and in the papyrus she gave legal precedents that a father could not take away a daughter from a marriage in which she desired to stay. Although the outcome was uncertain, clearly women did have some legal recourse to maintain their marriage.

Christians would have found this legal tradition reassuring, since not only were they against divorce, but it protected a converted daughter from her pagan father. Of course, before Christianity was legalized, a Christian wife could have been denounced for her beliefs. In Roman, and for that matter, most Mediterranean societies, the man controlled the family. The paterfamilias had complete control over all members of the household. While wives were seen as partners in the family structure, in charge of the household and its running, husbands had ultimate power. The Jewish writer Philo stated that the Jewish family was based on three concepts: love and kinship, superiority of parents, and the dominance of men over women. Like the prevailing norm of Jewish and pagan bias in favor of the husband, early Christian writers maintained the same prejudices. The letter from Peter presented the same idea where women were seen as the weaker partner. In the Epistle I Clement the husband again was in charge. Finally, in the late 1st-century writing, the *Shepherd of Hermas,* Hermas controlled his house and bore the ultimate judgment of his household's behavior. Hermas was being punished for his family's actions, as well as his fantasy of being married to his former owner Rhoda, clearly an allusion to his challenging of the traditional social norms and hierarchy.[3]

Wives in these relationships were expected to maintain a set of standards related to their station. Pagan writers argued that the wife should accept her husband's household gods. While faithfulness was encouraged, for Roman families it was usually one way. Wives were to be above reproach; adultery was punishable even by death. Husbands on the other hand could engage in extramarital relations. In the event of divorce among Roman citizens, the husband received custody of the children. For the lower class families, especially those involving noncitizens, the mother received custody. It was probable that many families among the lower classes had single mothers raising their children.

In Christian writings wives were expected to be chaste, show deference to her husband, be meek, and run the household in a just and upright fashion. Since mothers in antiquity typically oversaw the education of their children, especially daughters, Christian mothers had immense influence over the family's moral and educational direction. While fathers disciplined their children, making sure they did not become unruly, mothers instilled the family's traditional morals. For the children life was hard. For lower-class families children went to work as soon as possible. On farms and in shops children were expected to help out in some fashion. Children were to be obedient, show courtesy, and ultimately help provide for the parents. The idea of a "normal" childhood was fantasy.

Pagan and Christian children went to the same schools, read the same texts, and received the same instruction. Since church leaders mainly came from the same social class as government officials and administrators, the middle class, they were familiar with the same texts. This was clearly seen in the constant references to the great classical writers Plato, Cicero, and Virgil. Christians did not suggest altering the Roman educational method and school structure. The ancients traditionally saw the education of children from infancy to age 7 as not crucial. From 7 until 12 they went to elementary school, where they learned the rudiments of reading, writing, and counting. The next level, the *grammaticus,* occurred from 12 to 18, when they studied the great classical writers. Finally, at 18 they went to higher education, devoted to rhetoric. Unfortunately most of the surviving information concerned this latter phase. Teaching and upbringing were not linked; one had a schoolmaster for education, a nurse to keep the child well, and a pedagogue, usually a slave, to ensure the child was kept in line and protected.

A part of the family that is nonexistent in today's environment was slavery, which permeated ancient society. Manpower and not industry built ancient society. While it may be true that slavery slowed down the development of industry, it must be remembered that ancient society and economics revolved around agriculture. Construction projects and large agricultural estates required extensive amounts of manpower, with slaves being an important and integral part. Slaves loaded and unloaded the barges that brought the grain, oil, and wine to Rome to feed the urban poor. Slaves constructed the monuments, aqueducts, and roads that linked Rome with Italy and beyond. Slaves did the menial tasks no one desired, like cleaning the streets and sewers. Families likewise had slaves to cook, clean, carry the litters (taxis), run the household, and look out for and educate the children. Slaves could be freed, or even buy their freedom and become freedmen, with their children becoming Roman citizens. Christians accepted slavery because it had always existed and was part of everyday life. The sayings of Jesus and the early missionaries did not propose to end slavery; rather, some merely said that slaves should be obedient while masters should be humane.

Christianity did not propose to radically alter society; rather, it attempted to become a mainstream religion. The daily life of Christians involved religion. The rigors of Christian practices required the family to keep a balance between fanaticism and reality. Although some would have been devout and pious, most Christians just tried to make ends meet while believing. Christians in their family life attempted to provide the best family environment. Although expected to fast and pray on certain days, most Christians spent a majority of their time just trying to survive. Like other religions and cults Christianity had its core of followers and numerous members who merely belonged.

Christianity attempted to have a basis of moral teachings that existed inside and outside the home. Inside, the family was expected to maintain high moral standards. Outside the family the church further demanded the continual policy of helping community, especially stressing the giving of alms to the poor. Charity was important, and with the decline of the empire in the 4th century, the church fathers viewed almsgiving as a victory over greed.

Since Christianity originally grew up in different regions, often in isolated areas without contact with other Christian communities, variant forms existed. As these separate communities began to encounter one another it was only natural that divergent opinions had to be addressed. These divergent views often led to infighting. The continual infighting that occurred within the church by different groups had a profound influence upon Christianity. Two of the most important fights involved the Donatists and the Arians, both occurring after the legalization of Christianity.

DONATISM

During the persecutions in North Africa there arose particular cases surrounding individuals, "traditors" (traitors) handing over sacred texts (the Bible, letters from early officials, and so forth) to pagan Roman officials. After the persecutions some Christians argued that a local bishop, Felix, was a "traditor," and that his acts, including the sacraments of baptism, marriage, and holy orders (ordination of priests) as well as consecrating a new bishop, were invalid. A new bishop, Caecilian, was consecrated by three bishops, one of whom was the accused bishop, Felix. Caecilian's rival Majorinus was consecrated bishop after the Numidian bishops deposed Caecilian. Caecilian's accusers based their position upon the rumor that Felix had been a "traditor," arguing that since Felix was guilty of such a mortal sin, his sacraments, specifically his consecration of Caecilian, were invalid. The controversy then settled on two questions: Was Felix a traditor, and were the sacraments valid if he was? The supporters of Caecilian, the Catholics, argued that the sacraments were valid regardless of Felix's guilt, and that Felix was innocent anyway.

Both groups appealed to Constantine, the new emperor, who through his counsel, Bishop Ossius of Cordova (Spain), sided with Caecilian. Majorinus soon died and Donatus, who supplied the movement's name, took up the cause. In 313 the Donatists again appealed to the emperor, asking that the bishops of Gaul, who had not been persecuted and therefore did not have a vested interest in the outcome, decide the matter.

Constantine delegated the matter to Miltiades of Rome, a bishop from Africa who decided in favor of Caecilian. In August 314 the Council of Arles, composed of Gallic bishops, also decided in favor of Caecilian, expressing their disgust at the Donatists' violence. With Felix's acquittal in 314 of being a "traditor," the matter should have ended. The Donatists, however, continued to argue that the Catholic bishops and priests were not entitled to their offices. Setting up counter bishops and priests, the two sides fought continuously for two centuries, each saying that the others' original founders were "traditors." Within a short time many North

African regions were partisans of one side or the other, with some cities having both groups of priests and bishops.

But why did the council rule against the Donatists? Their decision may lie with Roman law. One duty of a priest was sanctifying a marriage. As the new religion, now free from the constraints of persecution, began to grow and obtain a favored position in Constantine's new government, the church validated marriages. In Roman law, marriage was a civil issue to determine the legitimacy of one's heirs. A child was legitimate, and able to inherit, only if its parents were married to each other at the time of its birth. If a couple's priest was not valid, and the sacrament of marriage was not valid, then the offspring of this invalid marriage could be viewed as illegitimate, having no legal standing to inherit property. Even if the couple were then "remarried," the original children would still be illegitimate. Thus, councilors to Constantine and the bishops may have foreseen the tremendous problems associated with backing the Donatists. Further, if these priests were deemed invalid, all of the marriages, baptisms and other rites they had performed would be invalidated, undermining the new religion and its recently gained political position.

The Donatists' refusal to accept the ruling led to continual fighting within the church. Constantine, growing impatient over the situation, attempted to compel the Donatists to accept his decision by sending in officials to arrest them. This led to a new persecution, that of Christian against Christian. Constantine ended his overt attacks on the Donatists by 321, allowing the Donatists to gain ground and even claim victory in the matter.

During the 390s all of this changed due to political turmoil and the rise of one of the Orthodoxy's greatest champion, Augustine of Hippo (Tunisia). From 393–398 the Donatists supported Gildo, a local military commander, who rebelled against Theodosius and Honorius, thereby losing official support. Appealing to the emperor Honorius, the Catholics successfully revived legislation against the Donatists, who lost power over the next 10 years. At the same time, Augustine produced a solid theological argument against Donatism; his analysis remains the basis of Catholic theology in its premise that the sacrament is sacrosanct or valid regardless of the grace of the minister who bestows it. In other words, the fact that a priest is guilty of a serious sin does not invalidate the sacraments he has bestowed upon the faithful. Augustine and his theological argument reinvigorated the Catholic movement, curtailing the Donatists. The movement was further diminished by the arrival of the Arian Vandals in the 430s, who persecuted both Orthodox Christians and Donatists. Finally, in the 8th century, Islamic forces extinguished Donatism.

ARIANISM

In the East, a different controversy arose, concerning God's nature. Orthodox, or Catholic, theology maintained that Jesus and God the Father are coeternal, of one nature. Around 320, Arius, a priest in Egypt, preached that Jesus, being the son, must have come after God the Father; therefore, he could not be considered coeternal. Arius' analysis seemed logical to many Christians and pagans, for how can a son be equal in age, and therefore power, to his father? Finding many adherents in the East, Arius won over bishops including Eusebius of Nicomedia (Turkey) and Eusebius of Caesarea (Palestine), the great church historian. His argument, however, went against the Orthodox views espoused by Athanasius in Alexandria. For the next few years Arius successfully promoted his cause throughout the East, splitting the Eastern church.

Constantine was drawn into the controversy after defeating Licinius in 324. Calling the Council of Nicaea (Turkey), composed mainly of Eastern bishops, Arius and Athanasius presented their cases before the emperor and bishops. Outnumbered, Arius was attacked by Athanasius, who used his great oratorical skill to undermine Arius' argument. The result was the Nicene Creed, reaffirming the Catholic view that God, the Father, and Jesus, the Son, are coeternal.

But the controversy raged on, with Arius preaching under the protection of Constantine's advisor, Eusebius, the Bishop of Nicomedia. While affirming the Nicene Creed, Constantine at first refused to curtail Arius and his followers, perhaps because of his failures with the Donatists in Africa. Constantine eventually condemned Arius, sending him into exile in Illyria late in 325 and exiling Arius' ally, Eusebius of Nicomedia, to Gaul from 325 to 328. Upon his return, Eusebius pursued the Arian cause, first as advisor to Constantine and then, after 337, as the bishop of Constantinople, securing Arius' recall in 337. Athanasius was, at the same time, fighting another heresy, the Melitian Schism, which centered on how to readmit Christians who had fled or committed apostasy during Diocletian's persecutions, and could not protect himself. After being condemned and stripped of his See he was exiled to Trier (in Gaul) in 335. Arius returned from exile after Athanasius' deposition and was restored to his old position, but he died before reentering Alexandria, and his followers claimed that he was murdered. Arius' movement, however, did not die, as his followers preached his message, especially in the north, and converted the Goths and Vandals. For his part, Eusebius of Nicomedia influenced Constantius, the emperor's son and future ruler in the East, using the controversy to maintain the independence of the Eastern church from Rome.

With Constantine's death, the Eastern Arian emperor Constantius persecuted many Orthodox bishops. In the West, however, the exiled Athanasius found protection with the Catholic Emperor Constans, Constantius' brother. Civil war nearly erupted between the Catholic and Arian emperors until Constantius allowed Athanasius to return to his See in Alexandria in 341. With the murder of Constans in 350, Constantius became emperor of a united empire, once again attacking Athanasius and the Catholics in both the East and West and forcing Athanasius to flee into the Egyptian desert in 356. For a short time the radical Arians held power, but upon Constantius' death, all of this changed with the rule of the pagan Julian, who had no partisan interest in these struggles, but who allowed the exiles removed by Constantius to return to their posts. Julian profited by the continuing struggle between the Arians and Catholics, since it distracted many Christian leaders from his pro-pagan policies.

After Julian's death and the return of a Christian Emperor, Jovian, the Arians remained strong in the East, not because of their position, but because of the divisions in their opposition. This situation changed in the 370s with Basil of Caesarea in Cappadocia, who sought to reunite the various Eastern groups. Further, with the accession of Gratian and Theodosius I, both of whom strictly followed the Orthodox Nicene Creed, the Arians lost their political and official strength. The struggle between Arianism and Orthodox Christianity had weakened the church and the East, which impacted late Roman society. The Arians greatest impact occurred in Africa, where the devout and avid Arian Vandal kings Genseric, Huneric, and Thrasamund persecuted the Catholics and Donatists for nearly a century (428–523). Although many of the other tribes in the West were Arians, they did not produce the same ferocity as the Vandals.

By the 6th century, Catholicism had supplanted Arianism, but their struggle profoundly affected the empire. Not only did the beginning of the split between the East and the West, both theological and political, occur, but many in the West now viewed the East with suspicion, since the Arians converted the barbarians. The East also viewed the West with suspicion, since the pope and others had asserted the Western supremacy over all other bishops.

Both of these struggles directly affected everyday Christians. For example, in North Africa, many cities had both Donatist and Catholic bishops and churches, producing fierce struggles between neighbors. In the city of Rome the Donatists were not a force, but after the conquest of Italy by the Germanic tribes, Arianism directly influenced the populace. In Rome the Church of St. Agnes was established as the Arian Church. The German rulers, Arians, and the Catholic pope constantly vied for the support of the populace. Ultimately both realized the influence the other side had and reached a truce. The normal Christian often faced important decisions when dealing with these groups. If they adhered to one side or the other they might be persecuted by fellow Christians. If they wished to advance in a particular bureaucracy it became important for them to follow one idea or the other, not out of sincere belief, but out of political, social, or economic advantage.

An example of how two leaders handled the Roman city and its leaders were Theodosius and Theodoric. Theodoric successfully used the upper class and religious leaders, even though he was a German Arian, to keep the peace, while Theodosius, a Catholic emperor, continually struggled with political and religious leaders.

Theodosius

Born in Cauca, Spain, about 346, Theodosius the Great (347–395), known as Flavius Theodosius, was the son of count Theodosius, who had previously and successfully defeated usurpers in Africa. Theodosius the Great established the House of Theodosius, ruling both the East and the West for over 50 years. He governed Moesia Prima or Superior in 373 or 374, where he defeated Rome's perennial problem the Sarmatians along the Danube. After his father, a successful general under Valentinian, was executed in 375, Theodosius retired to his family estates in Spain until 378. After the battle of Adrianople Gratian recalled Theodosius, making him general and then emperor in the East after some initial successes against the Visigoths in January 379. Theodosius created a new prefecture, Illyricum, placing parts of the Balkans, notably Macedon and Moesia, in the hands of the East. This provided for numerous conflicts between East and West during the next few centuries.

Theodosius campaigned against the Visigoths for several years. After realizing that it was impossible to defeat the Visigoths, Theodosius decided to negotiate a treaty in 380 and celebrated a triumph at Constantinople. The treaty allowed the Visigoths to settle in the empire en masse and be under their own leaders. In the West Magnus Maximus removed Gratian in Gaul, and when Maximus invaded Italy in 382, Theodosius used barbarian units, probably Visigoths, headed west and defeated him. Theodosius placed Valentinian II, Gratian's brother, under the control of the German Arbogast. Valentinian tried to exert more control and was found dead in 392. Arbogast promoted Eugenius as emperor until 394 when Theodosius defeated them, unifying the Roman world for the last time. This unity lasted only a few months, for in January 395 Theodosius died in Milan.

Theodosius expelled Arians from Constantinople and ordered their churches closed in the East. He likewise took actions against paganism, refusing to restore the Altar of Victory in the Roman Senate, and outlawed paganism in 392. During his reign Theodosius was known for his harshness. In 390 he massacred 7,000 citizens in Thessalonica for civil disorder. Later, in 390, while visiting Italy Ambrose ordered him to do penance under threat of excommunication. After doing penance Ambrose exerted even more influence, culminating in a degree in 391 outlawing paganism.

With Theodosius' death power passed to his sons Arcadius and Honorius. In the West, Arcadius was not able to stop the invasion and sack of Rome in 410. In the East, Honorius' son Theodosius II succeeded, ruling from 408 to 451.

Theodoric the Great

Theodoric the Great (c.a. 454–526), was an Ostrogoth who, at the age of eight, became a Roman hostage in Constantinople and received a classical education. At the age of 18 he returned to the Ostrogoths, where he became leader of part of the tribe. He was made consul and master of the soldiers by the emperor in 484. Theodoric then marched against Odaocer in Italy, forcing him to surrender in 493. Ruling Italy, Theodoric attempted to fuse the Ostrogoths and Romans with the help of ministers like Cassiodorus. He attempted to unite the regions of the West, giving aid to the Franks against the Visigoths and maintaining that the Roman Empire in the West still continued. To the Goths he ruled as king, while to the Romans he was a patrician. Being an Arian, he tried to help the Arians in the East, and he intervened in the election of pope. His health declined after he realized he could not bring about reconciliation within the various religious problems. He died in August 526.

The daily life of Christians in Rome was likewise directly influenced. When the Arian Germans took over the city they did not have enough troops to keep complete control. If riots broke out there would have been the potential for popular revolution. To help avoid this situation, the German kings, especially Theodoric, attempted to placate the populace by continuing the games and grain distribution. Like the emperor Augustus, who was forced to continue the bread and circus to keep the pagan mob peaceful, the Christian Arian Theodoric continued to provide bread and circus to the Christian mob to maintain peace and security.

NOTES

1. L. Michael White, *Building God's House in the Roman World* (Baltimore: Johns Hopkins University Press, 1990).

2. Bernard P. Grenfell and Arthur S. Hunt, *The Oxyrhynchus Papyri,* Part III (London: Egyptian Exploration Fund, 1903), no. 407, p. 12.

3. James S. Jeffers, "Jewish and Christian Families in First-Century Rome," in *Judaism and Christianity in First-Century Rome*, ed. Karl P. Donfried and Peter Richardson (Grand Rapids, MI: Wm. Eerdmans, 1998), pp. 128–150.

9

AFTERLIFE

How an individual and society view death often determines how they live their life. This chapter explores not only the Christian beliefs concerning death and the afterlife, but the day-to-day procedures for dealing with the dead and how they differed from those of pagan society. The complex set of laws from both groups concerning the place of burial, touching a corpse, and how the departed were remembered are examined. Crucial to understanding this distinction are examples of funeral inscriptions concerning the departed and the remembrances they were offered.

DEATH IN THE ANCIENT WORLD

As the popular saying goes "you cannot avoid death and taxes." While some may evade taxes, you cannot escape death. In antiquity societies and individuals fretted and debated the concept of death and the afterlife. Societies throughout the Mediterranean world developed an ideology for exploring and understanding the afterlife. The central question that everyone grappled with was, how does one explain their worth or life existence? This became fundamental, for if one's life has no meaning than why should humanity even exist? If one's life is so miserable now, is there going to be any change after death? In Egypt various philosophies existed concerning the afterlife. For some, the individual would be resurrected and have eternal life—the belief in Osiris— others considered the body a vessel to take the soul to the afterlife. For the Egyptians, the body and soul continued after death.

Funerary: Busts of a Man and Woman. The Walters Art Museum, Baltimore.

In the Homeric legends all individuals upon death went to Hades or the underworld. In the Odyssey, Odysseus traveled to the underworld and met the dead hero Achilles in Hades, who told Odysseus that he would rather be the lowest slave alive on earth than king of the underworld. A few centuries after Homer the Greeks developed the concept of apotheosis, where a human could be elevated to the status of a god upon death, thereby bypassing Hades. The best example was Hercules, the son of a god, Zeus, and a mortal. His struggles with Zeus' wife Hera and his extraordinary accomplishments allowed him to become a god after his tragic death. The next logical step was the elevation of a purely historical human, the best example being Alexander the Great. Finally, during the Hellenistic age, living humans were hailed as gods, producing the concept of the ruler cult. This ruler cult was then transferred to Rome where during the empire it became the imperial cult. The original concept of all individuals going to Hades remained, however, since only extraordinary individuals were gods, and this continual philosophy created a pessimistic outlook. The later mystery religions transformed this bleak view, but these religions dealt more with life on earth and less with the afterlife. Judaism instilled the belief in the concept of heaven, where the soul would be rewarded for living a good moral life, although even in Judaism that concept was not universally accepted. The Christian New Testament envisioned a completely new and different philosophy, salvation in the afterlife. In the Gospels Jesus constantly referred to a heaven. While dying on the cross, Jesus related to one of the criminals that they would both be in heaven that day. Christianity seemingly borrowed from all of these ideas, a concept of heaven and hell, salvation based on one's life, a possible glorious afterlife, and resurrection. This is not to say that Christianity was merely a conglomeration of all these religions; rather, this period and the Mediterranean region produced variant religious philosophies that intersected and allowed for synergy.

Pagans viewed death as the end of all existence, while Christians viewed it as another step in the soul's journey. These beliefs in turn shaped Christian rituals, beliefs, and practices concerning the dead. Christians viewed death as sleep, not the end of life, with the promise of resurrection leading to an awaking. Death was therefore a temporary state, unlike the traditional Roman view of death as a permanent unchanging state. Since death was only temporary, it should not be an occasion for sadness and mourning. Christians therefore used terms such as "rest" and "sleep" in describing those who had died, in contrast to pagans, who stated that death, as Fate, snatched their beloved from life, causing great sorrow, fear, and alarm.

In funeral inscriptions the two opposing religious views showed their marked differences. Christian inscriptions merely referred to the departed as sleeping or resting in peace, whereas pagan inscriptions point to being bitter, and death being caused by an angry god. For example, pagans would state that X was snatched from life at such a young date or Y was taken from someone too early. Like the Egyptian idea of a voyage to the afterlife, Christianity also viewed death as a voyage to paradise. The phrase *"migratio ad Dominum"* or "journey to God," where the departed Christian now traveled to God, is seen in literature, funeral inscriptions, and even art in the form of a boat. Christianity in many ways was closer to the Egyptian concept than the Greek in terms of death and afterlife.

Finally, Christianity viewed death as a rebirth, for the individual dying was no longer bound by the world's sins. Free from earthly vices and corruption the individual now was reborn into paradise, better than anything here now on earth. Death gave the individual freedom, paradise, and salvation. This is not to say that family members did not grieve; rather, the theology of Christian optimism differed from the pessimism of paganism. Finally, Christianity argued for the body's resurrection after the return of Jesus.

Over time the development of the concept of the resurrection of the individual went from the deceased being compared to angels, as seen in the Gospels with Jesus (Matthew 22; Mark 12), to being like Jesus in his Resurrection (witnessed in Paul's letter to I. Corinthians), to a spiritual body (argued by Origen), to finally a spiritualized flesh (argued by Augustine).[1] But did an individual really have their body raised from the dead? Although the answer was yes, the philosophers argued that the body was not crucial, but rather the soul. But the two were in fact connected, and under Augustine the resurrection of the individual was viewed as a perfect body with a pure soul living with immortality.

This development of the resurrection influenced how early Christians viewed death, the afterlife, and their burial rites. In early Christianity the followers of Jesus expected his immediate return and the end of the corporal world soon after his death, Resurrection, and ascension. Their view that his return was imminent led to the followers not worrying about long-term planning. For the first 30 years or so Christianity in many ways stagnated; the end of the world expected so soon gave hope for imminent salvation. Witness Jesus' comments not to worry about burying the dead, for the dead will take care of the dead (Luke 9). When Jerusalem was destroyed in 70 C.E., the end did not occur; the earth continued and now a shift in Christian philosophy concerning death occurred. All of these interactions gave rise to a new philosophy in burial, or how to deal with the dead.

DEATH AND BURIAL

Over time Christianity developed specific rituals for burial different from Judaism and paganism. Before dying, Christians would administer the *viaticum,* or Christ's body (bread) and blood (wine), to the individual in a farewell banquet. Later, Christians began the practice of putting the Eucharist into the mouth of the deceased, paralleling the pagan rite of putting a coin in the mouth of the deceased for the ferryman. This practice may have been borrowed to placate recent pagan converts, but as early as 393 C.E. at the council of Hippo (in North Africa) the church forbade it. Also important, Christians caught the dying gasp and imparted a final kiss to those near death. Catching of the dying gasp again borrowed an ancient pagan custom and philosophy, which argued that the soul exited through the mouth at the time of death. Christians as part of the burial service would not only catch the gasp but impart a final kiss to the deceased to show their love. This latter act contrasted with Judaism and paganism, which forbade contact with a corpse since it defiled the living. Christians deliberately made this a sacred sign and not profane. The final act, one that could be performed before or after death, was the arrangement of the limbs; the so-called stretching out of the feet and hands, preferably done before dying, symbolized the Crucifixion.

After death a series of rituals were performed with the body. First, the relatives closed the eyes and mouth, followed by the *conclamatio mortis,* or the lamenting, ensuring that the deceased was actually dead. Finally, they rearranged the hands and feet, with the hands now crossed over the torso. The mourners washed and then embalmed or at least anointed the corpse, and then clothed it. The Christians abandoned the pagan custom of

Sarcophagus with Garlands Supported by Two Cupids, Female Portraits, and Theatrical Masks. The Walters Art Museum, Baltimore.

crowning the dead, viewed as a form of idolatry, and replaced the physical crown with the concept of God being the crown.

After preparing the body, Christians held a wake in the deceased's home, and again, it was a time of remembrance and joy different from the pagan custom of wailing and moaning. Christians then held a vigil or service at the grave site, whether in a catacomb or sarcophagus. In the 4th century they transferred the wake to the church due to the legalization of Christianity and to make it part of the public religious service. A struggle soon developed between Christians, recent converts after Constantine's legalization and endorsement, and pagan/Christians, who held public mourning at the wake. These pagan/Christians continued their pagan ideas and beliefs, such as wild mourning, placing a coin (now Eucharist) in the mouth, and declaring that Fate had snatched the deceased, which promoted a negative view of the afterlife. The church tried to prevent some of these acts, such as forbidding the placement of the Eucharist in the mouth, and argued that the deceased were better off than the living and were reborn in Christ, but often to no avail.

After the wake a funeral procession occurred, a practice taken from paganism in which family members praised and glorified the deceased. Similar to the Roman custom of carrying the deceased to the tomb while displaying funeral masks of their ancestors, Christians proceeded to the burial site. But unlike Romans, Christians did not cremate but instead buried their dead in the manner of Christ, believing in the resurrection of the body. These burials occurred in the cemeteries or catacombs. The word cemetery, a Jewish and Christian term, meant burial; for pagans, cemetery, from *coemeterium*, denoted a bedroom. Therefore in Christianity cemeteries became a term used as a sleeping place for the dead. In the West it meant the whole burial ground, while in the East it could mean an individual tomb. The term catacomb was not used until the 11th century. As indicated, the catacombs were not used for places of worship or living during the persecutions, and in fact the word meant a structure above ground that was attached to the cemeteries. Since inhumation was costly and required a lot of land, the wealthy purchased and used the earliest cemeteries and then made their facilities available to fellow Christians, a form of charity. Valerian seized the cemeteries in 258 during his short persecution, but his son Gallienus restored them to the church, indicating that Rome recognized them as Christian "property."

Conversion to Christianity did not mean that all were strong believers, since often the impetus was not religious. The problem for the church would often center on continual pagan activities that contradicted Christian ideology, issues that would never really be settled for over a millennium.

How society deals with its dead can indicate how they view their position now and in the afterlife. Wealthy Romans had elaborate funerals and tombs, declaring for all to see that they were important, at least in their own eyes. These tombs included limestone sarcophagi that allowed for the body to be interned and then break down and decay due to the limestone. An individual could also be cremated, the most common method during the early empire, with their ashes placed in an urn and then interned in a tomb or niche. In both instances an inscription declared who the person was, their achievements, dates of birth and death or at least their age, and typically who erected the inscription. These inscriptions could be elaborate, celebrating the person's accomplishments and allowing for the visitor to learn more about them, or could simply allow family members the opportunity to celebrate their loved ones' memory in peace. Wealthy individuals interned their dead for burial in the family's mausoleum, or *columbaria*. If not wealthy an individual could belong to a burial club, or *collegia*, where at least they received a funeral and a simple burial. The individual paid an initiation fee and a yearly maintenance fee for which in return his fellow members guaranteed he would receive a proper burial and a celebrated remembrance meal. The burial would be in an urn or cemetery with a simple marker. A peasant with some means may be buried in the mass cemeteries or the catacombs with a small plaque indicating their name, which again gave some public and eternal remembrance. At the lowest level of society the urban poor were buried in mass graves without any type of marker, unknown and unremembered. Christians would have fit into all of these social strata, with their burials corresponding to their social-economic position.

The early Christians buried their dead in the catacombs, which ultimately had 60 to 90 miles of tombs encircling Rome, since Roman law and custom prevented burials inside the city walls, or *pomerium*. Most Christians and Jews preferred to bury their dead in their own catacombs. The total number of catacombs—Christian, Jew, and pagan—ultimately approached 1,000 km of passageways on the different levels in the cemeteries, enough for about 6,000,000 burials. The Christians could purchase the sites, especially the *cubiculum*, before their death by buying it directly from a *fossor* (digger). With the construction of such a large and elaborate burial system, Christians did not hide their dead.

The earliest Christian catacombs were named for Domitilla, of the Emperor Domitian's household, Priscilla, also a noble Roman, and Callistus. These sites were located outside the city wall on family estates. These catacombs originally were private burial places in their estate's gardens for the family and their household and were later given to the church. Dug into the volcanic ground the narrow corridors were lined three graves high on each side with oblong box-shaped niches, *loculi*. These *loculi* were then sealed with a thin limestone or marble plaque with an inscription. After one corridor was full the fossores would dig down and start a new corridor. For wealthier patrons the family had a *cubicula*, or a carved-out room holding several graves, and *arcosolium*, more expensive bins with an inscribed slab on top, instead of the vertical ones on the *loculus*. For those who could afford the cost, a sarcophagus was placed in the cubiculum. These cubiculum were often decorated with mosaics or frescoes; in effect these rooms became private burial chapels. The catacombs, especially the cubicula, were often decorated with art with scenes from the Old and New Testaments, such as Jonah and the whale, Daniel, Susanna, and Noah from the Old, and Lazarus, the three kings, the marriage feast, the multiplicity of the loaves, and the baptism of Jesus from the New.

It has been estimated that during the period 150–400 c.e., the time when the catacombs were used, about 500,000 to 750,000 Christians were buried. Although this number may seem small, one must remember that Christians did not become a large percentage of the population, especially in Rome, until well into the 4th and 5th centuries. Furthermore, by the end of the 4th century Christians abandoned the catacombs and interned their dead above ground at sites where individuals had been martyred and where churches, now used as administrative centers, began to be built.

The commemoration inscriptions can provide the modern reader with a picture of society and early Christian beliefs. These inscriptions were usually simple, often no more than a name and age. Like many pagan inscriptions they often recorded the deceased's exact age: year, month, and day. Some of the inscriptions, however, recorded more, for example displaying theological ideas such as the Trinity: "Oh Father of all, thou that has created Irene, Zoe, and Marcellus, receive them to thyself. To thee be glory in Christ."[2] The use of Jesus' name was rare in inscriptions, with a figure of a fish used instead of his name. Some inscriptions had messages not to disturb the tomb: "May he, who wishes to violate the tomb, incur the fate of Judas" or "All you Christians, keep this tomb safe to the end of the world, so that I may return to life without impediment, when He who comes will judge the living and the dead."[3] This last inscription is not only a good example of a command for not disturbing the tomb, but shows the idea that the resurrection was crucial.

Funeral inscriptions provide a glimpse as to how individuals wished to be remembered. The accompanying inscriptions in the Point in Time, from various times and places, show how these individuals presented their lives, with some interesting insights, for example, the accompanying inscription from the tomb of Abercius Marcellus, Bishop of Hieropolis in Phrygia in Asia Minor during the reign of Marcus Aurelius.

Abercius' inscription contains some interesting points. First, Abercius, a bishop and an important individual in the community, had the tomb constructed during his lifetime, making the conscious effort to tell his life story. Second, Abercius had traveled extensively: to Rome, Syria, and even Persia. Finally, he warns others not to try to set up another tomb or else pay a hefty fine, 2,000 gold pieces or over 44 pounds to the Roman treasury and 1,000 gold pieces or about 22 pounds to Hieropolis. Given that there was this warning, it must have been common in antiquity for people to reuse tombs. Also of interest is that the tomb was erected when

FUNERAL INSCRIPTIONS

BISHOP ABERCIUS' TOMBSTONE

The citizen of a notable city I made this [tomb] in my lifetime; that in due season I might have here a resting-place for my body. Abercius by name, I am a disciple of the pure Shepherd, who feedeth His flocks of sheep on mountains and plains, who hath great eyes looking on all side; for He taught me faithful writings. He also sent me to royal Rome to behold it and to see the golden-robed, golden-slippered Queen. And there I saw a people bearing the splendid seal. And I saw the plain of Syria and all the cities, even Nisibis, crossing over the Euphrates. And everywhere I had associates. In company with Paul, I followed, while everywhere faith led the way, and set before me for food the fish from the fountain, mighty and stainless (whom a pure virgin grasped), and gave this to friends to eat always, having good wind, and giving the mixed cup with bread. These words I, Abercius, standing by ordered to be inscribed. In sooth I was in the course of my seventy-second year. Let every friend who observeth this pray for me. But no man shall place another tomb above mine. If otherwise, then he shall pay two thousand pieces of gold to the treasury of the Romans, and a thousand pieces of gold to my good fatherland Hieropolis.

Abercius Marcellus, Bishop of Hieropolis, translated by J. B. Lightfoot, in *Documents Illustrative of the History of the Church*, Volume 1 to A.D. 313, ed. B. J. Kidd, translation of Christian Literature Series VI select passages (London: Macmillan, 1920), p. 111.

Christianity was still illegal. A second inscription comes a century later and concerns the life of a military man.

The Christian soldier's inscription recorded his career, serving during Diocletian's era and traveling extensively throughout the empire. Not only did he commemorate his career, but he honored his family. What is striking in this inscription is the number of places Aurelius Gaius visited throughout the Roman world. Even this late in the empire's history one could and did travel extensively. Another element of this inscription is the Christian philosophy of the Resurrection proudly displayed. Finally, the inscription points to the fact that Christians during the 3rd century had risen in the ranks of military, becoming officers. The final inscription concerns Marcus Julius Eugenius, who likewise served in the military, suffered during the persecutions of Maximinus Daza, and afterwards became bishop.

Eugenius' inscription again relates several interesting points. First, Eugenius was a member of the upper class, so that by the time of Diocletian, Christianity was no longer just a lower-class phenomenon. Second, service in the military was acceptable; this was in opposition to the second century, when military service was derided. Third, the inscription points to the structure of a church building with porches, art, and significant structures by the early 4th century. Finally, the inscription continues the idea of the previous two examples of detailing one's life on a funerary monument for future generations.

CHRISTIAN SOLDIER'S TOMBSTONE

Aurelius Gaius, son of Gaius, having served as a soldier, a legionnaire of the 1st Italica in Moesia, having then been chosen for the 8th Augustan in Germania, then in the provinces of Scythis and Pannonia in the Legion Iovia Scythiaca. Having served as recruit as a beginning cavalryman, then cavalry lancer, then orderly of a centurian of the third rank, orderly of senior centurian, orderly of [chief centurian?], orderly of imperial companions of the Emperor as a soldier of the 1st Iovia Scythica. Having traveled in our empire (through) Asia Caria [Lycia Phrygia] Lydia Lycaonie Cilicia [Armenia] Phoenicia Syria Arabia Palestine [Aegypt] Alexandria India [Libya ?] Mesopotamia Cappadocia [Persia] Galatia Bithynia Thrace [Rhodope or Haeminmonus] Moesia Carpi [Scytia or Dacia] Sarmatia 4 times at Viminacium [Dacia] Goths twice Germania [Quades and Macromans] Dardania Dalmatia pannonia [Noricum] Gaul Spain Mauretania [Numidia or Tripolitania]. Then having moved on after having labored at all these things I returned to my homeland, Pessionote [...], in the village of Kotian leaving behind my daughter Macedonia, I place upon the grave of my son Julius [...] and Areslous, my beloved wife, this stele by my own hands as a remembrance of her labors with Joy. Until the Resurrection Rejoice Always.

L'Annee epigraphique (Paris: Presses universitaires de France AE, 1981), no. 777.

EUGENIUS' TOMBSTONE

I, Marcus Julius Eugenius, served in the army of Pisidia as a member of the forces of Cyrillus Celer the senator; I was the husband of Julia Flaviana, daughter of the senator Caius Nestorianus, and I completed my military career with honour. Then, Maximinus issued an order compelling Christians to do sacrifice but without abandoning their service in the army; and have suffered many annoyances from the General Diogenes, I resigned my military commission, holding fast to the Christian faith. After dwelling for a short time in Laodicea, I was by the will of God made bishop, and for twenty years I laboured in the episcopate with honour: I built the church from its foundations upwards, to wit, the porches, the fore-courts, the paints, the sculptures, the font, the vestibule, etc.; and having completed all this, I renounced the life of man, and wrought myself a marble sepulcher; and I ordered that the aforesaid matter would be inscribed on the tomb built for myself and my issue.

Orazio Marucchi, *Christian Epigraphy,* trans. J. Armine Willis (Cambridge: Cambridge University Press, 1912), p. 323.

Inscriptions were not the only celebration of the departed. Christian writers commemorated the dead in poems and prayers. Two important figures who sought to preserve the memory and deeds of earlier Christians were Damasus and Prudentius, who wrote at the end of the 4th century.

Damasus (c. 304–84)

Of Spanish descent, Damasus was born in Rome. His father was a priest, and Damasus became a deacon to Pope Liberius and in 366 was elected pope to succeed him. Liberius had attempted to bring about peace in the church by dealing gently with the followers of the anti-pope Felix. A small group of three deacons and seven priests attempted to prevent Damasus, an ex-Felician, from being elected. His election, however, by the people at S. Lorenzo, was not peaceful, since a rival candidate, Ursinus, was consecrated in S. Maria in Trastevere, and a violent struggle took place. Followers of Damasus crossed the Tiber and began a three-day riot ending with numerous killings and wounding. The Emperor Valentinian supported Damasus, and Ursinus was exiled. On Sunday, October 7, protected by Roman soldiers, Damasus was anointed pope at the Lateran Church, the traditional parish for the pope. Unfortunately for the new pope, the memory and violence of his struggle with Ursinus did not end and his hope of a peaceful tenure did not exist. During his pontificate Damasus strongly attacked the Donatists and Arians, especially when the Emperor Theodosius proclaimed that the Catholic religion practiced in Rome and Alexandria was to be supreme. Damasus is also well remembered for his urging Jerome to produce a standard Latin translation of the Bible, the Vulgate, so that the church would have one universal and standard Bible instead of various translations. Damasus, however, was best remembered for his epigrams concerning the martyrs and his restoration of martyrs' relics and tombs. Damasus died in 384 and was buried in the church of SS. Marcus and Marcellianus on the Via Ardeatina, which he had built.

Prudentius (348–post 405)

Marcus Aurelius Clemens Prudentius, chief Christian poet of his time, was born in 348 in Northern Spain. His name and subsequent career indicated his noble birth and education. Educated in rhetoric and law, his knowledge of Latin Classical poets shined through his poems. He seems to have known little Greek or Hebrew, again indicative of his provincial training.

His early life had much carousing; nevertheless he held important civil offices and even rose in the emperor's court. Late in life he received some religious conversion and gave up his public life, perhaps joining a religious community. He seems to have had no money to help the poor, but instead devoted his life and work to God and the poor.

He made it his mission to provide a thorough understanding of Christianity to all, especially concerning the martyrs, so as to honor them. He visited Rome, but an illness increased his anxiety. He prayed to Hippolytus to intercede, and he soon recovered. At Rome he was impressed with the martyrs' memorial in the catacombs and churches, and he became acquainted with the poems of Pope Damasus, which influenced his own writings. He returned to Spain and wrote poems on St. Cassian and St. Hippolytus. In 403 he wrote against Symmachus (concerning the pagan statue of Victory in the Senate House in Rome). His later life is unknown.

From his writings he seemed to be a lovable and loyal Roman, proud of the empire. He had a fondness for art and wished to preserve pagan statues as art. He was loyal to the church and abhorred heresies.

WILLS

After an individual's death their will was publicly read. The last will and testament was crucial in the death of every Roman and impacted the family's daily life. The will represented the individual's accomplishments during their life and how they wished to be remembered. The will not only left behind the legacies and bequests but gave the opportunity for the deceased to praise or condemn individuals such as the emperor, imperial freedmen, family, and friends. For most inhabitants the will was the avenue to legitimize their heirs and to give heirs their legal rights and bequests. In order to inherit property an individual had to be recognized in the will. For most inhabitants the amounts were small and the procedures were routine. For some, however, the wills were contested. In such cases local judges heard the petitions and made judgments. Such petitions could center on the deceased's capacities, the legitimacy of the heirs, the validity of the documents, creditors' claims made on the estate, or even prior arrangements made between the deceased and relatives. The judge had to determine if the will was legal, meaning that all the proper arrangements had been made, and ensure that the deceased's motives were legal and were fulfilled. As in modern times contesting the will's validity usually involved money. If the estate owed money, creditors had the right to make claims, and of course, if the imperial treasury was owed money, it received its share first.

Powerful individuals could also find their wills contested by the emperor, who may have desired the money himself. Many of these individuals made the emperor their first heir in hopes that their family might receive some of the estate. Although these instances were confined to the powerful nobility in Rome, as time progressed and Christianity became more pronounced, especially after its legalization, Christians had to concern themselves with this possibility.

Examples of wills exist both in the legal codes of Justinian and in numerous papyri, indicating that individuals of all classes and regions created them in order to pass on their possessions. The wills made it possible for individuals to secure a position in their family's history and to portray how they had lived to their fellow citizens. Likewise for Christians the will represented the final component of the afterlife, and it hoped to guarantee that the individual was worthy of Christ's love. Christians ultimately viewed wills as religious testaments to the deceased's memory.

Christians' daily life encompassed all aspects of society in the Mediterranean world. What is amazing is how this small offshoot of Judaism not only survived but continually grew when nearly all aspects of its philosophy on how to live were being challenged. Persecuted by pagans and Jews, Christianity took hold in the 1st century, and its core religious tenets never compromised. Instead, Christians were a clearly identifiable group, often standing out, who argued against the mainstream lifestyles of the Mediterranean world. Within three centuries this small isolated group found a political protector, Constantine, which allowed the religion to flourish. A century after Constantine, Christianity had replaced traditional paganism in all aspects of daily life: meals, worship, family life, work, and death. Christians had adopted and changed customs from Judaism and paganism to suit their needs and in the end created a new ethos for society.

NOTES

1. Bruce Chilton, "Christianity," in *Death and the Afterlife,* ed. Jacob Neusner (Cleveland, OH: Pilgrim Press, 2000), p. 96.

2. Orazio Marucchi, *Christian Epigraphy,* trans. J. Armine Willis (Cambridge: Cambridge University Press, 1912) #38.

3. Laurence Keppie, *Understanding Roman Inscription* (Baltimore: Johns Hopkins University Press, 1991), p. 122.

10

IMPACT OF CHRISTIANITY

This chapter examines Christianity's impact on the daily life of Rome's inhabitants after Constantine legalized the religion. After a brief Biography of Rome's first Christian emperor, his endowing of early Christian basilicas, and the evolution of legislation restricting and ultimately outlawing paganism, a discussion of the organization and history of the papacy occurs, centering on Pope Leo and his role in protecting and leading the city after imperial abandonment. This discussion leads into the rise of pilgrimages, already existing in pagan society, which revitalized the city of Rome and provided an important component of the city's economy, even under the Arian Germanic kings, up to the modern age.

The Vatican, Pope John Paul II, and Catholicism celebrated the Jubilee in 2000 C.E. with great fanfare witnessing not only the regular 25-year celebration of the Holy Year, but also the era of a new century and more importantly a new millennium. Millions of visitors and pilgrims streamed into Rome to visit, celebrate, and venerate the center of Catholic Christianity. Catholics and non-Catholics journeyed to shrines to view early Christian relics in acts of piety and commemoration as the ancient imperial capital now played host to the papacy's power. This was not the first time Rome witnessed a major *jubilee;* 1,000 years earlier the Christian West celebrated the Golden Year with pilgrims, many fearful the end of the world was imminent, visiting the medieval city. The church promised those pilgrims traveling to Rome help in their journey to the afterlife for eternal salvation. In return pilgrims gave prayers, alms, and devotion, enriching and promoting the church. Christian pilgrims affected the daily lives of Romans after Constantine.

TRIUMPH OF CHRISTIANITY

With Constantine's triumph over Maxentius in 312 c.e. and his promulgation of laws tolerating, favoring, and endorsing Christianity, Rome witnessed a dramatic shift in its daily life. Christians no longer feared celebrating their religion openly. While probably caring no more or less than other emperors for the general welfare of his subjects, Constantine's beneficial policies toward Christianity changed the lives of this one group. Constantine needed a strong church leader to help transform and control Rome's political and religious life; the pope fit this role and was recognized in the West as Christianity's leader.

Constantine

Born about 285 in Serdicca (in modern Serbia) to Constantius and his concubine Helena, Constantine (285–337) grew up and was educated at Diocletian's imperial court. He served in Galerius' Persian campaign, perhaps as an aide. With the retirement of Maximian and Diocletian, Constantine became a hostage of Galerius. Escaping to the West, Constantine joined his father in Britain. When Constantius died, his troops hailed Constantine emperor. Galerius, forced to recognize him, allowed Constantine the title of Augustus. When Maxentius, with the help of his father Maximian, rebelled, Constantine at first supported him. To seal the relationship Constantine married Fausta, daughter of Maximian and sister of Maxentius. Maximian attempted to supplant his son in Rome but lost and was forced to flee. When Maximian fled his son Maxentius to Constantine, his son-in-law, and then tried to murder him, Constantine executed him in 310. In 312 Constantine, now in control of Britain, Gaul, and Spain, defeated Maxentius at the battle of the Milvian Bridge near Rome, winning the West, supposedly by invoking the name of Christ.

With the control of the West, Constantine made an alliance with Licinius in the East, giving him his sister as wife. Constantine began a series of reforms that transformed the army and the state. He separated the military command into two groups, the cavalry and the infantry. He placed the cavalry as mobile central reserves away from the frontier. He began his economic policies by reducing the weight of the gold solidus, producing the standard for nearly 1,000 years. Constantine's greatest difficulty lay in the religious problems in North Africa with the Donatists, where he backed the Catholic or Orthodox side against them.

Relations with Licinius began to sour in 316. Constantine defeated him in the Balkans, taking the lands west of the Hellespont. In 323 Constantine defeated Licinius and seized the remainder of the Roman Empire, executing him and his son. With this victory Constantine carried out reforms in the East. In 324 he announced the moving of the capital to Byzantium, now renamed Constantinople, officially founded in 330. This new capital, completely Christian, superseded Rome. At the same time Constantine had to deal with the controversy of Arius and his followers. In 325 he assembled the council of Nicaea, which denounced Arius despite Arius still holding sway over many in the government.

In 326 Constantine executed his eldest son and heir designate, Crispus, and in 327 executed his own wife, Fausta, for adultery. The two events may be connected, since Fausta may have attempted to supplant Crispus with her own children. Constantine attempted to formulate a policy in which his family would inherit his kingdom but failed. Although Constantine did not officially make Christianity the state religion, he did favor Christianity by granting lands and funds to the church. He ordered the Christian churches to be rebuilt by using funds from pagan temples. He granted tax exemptions to church officials and promoted churchmen into his bureaucracy. Although called upon to arbitrate religious controversies, he had little religious training and sought to make decisions that promoted imperial unity and peace rather than theological discernment. In 337 Constantine planned to march off to war against the Persians, but he fell ill and died.

CHRISTIANITY AFTER CONSTANTINE

When Christians could suddenly celebrate their faith by no longer meeting in secret or fearing imminent arrest, they began to view their new position not only as favored, but as providential. Christians had survived the persecutions, arguing that their survival was special, which now translated into various new initiatives by both the church and the state: buildings, organization, and the economy.

BUILDINGS

Before legalization, Christians worshipped in a state of semisecrecy, during some periods being tolerated or at least not persecuted while their worship places were often well known to local officials. Due to their tenuous situation, Christians could never expect permanency in their worship structures. The earliest Christian worship places were the house churches, private homes, some of which came down as the *titulus* or beneficence of wealthy Christians. There were 25 *tituli* in Rome at the time of Constantine's conversion, some of which became churches and were now enlarged. Typically a house or part of the house had been used by Christians, and when the owner died the house or title (in Latin *titulus*) was given to the church and became a parish; for example, the *Titulus Ceciliae* became St. Cecilia in Trastevere. The evolution of terminology proceeded from titulus, later to *domus,* Latin for "house of God" (Domus Dei), with finally the Greek word *ecclesia,* or church, superseding *domus* for the buildings.

Alternatively, during the 2nd century some Christians organized themselves into *scholae*, or associations, modeled on the pagan burial clubs as witnessed in the organization of the catacombs of Soter. The houses of confessors and martyrs also became churches, for example Ss. Giovanii e Paolo on the Caelian, a unique place, since the tomb was located inside the city walls.

A third situation existed where pagan monuments and temples became Christian churches, for example the Coliseum had the church S. Salvator in Tellure, and the Temple of Antoninus and Faustina in the Roman Forum was dedicated to St. Lorenzo. Finally, there were memorials of historical events, for example, the *oratorium Sanctae Crucis* (oratory of the Holy Cross), commemorating Constantine's victory over Maxentius.

After legalization, Christians constructed their own religious buildings, oratories, and churches now placed above ground over martyrs' tombs and catacombs, such as St. Peter's on the Via Cornelia, St. Paul on the Via Ostiensis, and St. Sebastian on the Via Appia, all originally outside the city walls. Additionally, Christians erected many structures on previously revered sites, for example, the Basilica of St. Paul Outside the Walls, where in the 4th century a new large church replaced the previous shrine. Another important site included St. Peters; Pope Anacletus (78–88 C.E.) built the original simple chapel on his tomb built by and now in 320 On Constantine and his mother Helen endowed wishes the first basilica here. San Giovanni in Lateran, the cathedral and bishop of Rome's seat, was built on a site occupied by the Laterani family in the 3rd century, giving the church its name Lateran. Originally the site was the headquarters of the imperial guard in the late 3rd/early 4th century. Constantine subsequently destroyed the building when he disbanded the guard after defeating Maxentius and proceeded to build the basilica. In 455 Genseric looted the church, stealing its treasury. Pope Sylvester built another great basilica, Santa Maria Maggiore, on the initiative of the Roman people, perhaps signaling his independence from the emperor who had founded the other great basilicas. Here, the pope may have desired to show his emerging political power.

Wealthy church members, who could now openly provide beneficence to the recently legalized religion, gave expensive gifts and adorned these new buildings with mosaics and art. Like earlier pagan temples, Christian churches now became repositories of Christian wealth, allowing individual Christians to display their social position in the community. By giving these gifts the traditional social hierarchy of patronage could continue within the realm of this new religion.

Many of the old pagan temples converted into churches became the new "temples" for ordinary Christians, the most famous being the Pantheon, which was rededicated as S. Maria ad Martyres in 609 C.E. Sources indicate that the Roman population swarmed into these structures to hear the gospels and homilies of local clergy testifying to the new religion's popularity. At the same time the old pagan temples suffered. The population stopped going to them, and later the state outlawed pagan rites, seized temple property and assets, and ultimately abolished pagan public celebrations. It is estimated that perhaps as many as 50 percent of the early Christian churches were former profane public buildings and pagan temples. The process began in the 4th century, with the profane sites converted into churches, while in the 5th and 6th centuries pagan temples were transferred. After Constantine's victory, the period from the Edict of Milan (313) to 394 witnessed Christianity exerting more influence over pagan religion. With the backing of the imperial family, Christianity proceeded from a favored to the official state religion within a century. Imperial policy now affected pagan temples, ancient places of worship, and museums of art, similar to the Renaissance church. The progression of moving from paganism to Christianity began in 319 when Constantine forbade private pagan sacrifices but still allowed public pagan sacrifices.

[H]aruspices and priests and those accustomed to serve this rite we forbid to enter any private house, or under the pretence of friendship to cross the threshold of another, under the penalty established against them if they contemn the law. But those of you who regard this rite, approach the public altars and shrines and celebrate the solemnities of your custom; for we do not indeed prohibit the duties of the old usage to be performed in broad daylight. (CT 9.16.2; 319 C.E.)[1]

Then in 320 Constantine suppressed Oriental cults, the direct competitors of Christianity. A Constantinian law, now lost, seemed to indicate a mild persecution of minor pagan temples, but not the great temples in Rome or major sites in other cities; the attack appeared to have been directed at rural sites, traditional strongholds for paganism. It appears from a later law by his son Constantius that at the time of his death Constantine may have been moving more towards persecuting paganism.

Let superstition cease; let the madness of sacrifices be abolished. For whoever, against the law of the divine prince, our parent [Constantine] and this command of our clemency, shall celebrate sacrifices, let a punishment appropriate to him and this present decision be issued. (CT 16.10.2; 341 C.E.)[2]

His other son Constans, however, realized the power of paganism, for he allowed the rural peasants the right to celebrate their festivals.

Although all superstition is to be entirely destroyed, yet we will that the temple buildings, which are situated without the wall remain intact and uninjured. For since from some have arisen various sports, races, and contests, it is not proper that they should be destroyed, from which the solemnity of ancient enjoyments are furnished to the Roman people. (CT 16.10.3; 342 C.E.)[3]

The sacred groves, regions of animism, were not protected and were now destroyed. In 356 Constantius closed pagan temples, even though earlier he had ordered them protected.

Mosaic: Medallion with Mithraic Scene. The Walters Art Museum, Baltimore.

It is our pleasure that in all places and in all cities the temples be henceforth closed, and access having been forbidden to all, freedom to sin be denied the wicked. We will that all abstain from sacrifices; that if any one should commit any such act, let him fall before the vengeance of the sword. Their goods, we decree, shall be taken away entirely and recovered to the fisc, and likewise rectors of provinces are to be punished if they neglect to punish for these crimes. (CT 16.10.4; 346 c.e.)[4]

In 408 Theodosius II issued a law (CT 16.10.9) stating that pagan temples could be reused for other purposes, including for Christian churches. And finally in 426, Theodosius II in the East, with probably a similar law in the West, ordered that temples, shrines, and altars be either destroyed or purified and given to the church. An example of the latter comes from the East, where an inscription in a pagan temple showed the conversion of a pagan temple into a Christian church: "The assembly of devils has become the house of God: The Life giving light shines where there reigned darkness."[5] In Rome more of the pagan temples remained intact than other cities, since many of these temples had historical value and were viewed as museums or historical relics by the population.

Ancient temple statues like the temples themselves underwent a similar process of survival. Some artwork remained in the original temples such as the statue of Rhea (Vestal) in her temple of the Vestal Virgins; some statues were transferred from temples to civic buildings—markets, theatres, and baths—and prominently displayed; and pagans purposely buried or concealed some statues for protection, and they were not desecrated by Christians as archaeologists originally thought.

ORGANIZATION

The early church, highly organized with different offices, was originally structured along the lines of the Jewish synagogues, which had a liturgical ruler who presided over the synagogue and its services. There was also a political group, the council or Sanhedrin, which had the power to punish members. The synagogues were not centrally controlled, but were independent. The independence of the local synagogues helped Christianity spread in its infancy, since there was no central Jewish control. The Christian use of Jewish structure and practice was only logical, since the early leaders grew up within the Jewish community. After its initial growth and subsequent break from Judaism, the Christian organization moved more to a central hierarchy, although not completely centralized, as seen later. With Christianity's legalization the church further developed and refined its organization, becoming more visible and active in the city life, not only in religion but in politics, economics, and society. The pope, taking the title Pontifex Maximus from the ancient Roman religion, stood at the top of the Western organization ruling the church spiritually and later politically. Popes argued they were Peter's successor, speaking for all of Christianity. Other bishops, especially in the East, disputed this claim, arguing that a council or a group of bishops from a particular district, region, or even all of Christianity had ultimate authority. This difference of spiritual power and interpretation often pitted the Eastern and Western churches against each other, at odds over matters of faith lasting even until the present age.

Although not completely centralized, the separate regions usually had similar ecclesiastical doctrines. Local leaders, who kept minutes of their meetings, possessed great influence, but this power was always limited by the universal doctrines of the faith and in the West the leadership in Rome. These local decisions often led some into conflict with mainstream or Catholic ideas. The region's local authority came from its bishop, but if problems arose in a region, a group of local bishops might meet to discuss, debate, and decide a course of action at a council. The early church through these councils issued constitutions, which local churches and sometimes the entire church followed. The church adopted the term diocese, a Roman political term for several provinces grouped together, which Christianity now used for a group of parishes in a region, organized together under the control of a bishop. The term parish, individual churches, called *titulus* (pl. *tituli*) in Rome, occurred first in 341 and was under the control of a priest.

PAPACY

Since the mid-3rd century emperors no longer ruled from Rome, but instead, moved their court to the frontiers as they fought foreign enemies and rival Roman generals. With Diocletian's restoration of the empire, the capital was not Rome but in Nicomedia. Constantine's victory in 324 over Licinius, the ruler in the East, allowed him to establish a new capital, Constantinople, modern-day Istanbul in Turkey. With this move Rome lost its claim to imperial power. Even when the empire split into Eastern and Western powers, the Western capital was not Rome but Milan or Ravenna. With the absence of imperial power in Rome the political vacuum needed to be filled. Two forces emerged: the fragmented, mainly pagan Senate; and the united church favored by the Christian emperor ruled by the pope. The pope, with help from the emperors, became a political figure in Rome and the West where the church's political power rose dramatically during the 4th century.

As the church's spiritual leader, the pope traditionally viewed himself as God's spokesman to the faithful, similar to pagan priests who had argued that they interpreted the gods' signs and reconciled humans with the divine. For everyday Romans nothing really changed except the leadership. The papacy's early period, as well as the foundation of the pope's supremacy, is problematic. Before Peter and Paul had arrived, unnamed Jewish Christians residing in Rome had already established the church. The Roman Church had already become important by 57 C.E., as seen in Paul's letter to the Romans. The letter of I Clement from 96 C.E. pointed to the principle of papal succession, and by 200 C.E. the pope began to take on the trappings of a monarch modeled on the Roman emperor.

The papacy, beginning in the 4th century, actively increased its power through a series of initiatives, becoming the spokesperson and defender of Rome and its inhabitants. First, popes exerted their religious power, continually stressing the authority of Christianity over other religions; the papacy even challenged emperors, who since Constantine had viewed themselves as Christianity's protectors and leaders. Second, popes increased their political and religious power through the church's traditional mission to help the poor. The giving of alms and goods reinforced the church's position in everyday lives. The state no longer could or cared to provide sustenance for the city poor, but the church could and did. Finally, the pope controlled the local parishes throughout Rome, using their administrative system to reach all levels of society. An example of the power of the papacy can be seen in the rule of Pope Leo, who saved Rome from Attila.

Leo (?–461)

Leo's birth and early life are obscure. Born in Italy, probably in Tuscany, Leo achieved fame for his diplomatic skills and his unwavering insistence on orthodoxy, earning him the titles of "the Great" and "Doctor of the Church." He was a deacon in Rome from 422 to 440 during the pontificates of popes Celestine I and Sixtus III. Sixtus in 440 sent Leo to Gaul to negotiate between two rival generals, Aetius and Albinus. After Sixtus' death in 440 delegates arrived from Rome and informed Leo of his election to the papacy.

Leo energetically endorsed the Orthodox faith by persecuting the followers of Pelagius throughout Italy. Leo also attacked the Manichaeans in Rome, urging the emperor Valentinian III to crack down on the sect. He sent a long refutation to the Spanish bishop Turibius concerning the heresy of Priscillianism, which combined astrology and fatalism, two traditional pagan attributes, with Manichaean beliefs on the evil of matter. This sect was growing in popularity among the Spanish population and even among the clergy, and Leo urged local bishops to eliminate it.

Leo asserted the pope's authority, especially in the West. This can be seen in his relations with Hilary, bishop of Arles, who had removed and replaced two bishops in Gaul. Leo accused him of exceeding his power, and with the aid of the emperor Valentinian III he denounced the bishop in 445, asserting the pope's authority in the West. Leo in 446 wrote to the African Church in Mauretania forbidding the election of a layman as bishop, or one who was twice married or married to a widow, as well as an ex-slave or those from an unsavory profession. Leo was also asked by some Eastern bishops to help suppress a revival of Nestorianism and was involved in a series of disputes in the East over papal supremacy.

Leo again was called upon to use his diplomatic skills when Attila invaded Italy in 452. Leo, accompanied by the counsel Avienus and the prefect of the city Trigetius met Attila near the confluence of the Po and Mincio rivers. The three negotiated with the Huns, and it is probable that the three bought off Attila. Immediately afterwards Attila withdrew and returned north.

A few years later the Vandal Genseric attacked Rome, and Leo once again used his negotiating abilities to keep the Vandals from burning the city and killing indiscriminately, although he could not save the city. For 10 days the Vandals systematically looted the city and returned to Africa with captives and booty. Leo began to repair the damage brought about by the invasion. After 21 years of rule, Leo died on November 10, 461. Throughout his rule he was known for his alms giving and caring for the poor. He was recognized not only for his concern for the city of Rome, but for his unswerving commitment against heresies and his position on papal supremacy.

PILGRIMAGES

After Constantine's conversion and the favoring of Christianity, Rome changed dramatically, becoming the church's political center in the West. Visitors throughout history came to Rome in search of wealth, trade, power, and religion. With Christianity openly practiced, Christians from all over the empire desired to see the sites where the Romans executed the early apostles Peter and Paul as well as other martyrs and their burial sites. Chief among the sites visited were the catacombs holding the martyrs' bodies, and recently erected churches, often placed on top of the catacombs. Christian pilgrims sought spiritual guidance and help—medicinal, psychological, or spiritual.

Before Christianity's supremacy, however, pagans traditionally visited their own sacred shrines. For example, the Greek city of Delphi had established its reputation as an oracle during the classical Greek age, likewise the Italian site of Cumae, with the Sibyl, became renowned for its pronouncements. Numerous sites throughout the ancient world had shrines celebrating curative powers and honoring gods such as Asclepius and Apis. Pagan pilgrims visited these sanctuaries for sacrifice and afterwards deposited votives, gifts to the gods. In addition they pleaded for help or asked for their questions to be answered. These religious sites increased in popularity if petitions were granted. The pilgrim would pay for animals to offer sacrifice of blood and flesh. An inscription from Rome has the prices of animals for sacrifices at a pagan religious shrine:

For the blood of _____ (perhaps a bull)	_____
And for its hide	_____
If the victim be entirely burnt	25 asses
For blood and skin of a lamb	4 asses
If the lamb be entirely burnt	6 1/2 asses
For a cock (entirely burnt)	3 1/2 asses
For blood alone	13 asses
For a wreath	4 asses
For hot water (per head)	2 asses[6]

Paganism was not the only religion before Christianity with revered sites and animal sacrifice. Jews revered, made pilgrimages, and offered animal sacrifices in the Jewish temple in Jerusalem, until its destruction by Vespasian and Titus during the Jewish revolt. Pilgrimages should therefore be seen not as a peculiarity of Christianity, but as existing throughout the ancient world.

TOURIST ECONOMY

With these pilgrimages an entirely new economy grew up affecting Christians and influencing the daily lives of everyday Romans. These pilgrims were not just individuals viewing graves; they were in fact comparable to modern tourists on vacations. Like modern tourists going

Votive Sabazios Hand, Bronze. Saint Louis Art
Museum.

to Disneyland or amusement parks, individuals taking pilgrimages
spent money on housing, food, protection, enjoyment, and souvenirs.
To accommodate the influx of pilgrims, local inns and hostels provided
room and board for the different social and economic classes at varying
levels of amenities, much as they had to merchants and other visitors
under pagan Rome. What differentiated these Christian pilgrims from
earlier visitors to Rome was the distance and reason for the journey.
Before, visitors tended to be either local rural inhabitants coming to
Rome to buy and sell items in a small-scale economy or merchants who
frequented Rome providing bulk items such as grain, oil, wine, and
luxury goods for the wealthy or the occasional political power seeker.
Now, however, the visitors were tourists who had different needs, since
they often came from great distances, usually in groups, with little or

no knowledge of the city, with varying economic means, and usually staying only for a short period. Unlike many visitors during the imperial period, who often returned, Christian pilgrims tended to visit Rome only once.

At the same time that there was a rise in Christian pilgrimages, which was usually seasonal, there was an overall decline in the city's population. After Rome's sack in 410 C.E. and the subsequent raids by German tribes, the city's infrastructure declined. The aqueducts were damaged, the sewers no longer maintained, the baths fell into disrepair, and the grain supply became tenuous, producing problems for the city. With these civic problems and without imperial patronage, Rome sank and subsided from its former positions as a large imperial city.

At this point pilgrimages came to the forefront and breathed new life into the city's economy. Many of the large houses subdivided into small apartments were now transformed from local tenements to hostels to provide guest quarters. Likewise some of the insulae became hostels and houses for religious orders. These religious orders comprised men and women who lived separately in communities and provided medical, teaching, and social services for the city and its visitors in self-contained communities. The religious orders provided services for pilgrims in exchange for money.

Pilgrims could explore the city, taking in the religious sites using the numerous itineraries or travel routes written by contemporaries. Similar to modern guide books that tell tourists about what museums, nightclubs, or restaurants to visit, these itineraries pointed out the basilicas and other points of interest. For example, one of the earliest of these surviving pilgrim itineraries was the Einsiedeln Itinerary written in the 8th century and preserved in a monastery at Einsiedeln, Switzerland. The document gave routes from certain starting points, usually a gate in the city wall, to well-known sites, with a list of buildings on the left- and right-hand sides of the route that the walking pilgrim could see and visit. The itinerary encompassed not only Christian sites but well-known ancient structures still existing in Rome in the 8th century. The accompanying excerpt is from the 3rd route going east to west from the Numentana Gate to the Roman Forum, in modern Rome from near the train station towards the Coliseum and the Forum.

The itinerary merely listed sites, while the 12th-century *Mirabilia urbis Romae* was a compilation and description of the city structures and stories associated with Rome. Some of the sections dealt with the city wall, gates, milestones, arches, hills, palaces, theaters, bridges, cemeteries, Augustus' name, and columns, among other highlights. Although a guidebook, it was more of a synthesis than just listings like an itinerary. The accompanying excerpt relates where the saints suffered from Roman authorities throughout the city.

EINSIEDELN ITINERARY

3.1 From the Numentana Gate to the Roman Forum

2 On the left Diocletian's Baths	On the right Sallust's Baths
3 (churches of) St. Cyriaci; St. Vitalis	(church of) St. Susanna and the marble horse
4 (church) of St. Agatha in hospital	(church of) St. Marcellus
5 monastery of St. Agatha	near the Apostles
6 Constantine's Baths	Trajan's Forum
7 * * *	(church of) St. Hadrian
8 On the Numentana Road	Outside the Wall
9 On the Left (church of) St. Agnes	On the Right (Church of) St. Nicomedia

Latin text from H. Jordan, *Topographie der Stadt Rom im Alterthum,* Vol. 2 (Berlin: Weidmaunde Buchhandlung, 1871), pp. 648–49 (translated by author).

THE MIRABILIA URBIS ROMAE

12. OF PLACES WHERE SAINTS SUFFERED

These are the places that are found in the passions of Saints: without the Appian gate, the place where the blessed Sixtus was beheaded, and the place where the Lord appeared to Peter, when he said, Lord, whither goest thou, and the temple of Mars; within the gate, the Dripping Arch; then the region of Fasciola at Saint Nereus; the *Vicus Canarius* at Saint George, where was Lucilla's house, and where is the Golden Vail; the *aqua Salvia* at Saint Anastasius, where the blessed Paul was beheaded, and the head thrice uttered the word Jesus, as it bounded, and where there be yet three wells which spring up diverse in taste; the garden of Lucina, where is the church of the blessed Paul, and where he lieth. *Interlude,* that is, between two Games; the hill of Scaurus, which is between the Amphitheatre and the Racecourse, before the Seven Floors, where is the sewer, wherein Saint Sebastian was cast, who revealed his body to Saint Lucina, saying Thou shalt find my body hanging on a nail; the *via Cornelia* by the Milvian bridge, and goeth forth into the street; the *via Aurelia* nigh to the Ring; the steps of Eliogabalus in the entry of the Palace; the chained island behind Saint Trinity; the Dripping Arch before the Seven Floors; the Roman Arch between the Aventine and Albiston, where the blessed Silvester and Constantine kissed, and departed the one from the other; *in Tellure,* that is the *Canapara,* where was the house of Tellus; the prison of Mamertinus before the Mars under the Capitol; the *Vicus Latericii* at Saint Praxede; the *Vicus Patricii* at Saint Pudentiana; the basilica of Jupiter at Saint Quiricus; the *thermae* of Olympias, where the blessed Laurence was broiled, in Panisperna; the Tiberian place of Trajan, where Decius and Valerian withdrew themselves after Saint Laurence's death, where the place is called the Baths of the Cornuti; the *Circus Flaminius* at the Jews' bridge; in the *Transtiberim*, the temple of the Ravennates, pouring forth oil, where is St. Mary's.

Mirabilia Urbis Romae, *The Marvels of Rome or A Picture of the Golden City,* trans. Francis Moran Nicols (London: Ellis and Elvey, 1889), pp. 29–34.

IMPACT

These two excerpts detail how Christians in the Middle Ages viewed ancient Rome. Pilgrims had become an important component of everyday life in the ancient city. With the fall of the Roman Empire, the city of Rome was transformed from an imperial capital to a religious center, ruled at first by foreign Germanic kings. These kings, however, were not Catholic like much of the city or the pope, but rather, Arian Christians from the East. The theological difference consistently tested the patience of both the Arian kings and Catholic popes as to how the city should be ruled and protected. With the defeat of these German leaders by Justinian in the 6th century and the subsequent overrunning of Italy by pagan Lombards, the pope and the church now completely controlled the city. The power of Christianity and the church made Rome a Christian Catholic center, with everyone in the city beholding to the church in some fashion.

The influence of Christianity in everyday life continued to gain strength during the medieval and Renaissance world. Roman inhabitants, however, continued to live their lives much as their predecessors had during antiquity. Although the church replaced the collapsed Roman Empire, the city's infrastructure suffered, and daily life changed. With the city's aqueducts damaged and no longer repaired, residents no longer had fresh water and the baths where they could relax, socialize, and wash. For church leaders the latter was not disturbing, since the early church fathers had traditionally viewed the baths as immoral playgrounds; their demise was probably not mourned. For the normal resident the damaged aqueducts resulted in an increase in disease and generally unsanitary conditions, which increased mortality rates and produced pain and suffering.

With the end of pagan Rome everyday life changed for the family as well. Unlike the past, where divorce was easy for either party, under Christianity marriages were not readily dissolved. The freedom for upper-class Romans probably remained due to annulments, but for lower-class residents, marriages were not so easily ended. In addition, with the increase in family morality stressed by the church, nonsanctioned marriages, common during the pagan empire without any moral judgment attached, were not only frowned upon but actively punished by the church and the city government. The daily eating habits of residents also changed, since Christianity advocated fasting and the eating of certain foods on certain days, such as fish instead of flesh on Fridays. The end of paganism also ended the communal feastings that occasionally took place at pagan religious holidays after animal sacrifices. Finally, the average resident witnessed a change in relaxation, with not only the baths ceasing, but the games being ultimately abandoned.

CONCLUSION

The daily lives of Roman inhabitants changed dramatically with the supremacy of Christianity after Constantine. Throughout the medieval period the Christian Church exerted an almost complete monopoly on individuals' daily lives, not only in Rome, but throughout the West. Christians set their calendar by the saints' feasts and their daily hours by religious prayers. The church told Christians what to eat, how to act, and when to pray. The daily life of ordinary Christians was tied closely to the local parish and its clergy. The preeminence of Christian habits continued into the Renaissance, but was often questioned, leading to dissensions. The dissension in the Christian West during the Renaissance was rooted in theological difference, but often displayed itself in daily lifestyles. With the Reformation and the Counter-Reformation, these lifestyles often became crucial dividing points between Protestants and Catholics. The use of the vernacular in services and literature, the allowance of divorce, the changes in dietary rules, and other acts altered daily life. But the influence of early Christian daily life continued: fasting, prayer, and the remembrance of Christ. These manifestations, so strong in Christianity's infancy, remained throughout its history and continue to exert a strong influence on the daily lives of Christians today.

NOTES

1. Joseph Cullen Ayer, *A Source Book for Ancient Church History* (New York: Charles Scribner's Sons, 1922), p. 286.

2. Joseph Cullen Ayer, *A Source Book for Ancient Church History* (New York: Charles Scribner's Sons, 1922), p. 321.

3. Joseph Cullen Ayer, *A Source Book for Ancient Church History* (New York: Charles Scribner's Sons, 1922), p. 321.

4. Joseph Cullen Ayer, *A Source Book for Ancient Church History* (New York: Charles Scribner's Sons, 1922), pp. 321–322.

5. Rodolfo Lanciani, *Wandering through Ancient Roman Churches* (Boston: Houghton Mifflin, 1924), p. 29.

6. Rodolfo Lanciani, *Pagan and Christian Rome* (Boston: Houghton Mifflin, 1892), p. 57. The *as* was a small Roman coin.

GLOSSARY

Apostasy—The act of denying one's faith; in Christianity the voluntary abandonment of being a Christian.

Atrium—Central room in a traditional Roman house used originally as a sitting room and receiving room, usually had a *compluvium* in the ceiling to let in light and water and an *impluvium* in the floor to collect water.

Compluvium—Opening in roof of Atrium-style house where the roof sloped inward to allow rainwater to collect in the *impluvium*.

Decurions—Town councilors from which the local magistrates were chosen.

Diaspora—Term for Jews who left Palestine after the destruction of the Temple in 70 C.E.

Drachma (pl. drachmae)—Originally a coin from ancient Greece, during this period a coin in Roman Egypt worth one-quarter of a denarius.

Flamens—Pagan priests who officiated at the celebrations of a particular god, usually chosen for life.

Forum (pl. fora)—A place in a city used for commercial/legal activities. In Rome there were numerous fora.

Impluvium—Basin in the floor of a traditional Atrium-style house used to collect of water.

Insula (pl. insulae)—A city block or an apartment house occupying all or part of a city block; could be several stories tall.

Jubilee—A year-long celebration held every 25 years in the Catholic Church; special emphasis was placed on those commemorating centuries and millennium.

Limes—Imperial frontiers of the Roman Empire. The limes could be artificial or man-made, including walls, such as Hadrian's Wall, or palisades and forts as in Germany.

Ludi—Public festivals celebrated with games, which could be theatrical, chariot races, and gladiatorial games.

Pax Romana—The Roman Peace, a term applied to the period from Augustus to the death of Commodus (31 B.C.E.–180 C.E.), in which the empire enjoyed prosperity.

Persecutions—The active punishment of a group, usually a minority, by another group or state. In the Roman period the term applied to the Roman state's punishment of the Christians.

Polytheism—The belief in many gods.

Praetorian prefect—Commander of the Praetorian Guard, an elite unit of Roman troops created by Augustus, originally housed throughout Italy, and centralized by Tiberius, who built a new camp in Rome. Ultimately the prefect was second only to the emperor in power.

Subura—Poor and overcrowded region of Rome near the Coliseum where a large number of the city poor lived and worked; it was usually considered a dangerous district.

Synagogue—From the Greek meaning a place of assembly; a place for Jewish worship.

Synaxis—Greek word meaning a meeting; in Christianity it was used to denote a meeting for any liturgical function including the Eucharist.

Vicus (**pl.** *vici)*—Local wards in the city of Rome. There were 424 such districts, each composed of several city blocks and supervised by local magistrates.

Vigiles—Local watchmen who functioned as policemen and fire fighters. Augustus originally had seven units, each working in two regions. Each unit or cohort originally had 560 men, but later they were doubled in size.

BIBLIOGRAPHY

ANCIENT

Abercius Marcellus, Bishop of Hieropolis. Translated by J. B. Lightfoot. In *Documents Illustrative of the History of the Church*, Vol. 1, to A.D. 313, edited by B. J. Kidd. Translation of Christian Literature Series VI select passages. London: Macmillan, 1920.

Aelius Aristides. "The Ruling Power." Translated by James H. Oliver. *Transactions of the American Philosophical Society.* Philadelphia: American Philosophical Society, 1953.

Ammianus Marcellinus. *The Roman History of Ammianus Marcellinus.* Translated by C. D. Yonge. London: George Bell and Sons, 1894.

L'Annee epigraphique. Paris: Presses universitaires de France AE, 1981.

Augustus. *Res Gestae Divi Augusti.* Translated by Frederick W. Shipley. Loeb Classical Library. London: Heinemann, 1924.

Cassiodorus. *The Letters of Cassiodorus.* Translated by Thomas Hodgkin. London: Henry Frowde, 1886.

Cassius Dio. *Roman History.* Translated by Earnest Cary, on the basis of the version of Herbert Baldwin Foster. Loeb Classical Library, London: Heinemann, 1914–27.

Celsus. *De medicina.* Translated by W. G. Spencer. Loeb Classical Library. London: Heinemann, 1935–38.

Cicero, Marcus Tullius. *Letters of Marcus Tullius Cicero, with his treatises on friendship and old age.* Translated by E. S. Shuckburgh; *Letters of Gaius Plinius Caecilius Secundus.* Translated by William Melmoth. Revised by F.C.T. Bosanquet. With introductions and notes. The Harvard Classics Vol. 9, New York: P. F. Collier, 1909.

Constitutions of the Holy Apostles. *The Ante-Nicene Fathers' Translations of the Writings of the Fathers Down to* A.D. *325*. Edited by Alexander Roberts and James Donaldson. American reprint of the Edinburgh edition revised and chronologically arranged, with brief prefaces and occasional notes by A. Cleveland Coxe. Grand Rapids, MI: Wm. Eerdmans, 1886.

Eusebius. *The Life of Constantine,* with a revised translation by Ernest Cushing Richardson. In *Post-Nicene Fathers of the Christian Church,* 2nd series. Vol. I. Translated into English with prolegomena and explanatory notes. Vols. I–VII. Under the editorial supervision of Philip Schaff and Henry Wace. New York: The Christian Literature Company, 1890.

Jordan, H. *Topographie der Stadt Rom im Alterthum.* 2 vols. Berlin: Weidmaunde Buchhandlung, 1871.

Marucchi, Orazio. *Christian Epigraphy.* Translated by J. Armine Willis. Cambridge: Cambridge University Press, 1912.

Mirabilia Urbis Romae. *The Marvels of Rome or A Picture of the Golden City.* Translated by Francis Moran Nicols. London: Ellis and Elvey, 1889.

Musurillo, Herbert. *The Acts of the Christian Martyrs; Introduction, Texts and Translations.* Oxford: Clarendon Press, 1972.

Origen. *Contra Celsum.* In *Documents Illustrative of the History of the Church,* Vol. I, to A.D. 313, edited by B. J. Kidd. Translation of Christian Literature Series VI select passages. London: Macmillen, 1920.

The Oxyrhynchus Papyri. Part III. Edited with translations and notes by Bernard P. Grenfell and Arthur S. Hunt. London: Egypt Exploration Fund, 1903.

Pliny the Elder. *The Natural History.* Translated by John Bostock and H. T. Riley. London: Taylor and Francis, 1855.

Pliny the Younger. *Letters.* Translated by William Melmoth. Revised by Winifred Margaret Lambart Hutchinson. Loeb Classical Library. London: W. Heinemann, 1915.

Salvian of Marseilles. *A Treatise of God's Government and of the Justice of His Present Dispensations in This World.* Translated by Thomas Wagstaffe. London: Printed for S. Keble, 1700.

Schaff, Philip, ed. *A Select Library of the Nicene and Post-Nicene Fathers of the Christian Church,* 1st Series. Vols. 1–14. New York: Charles Scribner's Sons, 1886–1889.

Schaff, Philip, and Henry Wace, eds. *A Select Library of the Nicene and Post-Nicene Fathers of the Christian Church,* 2nd Series. Vols. 1–14. New York: The Christian Literature Company, 1890–1900.

Suetonius. *Lives of the Twelve Caesars.* Translated by J. C. Rolfe. Loeb Classical Library. London: Heinemann, 1913.

The Syriac Chronicle Known as that of Zachariah of Mitylene. Translated by F. J. Hamilton and E. W. Brooks. London: Methuen, 1899.

Tacitus. *Complete Works of Tacitus.* Translated by Alfred John Church, William Jackson Brodribb, and Sara Bryant. New York: Random House, 1873.

Tertullian, *Tertulliani Apologeticus.* Text of Oehler. Annotated with an introduction by J. E. B. Mayor and a translation by A. Souter. Cambridge: Cambridge University Press, 1917.

MODERN

Alfoldi, A. *The Conversion of Constantine and Pagan Rome.* Translated by Howard Mattingly. Oxford: Clarendon Press, 1958.

Allard, Paul. *Ten Lectures on the Martyrs.* Translated by Luigi Cappa Delta. New York: Benziger Brothers, 1907.

Aquilina, Mike. *The Mass of the Early Christians.* Huntington, IN: Our Sunday Visitor, 2001.

Ayer, Joseph Cullen. *A Source Book for Ancient Church History.* New York: Charles Scribner's Sons, 1922.

Balch, David L., and Carolyn Osiek. *Early Christian Families in Context.* Grand Rapids, MI: Wm. Eerdmans, 2003.

Bell, H. Idris. *Jews and Christians in Egypt.* London: British Museum, 1924.

Cabrol, Fernan. *The Prayer of the Early Christians.* Translated by Ernest Graf. London: Burns Oates and Washbourne, 1930.

Chadwick, Henry. *The Church in Ancient Society.* Oxford: Oxford University Press, 2001.

Chilton, Bruce. "Christianity." In *Death and the Afterlife*, edited by Jacob Neusner, pp. 79–96. Cleveland, OH: Pilgrim Press, 2000.

Cullmann, Oscar. *Early Christian Worship.* Philadelphia, PA: Westminster Press, 1953.

Curra, John R. *Pagan City and Christian Capital Rome in the 4th Century.* Oxford: Clarendon Press, 2000.

Davies, J. G. *The Early Christian Church.* Westport, CT: Greenwood Press, 1965.

Davies, Jon. *Death, Burial and Rebirth in the Religions of Antiquity.* London: Routledge, 1999.

de Kleijn, Gerda. *The Water Supply of Ancient Rome.* Amsterdam: Gieben, 2001.

Donfried, Karl P., and Peter Richardson, eds. *Judaism and Christianity in First-Century Rome.* Grand Rapids, MI: Wm. Eerdmans, 1998.

Elliott-Binns, L. E. *The Beginning of Western Christendom.* London: Lutterworth Press, 1948.

Frend, W.H.C. *The Archeology of Christianity: A History.* Minneapolis, MN: Fortress Press, 1996.

Frend, W.H.C. *The Rise of Christians.* Philadelphia: Fortress Press, 1984.

Hamman, Adalbert. *Early Christian Prayer.* Translated by Walter Mitchell. London: Longman, Green, 1961.

Hamman, Adalbert. *How to Read the Church Fathers.* New York: Crossroad, 1993.

Hobson, Deborah. "House and Household in Roman Egypt." *YCS* 28 (1985): 211–229.

Hunt, E. D. *Holy Lord Pilgrimage on the Later Roman Empire* A.D. *312–460.* Oxford: Clarendon Press, 1982.

Jeffers, James S. "Jewish and Christian Families in First-Century Rome." In *Judaism and Christianity in First-Century Rome*, edited by Karl P. Donfried and Peter Richardson, pp. 128–150. Grand Rapids, MI: Wm. Eerdmans, 1998.

Keppie, Laurence. *Understanding Roman Inscription.* Baltimore: Johns Hopkins University Press, 1991.

Kidd, B. J., ed. *Documents Illustrative of the History of the Church,* Vol. II, 313–461 A.D. Translation of Christian Literature Series VI select passages. London: Macmillan, 1923.

Krautheimer, Richard. *Early Christian and Byzantine Architecture.* The Pelican History of Architecture. Edited by Nikolaus Pevsnen and Judy Nain. Harmondsworth, UK: Penguin, 1975.

Laeuchli, Samuel. *Power and Sexuality.* Philadelphia: Temple University Press, 1972.

Lanciani, Rodolfo. *Pagan and Christian Rome.* Boston: Houghton Mifflin, 1892.

Lanciani, Rodolfo. *Wandering through Ancient Roman Churches.* Boston: Houghton Mifflin, 1924.

Lebreton, Jules, and Jacques Zeiller. *The History of the Primitive Church.* Translated by Ernest C. Messenger. 2 vols. New York: MacMillan, 1947.

MacDonald, Alexander. *Christian Worship in the Primitive Church.* Edinburgh: T and T Clark, 1934.

MacDonald, Margaret. "Was Celsus Right? The Role of Women in the Expansion of Early Christianity." In David L. Balch and Carolyn Osiek, *Early Christian Families in Context,* pp. 157–184. Grand Rapids, MI: Wm. Eerdmans, 2003.

Malherbe, Abraham. *Social Aspects of Early Christianity.* Baton Rouge: LSU Press, 1977.

Make, Emile. *The Early Church of Rome.* Translated by David Buxton. Chicago: Quadrangle Books, 1960.

McClean, B. H. *An Introduction to Greek Epigraphy.* Ann Arbor: University of Michigan Press, 2002.

Meeks, Wayne A. *In Search of the Early Christian Selected Essays.* New Haven: Yale University Press, 2002.

Momigliano, Arnaldo, ed. *The Conflict between Paganism and Christianity in the 4th Century.* Oxford: Clarendon Press, 1963.

Morrill, Richard, Gary L. Gaile, and Grant Ian Thrall. *Spatial Diffusion.* Scientific Geography Series. Vol. 10, pp. 21–22. Newbury Park, CA: SAGE Publications, 1988.

Neusner, Jacob, ed. *Death and the Afterlife.* Cleveland, OH: Pilgrim Press, 2000.

Nunn, Rev. H. P. *Christian Inscriptions.* New York: Philosophical Library, 1952.

Painter, K. S. *The Water Newton Early Christian Silver.* London: British Museum, 1977.

Patzia, Arthur G. *The Emergence of the Church.* Downer's Grove, IL: Inter-Varsity Press 2001.

Pestman, P. W. *Marriage and Matrimonial Property in Ancient Egypt.* Papyrologica Lugduno-Batava. Vol. 9. Leiden: Brill, 1961.

Quasten, Johannes. *Patrology.* 3 vols. Utrecht-Antwerp: Spectrum, 1975.

Ramage, Edwin S. "Urban Problems in Ancient Rome." In *Aspects of Graeco-Roman Urbanism,* edited by Ronald T. Marchese. BAR International Series 188 (1983) 61–91.

Ramsey W. M. *The Church and the Roman Empire before* A.D. *170.* London: Hodder and Stoughton, 1893.

Richardson, Peter. "Augustan-Era Synagogues in Rome." In *Judaism and Christianity in First-Century Rome,* edited by Karl P. Donfried and Peter Richardson, pp. 17–29. Grand Rapids, MI: Wm. Eerdmans, 1998.

Rusch, William G. *The Later Latin Fathers.* London: Duckworth, 1977.

Rutgers, Leonard Victor. "Roman Policy Toward the Jews: Expulsions from the City of Rome during the First Century C.E." In *Judaism and Christianity in First-Century Rome,* edited by Karl P. Donfried and Peter Richardson, pp. 93–116. Grand Rapids, MI: Wm. Eerdmans, 1998.

Schaff, Philip. *History of the Christian Church.* 8 vols. Grand Rapids, MI: Wm Eerdmans, 1910.

Schnabel, Eckhard J. *Early Christian Missions.* Vols 1–2. Downer's Grove, IL: Inter-Varsity Press, 2004.

Snyder, Graydon F. *Antepacem Archeological Endurance of Church Life Before Constantine.* Macon, GA: Mercer University Press, 2003.

Spence-Jones, H.D.M. *The Early Christians in Rome.* 2nd ed. London: Methuen, 1911.

Stevenson, J. *The Catacombs.* London: Thames and Hudson, 1978.

Stevenson, J. A. *New Eusebius Documents Illustrating the Identity of the Church to* A.D. *337.* London: SPCK, 1987.

Wallace-Hadrill. "Domus and Insulae in Rome: Families and Housefuls." In David L. Balch and Carolyn Osiek, *Early Christian Families in Context,* pp. 3–18. Grand Rapids MI: Wm. Eerdmans, 2003.

White, L. Michael. *Building God's House in the Roman World.* Baltimore: Johns Hopkins University Press, 1990.

White, L. Michael. "Synagogue and Society in Imperial Ostia: Archaeological and Epigraphic Evidence." In *Judaism and Christianity in First-Century Rome,* edited by Karl P. Donfried and Peter Richardson, pp. 30–59. Grand Rapids, MI: Wm. Eerdmans, 1998.

White, L. Michael. *Social Origins of Christian Architecture.* 2 vols. Valley Forge, PA: Trinity Press International, 1996.

Winter, Bruce W. *Seek the Welfare of the City: Christians as Benefactors and Citizens.* Grand Rapids, MI: William B. Eerdmans, 1994.

WEB SITES (NOTE: WEB SITES ARE SUBJECT TO CHANGE)

General

The Centre for Late Antiquity
http://www.art.man.ac.uk/cla/home.htm

Ramsey Library Research Guides
http://bullpup.lib.unca.edu/library/rr/early_xnty.html

The Hall of Church Fathers
http://www.spurgeon.org/~phil/fathers.htm

Bill Thayer: University of Chicago
http://penelope.uchicago.edu/Thayer/E/home.html

Texts

New Advent
http://www.newadvent.org/fathers/

Early Christian Writings
http://www.earlychristianwritings.com/

The Early Church Fathers
http://www.ccel.org/fathers2/
http://www.ccel.org/

Early Church Fathers—Additional Texts
http://www.ccel.org/p/pearse/morefathers/home.html
http://www.earlychristianwritings.com/fathers/

Maps

Forma Urbis Romae
http://penelope.uchicago.edu/~grout/encyclopaedia_romana/imperialfora/forma.html
http://sights.seindal.dk/sight/290_Lanciani_Forma_Urbis_Romae.html
http://formaurbis.stanford.edu/

Maps of the Roman Empire
>   http://intranet.dalton.org/groups/rome/RMAPS.html

Films: Films for Humanities and Sciences

http://www.films.com/
African Ascetics and Celtic Monks: Christianity in the 5th and 6th Centuries, c. 1999.
Jesus, Mary Magdalene, and Da Vinci, c. 2003.
Monks, Keepers of Knowledge, c.2004.
The Birth of a New Religion: Christianity in the 1st and 2nd Centuries, c. 1999.
Trials and Triumphs in Rome: Christianity in the 3rd and 4th Centuries, c. 1999.
Who Wrote the New Testament? c. 2003.

INDEX

About the Author

JAMES W. ERMATINGER is professor and chair of the Department of History at Southeast Missouri State University in Cape Girardeau, Missouri. He is the author of *Economic Reforms of Diocletian* (1996) and *The Decline and Fall of the Roman Empire* (Greenwood, 2004) as well as other articles on late Roman history.